The Music of Fantasy Cinema

Genre, Music and Sound

Series editor: Mark Evans, Macquarie University, Sydney

Over the last decade screen soundtrack studies has emerged as a lively area of research and analysis mediating between the fields of cinema studies, musicology and cultural studies. It has deployed a variety of cross-disciplinary approaches to illuminate an area of film's audio-visual operation that was neglected for much of the late twentieth century. This series extends the field by addressing the development of various popular international film genres in the post-war era (1945–present), analysing the variety and shared patterns of music and sound use that characterize each genre.

Published

Terror Tracks: Music, Sound and Horror Cinema
Edited by Philip Hayward

Drawn to Sound: Animation Film Music and Sonicity
Edited by Rebecca Coyle

Earogenous Zones: Sound, Sexuality and Cinema
Edited by Bruce Johnson

Forthcoming

Movies, Moves and Music: The Sonic World of Dance Films
Edited by Mary Fogarty and Mark Evans

Sounding Funny: Sound and Comedy Cinema
Edited by Mark Evans and Philip Hayward

The Singing Voice in Contemporary Cinema
Edited by Diane Hughes and Mark Evans

The Music of
Fantasy Cinema

Edited by
Janet K. Halfyard

SHEFFIELD UK   BRISTOL CT

Published by Equinox Publishing Ltd

UK: Unit S3, Kelham House, 3 Lancaster Street, Sheffield, S3 8AF
USA: ISD, 70 Enterprise Drive, Bristol, CT 06010

www.equinoxpub.com

Paperback edition published 2014.

The authors and publisher thank the following for permission to reproduce copyright material:

Warner-Barham Music for 'Double Trouble' (from *Harry Potter and the Prisoner of Azkaban*). Words and music by John Williams. © 2004 Warner-Barham Music, LLC. All rights administered by Warner-Tamerlane Publishing Corp. All rights reserved.

Hal Leonard Corporation for 'Flash's Theme' (words and music by Brian May. ©1980 Queen Music Ltd and Wide Music Inc.) and 'Who Wants To Live Forever' (words and music by Brian May. ©1986 Queen Music Ltd.). All rights for Queen Music Ltd. in the U.S. and Canada controlled and administered by Beechwood Music Corp. All rights for Queen Music Ltd in the world excluding the U.S. and Canada controlled and administered by EMI Music Publishing Ltd. All rights reserved. International copyright secured. Used with permission.

Hal Leonard Corporation for 'Princes of the Universe' (words and music by Freddie Mercury. ©1986 Queen Music Ltd.) All rights for the U.S. and Canada controlled and administered by Beechwood Music Corporation. All rights for the world excluding the U.S. and Canada controlled and administered by EMI Music Publishing Ltd. All rights reserved. International copyright secured. Used with permission.

ISBN 978-1-908049-93-3 (hardback)
 978-1-781791-00-4 (paperback)

British Library Cataloguing-in-Publication Data
A catalogue record for this book is available from the British Library.

Library of Congress Cataloging-in-Publishing Data

The music of fantasy cinema/edited by Janet K. Halfyard
 p. cm.—(Genre, music and sound)
 Includes bibliographical references and index.
 ISBN 978-1-908049-93-3 (hb)
 1. Motion picture music—History and criticism. 2. Fantasy films—History and criticism.
I. Halfyard, Janet K., 1966–
 ML2075.M8795 2012
 781.5'42—dc23
2011022248

Typeset by S.J.I. Services, New Delhi
Printed and bound in Great Britain by Lightning Source

Contents

Contributors

Lee Barron is a senior lecturer in media and communication at Northumbria University. His main research and teaching interests are in the areas of cultural theory, media and popular culture. He has published articles in *Fashion Theory*, *Journal of Popular Culture* and *International Review of the Aesthetics and Sociology of Music*, as well as contributing to other volumes in this Equinox series.

Alexander G. Binns is Director of Graduate Studies in Music at the University of Hull. His primary research deals with music in film, especially on the ways in which musical categories inflect and shape our understanding of culture. He is also interested in opera and, more generally, in music as an interdisciplinary phenomenon: its relations with space and geography, in particular the city, and its intersections with literature and visual culture.

Mark Brill is an assistant professor of music at the University of Texas at San Antonio. He writes on Latin American music, specializing in the Mexican Baroque, and is the author of a textbook entitled *Music of Latin America and the Caribbean*. He has also written on film music and composers, including James Newton Howard, Maurice Jaubert and Bernard Herrmann, and was the guest editor of an issue of the *Journal of Film Music* dedicated to the composer Leith Stevens.

Liz Giuffre is currently a PhD candidate at Macquarie University in the Department of Media, Music, Culture and Communications, as well as being a published writer and researcher for various popular music and media publications around Australia.

Janet K. Halfyard is Director of Undergraduate Studies at Birmingham Conservatoire. Her publications include *Danny Elfman's* Batman: *A Film Score Guide* (2004) and an edited collection of essays on *Music, Sound and Silence in* Buffy the Vampire Slayer (2009), as well as chapters and articles on film and television music, including contributions to the Equinox Genre, Music and Sound volumes on horror and animation.

Victoria Hancock first became interested in film music while studying with Janet K. Halfyard at Birmingham Conservatoire. Her undergraduate dissertation focused on the musical construction of women in twentieth-century Hollywood film. After graduating from the Conservatoire she gained a master's degree with distinction in magazine journalism at the University of Sheffield.

Philip Hayward is Director of Research Training at Southern Cross University, Australia. He has edited two volumes on screen sound – *Off the Planet: Music, Sound and Science Fiction Cinema* (2004) and *Terror Tracks: Music, Sound and Horror Cinema* (2009) – and, with a team of ARC Discovery Project researchers, is currently investigating uses of music in contemporary Australian cinema.

Scott Murphy is an associate professor of music theory at the University of Kansas. His research on the structures, syntax and meanings of music from the nineteenth and twentieth centuries, including but not limited to film music analysis and new perspectives on metre as applied to the music of Brahms, has appeared in numerous journals and books.

J. Drew Stephen is an associate professor of musicology at the University of Texas at San Antonio. His research interests include the cultural significance of the hunt in Romantic opera, the history and performance practices of the horn in the eighteenth and nineteenth centuries, Canadian music, film music and rock music. He is currently preparing a textbook, *Rock This Way*, for publication in 2012.

Jamie L. Webster received her PhD in musicology and ethnomusicology from the University of Oregon in 2009 with a dissertation on the music of the first five *Harry Potter* films. Other publications have focused on the phenomenon of American women singing Bulgarian songs, the periodic complexities of Romanian dance music, and the ways that cultural idealisms have affected choreographies and musical decisions for twentieth-century ballet and national ensemble productions.

Ben Winters is a lecturer in music at the Open University. He completed his doctorate at the University of Oxford in 2006 and was subsequently research fellow at City University, London (2006–8); an early career research associate at the Institute of Musical Research, University of London (2008–9); and a lecturer in music at Christ Church, Oxford (2009–11). He is the author of *Erich Wolfgang Korngold's* The Adventures of Robin Hood: A Film Score Guide (2007), and has published articles on film music in journals such as *Music & Letters*, *Music, Sound, and the Moving Image*, *Brio*, and the *Journal of the Royal Musical Association*.

Introduction
Finding Fantasy

Janet K. Halfyard

Over the past two years during which I have worked on this project, I have repeatedly found myself debating whether this volume of essays on music in fantasy cinema is timely or premature. The argument could be made for either case. The timeliness stems from the fact that there was a significant upsurge of interest in fantasy cinema from film-makers and audiences in the late 1990s that persisted throughout the first decade of the twenty-first century, and it was probably predictable that there would be corresponding interest from academics. Much of this, so far, has centred on Peter Jackson's *The Lord of the Rings* (2001–3), with edited collections of essays from Brennan Croft (2004), Mathijs (2006), Mathijs and Pomerance (2006), Margolis *et al.* (2008) and Barker and Mathijs (2008), and monographs on fantasy film from Bellin (2005) and Thompson (2007). This interest in fantasy cinema builds on an existing body of work on fantasy literature, with studies of J. K. Rowling's *Harry Potter*, in both book and cinema manifestations (for example, Whited, 2002; Heilman, 2003, 2009), and the beginnings of an academic literature looking at fantasy cinema as a whole (Worley, 2005; Butler, 2009; Fowkes, 2010).

The prematureness stems from the perennial problem of musicologists, our preference for looking at a 'complete' opus. Most of the work on individual composers tends to be done once the composer has died and his (or her) body of work can therefore be considered complete: film musicology is not immune from this, with much more academic writing dedicated to Bernard Herrmann than to John Williams, for example, although they have clearly been equally important in the shaping of film music over similarly extended periods of time.[1] This is not a problem we share with others involved in studying temporal arts and artefacts such as cinema and television, and the result is that music is generally under-represented in such studies. Three of the four edited collections on *The Lord of the Rings* contain one essay on music: 'Musical Middle Earth' (Donnelly, 2006), 'Enchantments of *Lord of the Rings*: soundtrack, myth, language and modernity' (Buhler, 2008) and 'Howard Shore's *Ring* Cycle: the film score and operatic strategy' (Bernanke, 2008); but there is a strong sense that the film industry is going to continue to make large numbers of fantasy films over the next decade and this alone makes me, as a musicologist, a little cautious. At the time of writing, Christmas 2010, the top three films at the UK box office are all fantasy films of one form or another: *Tron: Legacy* (Joseph Kosinski, 2010); *The Chronicles of Narnia: The Voyage of the Dawn Treader* (Michael Apted, 2010); and *Harry Potter and the Deathly Hallows, Part 1* (David Yates, 2010). The *Harry Potter* series (Chris Columbus *et al.*, 2001–11) is not due to finish until the end of 2011; the *Lord of the Rings* trilogy is set to be extended by a two-part prequel, *The Hobbit*, with the first film due for release in 2012. In 2011 a host of fantasy offerings are promised, including *Season of the Witch* (Dominic Sena), *Thor* (Kenneth Branagh), *Pirates of the Caribbean: On Stranger Tides* (Rob Marshall), *Your Highness* (David Gordon Green), *The Tree of Life* (Terrence Malick), *Sucker Punch* (Zack Snyder), *The Twilight Saga: Breaking Dawn, Part 1* (Bill Condon) and a remake of *Conan the Barbarian* (Marcus Nispel). Fantasy film is in no sense a finished opus but an energetic and lively ongoing saga that currently inhabits our cinemas, and this leaves any statement one might make on the nature of fantasy film music uncomfortably provisional and potentially unstable.

Nonetheless, there is an existing body of fantasy film and its music and so, ultimately, the argument for timeliness wins out – because, although work on the fantasy genre continues apace, not only is music under-represented in other collections of essays but the monographs tend to ignore the presence of music altogether. Both Worley and Fowkes make only the very briefest mentions of music in passing, even though Fowkes's opening chapter is on the musical *The Wizard of Oz*; and neither of them includes it as a term in the index, so little importance does it have for them in the construction of the fantasy narrative.

Fantasy as film genre

It need hardly be said that genre is a contested area in film studies. As Jane Feuer notes, "genres are made, not born ... a genre is ultimately an [analyst's] abstract conception rather than something that exists empirically in the real world" (1992: 144), while both Bordwell (1989) and Stam (2000) question the process by which genres are classified and defined. Bordwell lists some of the existing categories of genre used in relation to film to show how inconsistent the criteria for establishing a genre can be:

> by period or country (American films of the 1930s), by director or star or producer or writer or studio, by technical process (CinemaScope films), by cycle (the 'fallen women' films), by series (the 007 movies), by style (German Expressionism), by structure (narrative), by ideology (Reaganite cinema), by venue ('drive-in

movies'), by purpose (home movies), by audience ('teenpix'), by subject or theme (family film, paranoid-politics movies). (Bordwell, 1989: 148)

Stam makes a similar point, noting that "some genres are based on story content (the war film), others are borrowed from literature (comedy, melodrama) or from other media (the musical)" (2000: 14) – and one need only look at this Equinox series to see that genre is defined differently in the construction of different volumes, with animation (technique) standing alongside pornography (content) and horror (theme). One could, in theory, have a pornographic animated horror film, happily demonstrating that, as Stam identifies, the boundaries of genre are very flexible and are not monolithic (*ibid.*: 128). No single film is likely to belong to a single genre: King Kong is as much a part of fantasy as he is of horror.

The film industry itself, unlike film studies, takes a slightly more pragmatic approach to genre: in this context, it is a marketing rather than an analytical tool, and genre normally identifies narrative theme (action, drama, adventure, Western, horror, etc.) as an indicator of what the film is 'about', in order to guide (and entice) the potential viewer. Theme, however, seems to the theorists to be a particularly weak way of defining genre: "any theme may appear in any genre" (Bordwell, 1989: 147); and this is certainly true of fantasy, which seems to be one of the more difficult genres to pin down due to the diversity of the films that have this generic label thrust upon them. Both Worley and Fowkes devote their introductory chapters to a discussion on the nature, typology and problem of the fantasy film genre. For Worley, the problem is presented by fantasy's relationship with science fiction on the one hand and supernatural horror on the other, and he concludes that as a result it "feels poorly defined as a film genre, and often acts as a dumping ground for movies that fail the more recognizable dress code of sci-fi and horror" (2005: 8). The waters are further muddied by the extent to which theory itself elides these three genres: in their discussion of film genre Sobchack and Sobchack group fantasy, horror and science fiction together as the "fantastic genres" (1980: 258); while Lucy Armitt includes in her discussion of fantasy literature "Utopia, allegory, fable, myth, science fiction, the ghost story, space opera, travelogue, the Gothic, cyberpunk [and] magic realism" (2005: 1).

In attempting to define fantasy as a film genre distinct from science fiction, in particular, Worley and Fowkes reach similar conclusions. For Worley, the key ingredient is magic and magical events which defy explanation by scientific or rational means: they require a high degree of willingness on the part of the audience to suspend our disbelief and to trust that what we see is simultaneously fantastic and real rather than real because it is explicable (Worley, 2005: 10). For Fowkes, the key idea is that the audience must perceive a "fundamental break with our sense of reality ... an 'ontological rupture'"

(2010: 2), and again she emphasizes the importance of magic as opposed to science as the source of events that create that sense of rupture:

> The word 'rupture' distinguishes the fantastic elements in fantasy from those in science fiction, where fantastic phenomena are ostensibly extrapolations or extensions of rational, scientific principles. Thus in science fiction, the ability to instantly transport oneself to a distant location will be justified by extrapolating from scientific or quasi-scientific principles ("beam me up, Scotty"), while in fantasy it may be attributed to magic, as in the Harry Potter movies, where characters skilled in magic can use an old boot to 'disapparate' from one place to another. (ibid.: 5)

Another issue both writers identify is that fantasy elements occur in many films that might not immediately be thought of as fantasy films. The classic idea of a fantasy film is located somewhere quasi-medieval or exotic, involves swords, sorcery and quests and finds its paradigm in *The Lord of the Rings*. However, as they also both indicate, there are a great many other films that are also incontestably fantastic in their concept but do not bear any obvious resemblance to the high-fantasy model, such as *Big* (Penny Marshall, 1988), *Groundhog Day* (Harold Ramis, 1993) or any one of the comic-book superhero films from *Superman* (Richard Donner, 1978) and *Batman* (Tim Burton, 1989) to the enormous number of such films made in the last decade. Burton's *Edward Scissorhands* (1990) is equally far removed from high fantasy, while other films appear to be hybrids. *City of Angels* (Brad Silberling, 1998) is both a romance and a fantasy while *Bruce Almighty* (Tom Shadyac, 2003) is both comedy and fantasy. *Pan's Labyrinth* (Guillermo del Torro, 2006) combines fantasy with historical drama, much as *A Matter of Life and Death* (Michael Powell and Emeric Pressburger, 1946) did with wartime drama sixty years earlier; while *Beetlejuice* (Tim Burton, 1985) might be described as black-comedy horror-fantasy. Worley suggests a model to account for all the different types of film that might reasonably be included within the genre by proposing five sub-categories on a scale from the 'realistic' to the 'expressionist'. The most realistic fantasies (perhaps a little counter-intuitively) are the epic fantasies, in which the internal rules applying to magic and the fantastic are most rigid and therefore the ones where the audience is required to suspend its disbelief most completely. This is the type of immersive fantasy Tolkien referred to when he described what the fantasy writer should aim to achieve:

> He makes a Secondary World which your mind can enter. Inside it, what he relates is 'true': it accords with the law of that world. You therefore believe it, while you are, as it were, inside. (Tolkien, 1966: 37)

At the other extreme, the 'expressionist' end of his scale, Worley – again mixing terminology a little – places surrealist fantasies. These are visually flamboyant, fantasy "at its most chaotic" and fantasy here is "a mode rather than a subject" (Worley, 2005: 13) – that is, it becomes a technique or style as much as (or more than) a narrative theme. At that extreme, he places films such as Buñuel's *Un Chien Andalou* (1929) and *L'Âge d'or* (1930), but also Derek Jarman's *Jubilee* (1978); and one might add to this category films involving sudden, surreal ruptures to their narratives such as *Orlando* (Sally Potter, 1992) and *Lost Highway* (David Lynch, 1997). The other categories Worley identifies are fairy-tale, earthbound fantasy and heroic fantasy.

Worley's categories, like any categories, are not entirely discrete, but the 'earthbound fantasies' are slightly problematic, incorporating anything which is set on our own planet at a recognizable point in history, normally contemporaneous to when the film was made. This elides films that approach fantasy in very different ways: *Peggy Sue Got Married* (Francis Ford Coppola, 1986), *Highlander* (Russell Mulcahy, 1986), *Big* (Penny Marshall, 1988), *Meet Joe Black* (Martin Brest, 1998), the various *Harry Potters*, *King Kongs* and Santa movies are all fundamentally the same 'type' of fantasy in this construction.[2] Instead, I would suggest that there are three separate types of fantasy here. In the first, we have films in which the world is exactly as we know it but a single fantasy 'gesture' occurs with the introduction of specific characters, locations or objects that every one within the diegesis of the film acknowledges as fantastic, contradicting everything they previously believed was possible. These films are almost always comedies (or at least light-hearted) and the fantastic intervention is often transformative, allowing characters to learn something about themselves and to approach their lives (post-fantasy) in a new way. This accounts for all the 'age-swap' and time-travel narratives – *Big*, *Peggy Sue Got Married*, *Freaky Friday* (Gary Nelson, 1976), *Groundhog Day* (Harold Ramis, 1993), *The Family Man* (Brett Ratner, 2000), *17 Again* (Burr Steers, 2009), even *Bill and Ted's Excellent Adventure* (Stephen Herek, 1989) – and films where characters (normally children) discover magical objects, such as *The Indian in the Cupboard* (Frank Oz, 1995), *Jumanji* (Joe Johnston, 1995) and *Click* (Frank Coraci, 2006). Here, the fantasy is isolated, located in one specific area of the narrative's construction and recognized as abnormal by all those aware of its existence. Significantly, perhaps, this type of film is not represented in this collection. They are, at heart, human comedies (they always end happily) of self-discovery that use fantasy as a mechanism in the transformation and growth of the protagonists rather than narratives that explore the fantastic itself. In these films, we share with the characters a temporary suspension of disbelief before the world returns to normal.

Closely related to this, my second group is a range of fantasy subgenres in which long-standing human myths and beliefs turn out to have been true all along: again, this acts along much the same lines as the single fantasy gesture, the one thing introduced into the otherwise normal world, but which the audience might accept as 'real' in some sense because it accords with how we suspect (or wish) the world actually works. Some characters in the narrative already know this; others (along with the audience) are invited to discover it, whether it is witchcraft and magic (*The Witches of Eastwick* [George Miller, 1987], *Death Becomes Her* [Robert Zemeckis, 1992], *Practical Magic* [Griffin Dunne, 1998]); mermaids and other mythical creatures (*Miranda* [Ken Annakin, 1948], *Splash* [Ron Howard, 1984]); Santa Claus (*Miracle on 34th Street* [George Seaton, 1947] and countless others); ghosts (*Ghostbusters* [Ivan Reitman, 1984], *High Spirits* [Neil Jordan, 1988], *Always* [Steven Spielberg, 1989]); angels (*It's a Wonderful Life* [Frank Capra, 1946], *City of Angels, Meet Joe Black*) or devils (*Beetlejuice* [Tim Burton, 1988], *Bedazzled* [Harold Ramis, 2000], *Little Nicky* [Steven Brill, 2000]). Again, many of these are light-hearted, but there is also a good proportion that treat their subjects seriously and thoughtfully. There is a single essay in the current collection that falls into this category, Philip Hayward's examination of *The Last Wave*, where the myths-made-real are Aboriginal (or purport to be). Again, in these films, our 'belief' is not unduly challenged: we may already willingly or partially believe in angels or ghosts or mystic spirituality; and even if we do not, the fantastic supernatural as presented in these films taps into something that is nonetheless familiar and accepted as part of a wider cultural epistemology.[3]

By contrast, there are worlds which look very much like ours at the outset but which we rapidly discover hold marvels and horrors beyond anything we ever imagined: monsters (King Kong), immortals (*Highlander*), worlds-within-worlds that now cross into our own (*Last Action Hero* [John McTiernan, 1993], *Harry Potter*). In my third 'earthbound' group, the characters are forced to accept that these things are real, have always been real and will continue to be part of the ongoing reality of their world. As such, they move away from being 'earthbound', part of our own world, and into Tolkien's secondary worlds, with their own rules and natural laws that are now evidently quite different from our own – and hence they find themselves in the immersive waters of fairy-tales and of heroic and epic fantasy. What also sets them apart from the genuine earthbound fantasies is that they are much less uniformly light-hearted. Here, while the idea of self-discovery and transformation for the principal characters is still often an important feature, the exploration of the fantastic is at the core of the film. It is no longer an isolated narrative gesture but creates a rupture between our reality and the diegesis of the film that requires a suspension of disbelief far greater than in the other two types outlined above. This is the type of fantasy that the current volume is most interested in, the fairy-tales, heroic and epic narratives that present worlds fundamentally different from our own in which magic and monsters are both real and serious, and heroes are required to maintain order by controlling the fantastic.

Harry Potter is a good example of the way that epic, immersive fantasy has developed in recent years beyond the sword-and-sorcery model of *The Lord of the Rings* (although both swords and sorcery remain very much in evidence). J. K. Rowling's fantasy world has very rigid rules about the nature of magic, which would place it at the 'realistic' end of Worley's scale – it just so happens that this world exists alongside our own, mundane reality; but our world is thoroughly sidelined in the narrative, generally only appearing at the start of films before we make the rapid transition into the 'real' world of magic.

A recurring element in each episode of the series is the hero's journey (as defined by Joseph Campbell, 1949): the hero is called to adventure, crosses the threshold to the underworld, undergoes trials in order to complete a quest and then returns, bestowing a boon upon the world, which normally translates as making it safer for us all. This idea is reiterated in each one of the *Harry Potter* books and faithfully reproduced in the films. The transition from the 'Muggle' world to the world of magic is therefore an essential part of the quest, crossing the threshold between two realities; but it is further articulated in the way that each film at some point requires Harry to venture into a dangerous place – often underground or alluding to the underworld in some other way, such as the cemetery at the end of *Goblet of Fire* (Mike Newell, 2005) – in order to complete his final battle.

The hero's journey aspect of *Harry Potter* is one of the series' most significant influences on contemporary fantasy film-making. The *Lord of the Rings* trilogy and the *Harry Potter* films are two gigantic franchises that have dominated recent fantasy film, spanning – and extending beyond – the first decade of the twenty-first century. Between them, these two series are largely responsible for re-igniting a cinematic interest in epic, immersive fantasy, specifically in magic and mythology, that had largely lain dormant since the 1980s, although the development of CGI technology has also been a major factor in these developments. *Harry Potter* in particular has had an impact on the type of mainstream fantasy film being made, as is apparent in the basic conceit of many recent fantasy plots: a young person discovers that he or she has magical gifts and an important destiny and must learn how to control these gifts in order to save the day. This basic structure to the narrative of the *Harry Potter* films (where each film essentially reiterates the same process of Harry developing his gifts to defeat a new threat) is found in similar forms in films such as *Eragon* (Stefen Fangmeier, 2006), *The Golden Compass* (Chris Weitz, 2007), *The Seeker: The Dark Is Rising* (David L. Cunningham, 2007), *Stardust* (Matthew Vaughn, 2007), *The Secret of Moonacre* (Gabor Csupo, 2008), *Inkheart* (Iain Softley, 2008), *The Spiderwick Chronicles* (Mark Waters, 2008), *The Last Airbender* (M. Night

Shyamalan, 2010), *Percy Jackson and the Lightning Thief* (Chris Columbus, 2010) and Tim Burton's re-envisioned *Alice in Wonderland* (2010).[4] By contrast, *Lord of the Rings* has fewer obvious imitators – one suspects that film-makers are still very aware of how difficult it is for this type of film to attract an audience, as seen in the 1980s with films such as *Krull* (Peter Yates, 1983), *Ladyhawke* (Richard Donner, 1985) and *The Dark Crystal* (Jim Henson and Frank Oz, 1982). Films which obviously appeal to children, such as *Harry Potter* and its imitators, or which can attach themselves to another genre in addition to their fantasy elements (e.g., comedy, romance, action) generally appear to be more attractive propositions to the film-makers than the quasi-medieval immersive myths of a film like *The Lord of the Rings*.

Fantasy music

Film music, as Claudia Gorbman tells us, weakens our rational defences and "increases the spectator's susceptibility to suggestion" (1987: 5). It draws the spectator in: "film music lowers our thresholds of belief ... lessens awareness of the frame, relaxes the censor ... [and is often] a catalyst in the suspension of judgement" (*ibid.*: 6). If music is felt to be needed in realist cinema, it is clearly even more essential in fantasy cinema in order to draw the spectator into the fantastic secondary world: it is one of cinema's great ironies that something as artificial and extra-diegetic as musical underscore can be so necessary to an audience's belief in the 'reality' of a film narrative.

Perhaps the most surprising omission from this collection is what might be called, to refine Worley's terms a little, 'grand epic fantasy': film franchises in the fantasy genre that are in effect a single film, a single narrative that is on such a grand scale that it has been split into two or more films. The most famous are the two sci-fi fantasy trilogies of *Star Wars* (George Lucas *et al.*, 1977–83; 1999–2005) and *The Lord of the Rings* trilogy, but the *Pirates of the Caribbean* series (Gore Verbinski and Rob Marshall, 2003–11) and *The Matrix* trilogy (Andy and Lana Wachowski, 1999–2003) also fit this description.[5] This kind of epic is quite different from what might be called the serial fantasies of a franchise such as those surrounding Batman and Superman, where each film is self-contained; or even Harry Potter where, despite the connecting thread of his ongoing battle with Voldemort, nonetheless each film (other than the final ones) presents a self-contained narrative, a battle in the ongoing war, that is complete by the closing credits.[6]

The grand epic presents a particular challenge to a film-music scholar on a number of counts. The first is the fact that one is, in effect, dealing with a single film score that extends over two or three films – in all the examples of grand epic cited above, the same composer worked on the score for all parts of the extended narrative, which is not true of the serial fantasies. Tackling the film score for an 'average' 120-minute film can be challenging: the focused listening required, the aural ability to recall fragments of music across a two-hour period in order to make connections between what is happening at different points in the film and the score is, to put it bluntly, very hard work. To try and do this for a film extending over six hours (the first *Star Wars* trilogy) or nine hours (the cinema-release version of *The Lord of the Rings*) or indeed eleven hours (the extended edition) is quite a logistical test; but the logistics are only one part of the problem. The more significant part is the type of scoring strategy employed by films on this grand epic scale. The composers work extremely hard to help the audience navigate their way through the narrative; and they generally do this by writing rigorously thematic, leitmotivic scores. When Williams did this for *Star Wars*, it was widely regarded as innovative, a modern reinvention of a much older style of film scoring, but the problem that it presents to film-music scholars now is that once one has accepted the impressiveness of the composer's achievement, analysing the score becomes, essentially, a jigsaw puzzle of 'spot the leitmotif' and it can be unexpectedly difficult to extract an interesting and enlightening argument from the resulting map of themes. The score functions exactly as it is intended to: it anchors characters and places in a musical location that we recognize when we hear it, even if we do not do so consciously; and in doing this, it helps us to navigate the vast expanse of viewing time across which the narrative stretches. David Butler (2006) has examined the ways in which music operates in relation to time within film; one of his ideas is that music can help tell us *when* in a narrative we are, specifically in instances where the narrative is non-linear in some sense.[7] *Star Wars* is an extremely linear narrative, and there are relatively few non-linear aspects to *The Lord of the Rings*: flashbacks to the history of the ring, to Smeagol's life before he became Gollum; flashforwards as Arwen sees visions of her future with Aragorn; and several instances of Gandalf recounting things he has done and where he has been on occasions when he has been separated from the rest of the Fellowship. But for the most part, this is also a linear narrative. Nonetheless, Butler's ideas about time and musical navigation in relation to the non-linear apply here too, due to the extension of narrative time across films that, in addition to their own duration, were not originally designed to be viewed consecutively but would have been first seen by many viewers at least a year apart. The consistency of Howard Shore's themes becomes an essential part of navigating a narrative that, while fundamentally linear, potentially challenges a viewer's ability to follow what is happening. This is even more pronounced in *The Two Towers*, the middle film of *The Lord of the Rings*, where the Fellowship is divided into several groups, each pursuing its own goal, while the people of Rohan, Gondor and the elves are also all engaged in their own particular storylines. Whilst still linear on a macro-structural level there are multiple narrative arcs operating concurrently at the micro-structural level, all coming back together in the final film. The leitmotivic consistency which allows the viewer to navigate through these arcs by locating characters and places in specific musical environments is also the aspect that makes the scores difficult to discuss in the terms that film-music scholars are fond of: the music has a tendency to write its meaning in large letters rather than subtly exploring the subtexts that we musicologists are so eager to unpick.

The overall coverage of this volume does allow us to see clearly the manner in which fantasy and its musical strategies have changed over time, and this is one of the main reasons that they are generally presented in chronological order. In the opening essay, Mark Brill examines the films of Ray Harryhausen, the producer and master of special effects, who made his distinctive mark on fantasy cinema using stop-motion animation, a strategy emulated in more recent years by director and writer Tim Burton. Harryhausen's fantasies reflected the Hollywood Golden Age fascination with the exotic in his exploration of fantasy narratives drawn from Greek myths and the *Arabian Nights* tales, notably the various voyages of Sinbad, and Brill examines the musical construction of exotic Others in Harryhausen's output, with scores written by Herrmann, Rózsa and Rosenthal.

Coming from an entirely different perspective, Philip Hayward is also concerned with the musical construction of the Other, this time of Australian Aboriginal Otherness in Peter Weir's *The Last Wave* (1977), a film Hayward concludes could probably not have been made in a later, more politically correct, time, because of the way it constructs a fantasy on and around Aboriginal spirituality. The film also represents a significant point in fantastic music, with a move away from the orchestral timbres of classical Hollywood practice in the later 1970s into soundtracks characterized by synthesized, atmospheric and ambient sound. Several essays examine this shift away from orchestral scoring: Lee Barron looks at a specific moment of conflict between orchestral and electronic scores in the music for Ridley Scott's *Legend* (1985), where production company concerns about the audience reception of the film resulted in the UK release using the original orchestral score by Jerry Goldsmith and the US release having a different cut of the film with a score by the German electronica group Tangerine Dream. J. Drew Stephen examines the two scores contributed by Queen to *Flash Gordon* (Mike Hodges, 1980) and *Highlander* (1986), and the specific contribution that the songs and high-energy performances of the band members brought to the tone and reception of those films; while Liz Giuffre looks at David Bowie's performance in and music for *Labyrinth* (Jim Henson, 1984).

The trend towards pop-scoring in films from the 1980s is part of a wider trend in film music at the time, and the pop influence even on more conventional scoring of fantasy films can be heard in *The Princess Bride* (Rob Reiner, 1987), for example, where the main melodic instrument used for the Buttercup's theme is an acoustic guitar – practically the only acoustic instrument used, as the score overall is synthesized rather than played on orchestral instruments. The pop scores bring several added dimensions to the construction of the fantastic, however. On one level, they can counter the suturing function that Gorbman (1987) identifies as an aspect of orchestral scoring, and instead create a sense of distance. Where songs are used, we unavoidably attend to the lyrics of songs we may already know, sung by voices that are overwhelmingly familiar as belonging to Freddie Mercury, Brian May, Roger Taylor and David Bowie. The real world thus intrudes into the fantasy narrative in the form of these musicians and their music, and potentially disrupts our suspension of disbelief by presenting us with something that is unquestionably 'real' in the midst of a fictional narrative. And this intrusion works in the opposite direction as well, the fantastic encroaching on the real world by means of the musicians' pop music videos. The boundaries separating the real and the fantastic are transgressed in *Labyrinth* (discussed by Liz Giuffre in Chapter 5) when we hear Bowie's voice singing 'As The World Falls Down' in the hallucinatory ballroom scene: Jareth (the character he plays in the film) casts a spell to capture Sarah in a magical bubble in which a ball appears to be taking place and the presence of Jareth's voice in the soundtrack seems to reinforce his control of the situation; he is the author of this particular fantasy/spell, and the song signals that. But the voice is also Bowie's voice and Bowie himself is outside the diegesis of the film – yet he places himself within it in the video for this song, which uses colour sequences from the film alongside black-and-white sequences of Bowie in the persona of a 1950s crooner. Moreover, Hoggle – one of the Jim Henson creatures – is transported from the film into the black-and-white sections of the video, which therefore extends the fantasy outside the frame of the film's narrative, a genuinely fantastic transgression of the narrative boundaries that creates an interestingly equal relationship between Bowie and the character he plays as authors of their own fantasies. What Bowie does with this song inside the film and outside it with his video parallels what Jareth is doing with it inside and outside the ballroom.

This kind of fantastic transgression of narrative boundaries is something that popular music lends itself to in fantasy films. Queen's music from *Highlander*, discussed by Drew Stephen in Chapter 3, facilitates movement back and forth between the real and the fantastic on several occasions, whether it is Connor MacLeod in the film quoting the title of Queen's song as he says to the young Rachel "It's a kind of magic" or the astonishingly diegetically confusing video for another of the film's songs, 'Princes Of The Universe'. The video was shot on the *Highlander* set and, like 'As The World Falls Down', includes footage from the film; but then Christopher Lambert (or is it Connor MacLeod?) literally walks out of the film and into the video, crossing swords with Freddie Mercury (whose sword is his trademark microphone stand), while Brian May takes the place of the Kurgan on the stone steps of MacLeod's ruined Scottish castle. This is in direct contrast to other, non-fantastic films where song videos are shot on location and use footage from the film, such as Bryan Adams's 'Everything I Do (I Do It For You') from *Robin Hood: Prince of Thieves* (Kevin Reynolds, 1991), where there is no sense of Adams interacting with the narrative in any way (and, in fact, his voice is never heard in the film, only over the end credits). Fantasy is able to exploit the ambiguities of real musicians in a fantastic context to extend the fantastic beyond the boundaries that normally contain it.

However, despite the trend towards popular music scores in the 1970s and 1980s, one composer is credited with almost single-handedly reviving the sound of classical Hollywood orchestral scoring – John Williams – the first score in this revival being *Star Wars*, closely followed by *Superman* (Richard Donner, 1978). Ben Winters discusses musical romanticism in Chapter 6, and this paves the way for a discussion of orchestral scores from some of the composers most closely associated with fantasy scoring since then. Danny Elfman's score for *Edward Scissorhands*, which established a melancholy fairy-tale sound-world that was widely imitated and is still instantly recognizable today in both scoring and advertising, is discussed by Alexander Binns in Chapter 7; Elliot Goldenthal's *Final Fantasy: The Spirits Within* (Hironobu Sakaguchi and Moto Sakakibara, 2001) is examined by Scott Murphy in Chapter 8; and in Chapter 9 Victoria Hancock and I contrast John Williams's scores for the *Indiana Jones* films in the 1980s with Jerry Goldsmith and Alan Silvestri's music for *The Mummy* films in the 2000s. John Williams again comes to the fore in Jamie Webster's chapter on the first five *Harry Potter* films, which looks at how other composers worked with his themes in the subsequent films and how the different scores reflect the various directors' approach to the *Harry Potter* narrative. The final chapter of the volume looks at the most recent film under discussion and reflects another contemporary trend with the hybrid pop/orchestral soundtrack of *The Sorcerer's Apprentice* (John Turteltaub, 2010). This film continues Jerry Bruckheimer's successful relationship with that other stalwart of fantasy-film production, Disney, a relationship that has also given us the *Pirates of the Caribbean* franchise. Film musicology is still a little uncertain about Bruckheimer's powerhouse of film and television production and his stable of composers that includes Hans Zimmer's Remote Control (formerly Media Ventures): there is a lurking suspicion that their music lacks sophistication, but this chapter demonstrates that the music and sound of *The*

Sorcerer's Apprentice are as imaginatively realized as that of any of the older and more revered fantasy films discussed here.

Fantasy, for so long cinema's slightly embarrassing relative, has thoroughly come into its own in the last decade, and its influence is not restricted to film. The field of videogames offers another route into the immersive world of fantasy, and all the major fantasy films of recent years come with their own videogame versions. Indeed, certain videogames have themselves spawned films, as exemplified here by *Final Fantasy: The Spirits Within*, but other high-profile conversions include *Lara Croft: Tomb Raider* (Simon West, 2001) – an early attempt to model a female adventurer on Indiana Jones – and *Prince of Persia: The Sands of Time* (Mike Newell, 2010). Likewise, television has developed a thriving market for fantasy and fantasy/horror/science-fiction hybrids, such as *Buffy the Vampire Slayer* (Twentieth Century Fox 1997–2002), *Supernatural* (Warner Bros Television, 2005–), *Lost* (Buena Vista Television, 2004–10), *Haven* (Syfy, 2010–) and *Heroes* (NBC, 2006–10). Given the wealth of work currently being produced in fantasy genres, this volume is certainly timely, but there will undoubtedly to be much more to say for many years yet.

Notes

1. Bernard Herrmann composed for films from *Citizen Kane* (Orson Wells, 1941) to *Taxi Driver* (Martin Scorsese, 1976) – this was his final score, although *Obsession* (Brian de Palma, 1976) was released later. He composed just under 80 film scores in his thirty-five-year career and won one Academy award, for *The Devil and Daniel Webster* (William Dieterle, 1941). John Williams, who began composing for television in 1956, wrote his first film score for *Downbeat* (Lou Place) in 1958. He currently has over 130 scoring credits to his name in a career that has spanned more than 50 years. He has won five Academy awards (for *Fiddler on the Roof* (Norman Jewison, 1971), *Jaws* (Steven Spielberg, 1975), *Star Wars* (George Lucas, 1977), *E.T.: The Extra-Terrestrial* (Steven Spielberg, 1982) and *Schindler's List* (Steven Spielberg, 1993), and holds the record for the most nominated individual with almost 40 other nominations to date. There are at least five academic monographs dedicated to Herrmann as well as essays in academic journals, including a special edition of the *Journal of Film Music* (2003). There are currently no academic monographs dedicated to Williams and very little literature examining his music at all outside the popular press; a rare exception is Buhler (2000).
2. These films are all included in Worley's discussion of earthbound fantasy.
3. Many of these films have a foot strongly in the same camp as horror but seem closer to fantasy in that the essential ingredient of horror – fear – is taken out and replaced by comedy. The subject of horror comedies is discussed in Paul (1994); and the music of these films is examined in Halfyard (2010).
4. One of the most curious features of these films is that none of them has been as successful as one might imagine in terms of box-office receipts. Whereas all

the *Harry Potter* films broke even on their US box-office takings alone and made substantial profits overall, almost none of the other fantasy films listed here achieved this and some clearly made substantial losses, notably *The Secret of Moonacre*. Certainly, none of these films achieved box-office success on anything approaching the scale of *Harry Potter*.

5. In both these latter two cases, the first film of the sequence is self-contained but the second and third form a single extended narrative.

6. Again, the final two films present a single narrative which is simply suspended at the close of *Harry Potter and the Deathly Hallows: Part 1* (2010); although the negative outcome of *Harry Potter and the Half-Blood Prince* (Dumbledore's death) creates a far greater sense of continuity in the transition between this and the final story than in previous episodes in the series.

7. I am grateful to Rebecca Shepherd of Macquarie University for making the connection between Butler's essay and possible approaches to examining the music of *The Lord of the Rings*.

References

Armitt, L. (2005), *Fantasy Fiction: An Introduction*, New York: Continuum.

Barker, M., and Mathijs, E. (eds) (2008), *Watching* The Lord of the Rings: *Tolkien's World Audiences*, New York: Peter Lang.

Bellin, J. D. (2005), *Framing Monsters: Fantasy Film and Social Alienation*, Carbondale: Southern Illinois University Press.

Bernanke, J. (2008), 'Howard Shore's *Ring* Cycle: The Film Score and Operatic Strategy', in H. Margolis, S. Cubitt, B. King and T. Jutel (eds), *Studying the Event Film:* The Lord of the Rings, Manchester and New York: Manchester University Press, pp. 176–85.

Bordwell, D. (1989), *Making Meaning: Inference and Rhetoric in the Interpretation of Cinema*. Cambridge, MA: Harvard University Press.

Brennan Croft, J. (ed.) (2004), *Tolkien on Film: Essays on Peter Jackson's* Lord of the Rings, Alhambra, CA: Mythopoeic Press.

Buhler, J. (2000), '*Star Wars*, Music, and Myth', in J. Buhler, C. Flinn, and D. Neumeyer (eds), *Music and Cinema*, Hanover, NH: Wesleyan University Press, pp. 33–57.

Buhler, J. (2008), 'Enchantments of *Lord of the Rings*: Soundtrack, Myth, Language, and Modernity', in E. Mathijs and M. Pomerance (eds), *From Hobbits to Hollywood: Essays on Peter Jackson's* Lord of the Rings, Amsterdam/New York: Rodopi, pp. 231–48.

Butler, D. (2006), 'The Days Do Not End: Film Music, Time and Bernard Herrmann', *Film Studies*, 9, 51–63.

Butler, D. (2009), *Fantasy Cinema: Impossible Worlds on Screen*, London: Wallflower Press.

Campbell, J. (1949), *The Hero with a Thousand Faces*, Princeton: Princeton University Press.

Donnelly, K. J. (2006), 'Musical Middle Earth', in E. Mathijs (ed.), The Lord of the Rings: *Popular Culture in Global Context*, London: Wallflower Press, pp. 172–88.

Feuer, J. (1992), 'Genre Study and Television', in R. C. Allen (ed.), *Channels of Discourse, Reassembled: Television and Contemporary Criticism*, London: Routledge, pp. 138–59.

Fowkes, K. A. (2010), *The Fantasy Film*, Chichester: Wiley-Blackwell.

Gorbman, C. (1987), *Unheard Melodies: Narrative Film Music*, Bloomington: Indiana University Press; London: BFI.

Halfyard, J. K. (2010), 'Mischief Afoot: Supernatural Horror-Comedies and the *Diabolus in Musica*', in N. Lerner (ed.), *Music in the Horror Film: Listening to Fear*, New York: Routledge, pp. 21–37.

Heilman, E. (2003), *Harry Potter's World: Multidisciplinary Critical Perspectives*, New York: Routledge.

Heilman, E. (2009), *Critical Perspectives on Harry Potter*, New York: Routledge.

Margolis, H., Cubitt, S., King, B., and Jutel, T. (eds) (2008), *Studying the Event Film:* The Lord of the Rings, Manchester and New York: Manchester University Press.

Mathijs, E. (ed.) (2006), The Lord of the Rings*: Popular Culture in Global Context*, London: Wallflower Press.

Mathijs, E., and Pomerance, M. (eds) (2006), *From Hobbits to Hollywood: Essays on Peter Jackson's* Lord of the Rings, Amsterdam/New York: Rodopi.

Paul, W. (1994), *Laughing, Screaming: Modern Hollywood Horror and Comedy*, New York: Columbia University Press.

Sobchack, T., and Sobchack, V. C. (1980), *An Introduction to Film*, Boston: Little, Brown & Co.

Stam, R. (2000), *Film Theory*, Oxford: Blackwell.

Thompson, K. (2007), *The Frodo Franchise:* The Lord of the Rings *and Modern Hollywood*, Berkeley: University of California Press.

Tolkien, J. R. R. (1966), *The Tolkein Reader*, New York: Ballantine.

Whited, L. A. (2002), *The Ivory Tower and Harry Potter: Perspectives on a Literary Phenomenon*, Columbia: University of Missouri Press.

Worley, A. (2005), *Empires of the Imagination: A Critical Survey of Fantasy Cinema from Georges Méliès to* The Lord of the Rings, Jefferson, NC: McFarland & Co.

1   Fantasy and the Exotic Other
The Films of Ray Harryhausen

Mark Brill

Starting in the 1940s, the producer and visual effects designer Ray Harryhausen perfected the art of stop-motion animation and with it took the genre of fantasy film to new heights, producing several films that have become legendary. To complement the spectacle of these effects, Harryhausen, along with his producer Charles Schneer, sought the collaboration of some of the most important composers of their day. This chapter will examine the music of *The 7th Voyage of Sinbad* (1958; henceforth *7th Voyage*) and *Jason and the Argonauts* (1963; henceforth *Jason*), both scored by Bernard Herrmann;[1] *The Golden Voyage of Sinbad* (1974; henceforth *Golden Voyage*), scored by Miklós Rózsa; and *Clash of the Titans* (1981; henceforth *Titans*), scored by Laurence Rosenthal. Rather than analysing every cue from all four films, I shall attempt to identify specific musical and filmic elements and distinguish the trends common to fantasy films during this period of film-making.

Because of its narrative depictions of exotic places and unfamiliar cultures, and its emphasis on magic and the supernatural, the fantasy-film genre often provides composers with the occasion for writing spectacular – but rarely subtle – music. It is no accident that some of the finest film scores have been written for fantasy films, as well as (for the same reasons) the related science-fiction genre. Music critic Christopher Husted notes that:

> One of the great attractions of fantasy films for composers is that the numerous encounters with spectacle - a giant Cyclops, sword-wielding skeletons, giant birds, dragons - offer great opportunities for the musical expression of the sublime ... The sublime - the experience of overwhelming emotion, of awe - is at the heart of what Harryhausen's films are about. Spectacular 'sights' rely on the rhetoric that 'larger than life' music supplies.[2]

In particular, an elevated relationship emerged between stop-motion animation and prominent musical scores almost from the inception of sound film with the success of *King Kong* (Merian C. Cooper, 1933), arguably the most influential fantasy film of all. Max Steiner's score for *King Kong* set the bar high not only for fantasy films but for all films, and is probably the most widely imitated score of the first twenty years of the talking era. For its part, stop-motion animation remained at the forefront of fantasy film until the 1970s, when films such as *Westworld* (Michael Crichton, 1973), *Futureworld* (Richard T. Heffron, 1976) and especially *Star Wars* (George Lucas, 1977) ushered in computer-generated imagery (CGI). Even after CGI became widespread, stop-motion animation was never abandoned, and film-makers such as Tim Burton continue to use it with great success.

Fantasy film and Joseph Campbell

Many of the fantasy films of the past hundred years can be closely linked to the comparative mythology theories advanced by Joseph Campbell, who found that myths from diverse cultures, geographical locations and historical eras contain similar archetypal elements. Campbell's seminal work *The Hero with a Thousand Faces* (first published in 1949) posits an archetype story which can be summarized as follows:

> A hero ventures forth from the world of common day into a region of super-natural wonder: fabulous forces are there encountered and a decisive victory is won: the hero comes back from this mysterious adventure with the power to bestow boons on his fellow man. (2008: 23)

Though not all fantasy films follow Campbell's hero quest, many of them do, notably the more recent *Lord of the Rings* trilogy (2001–3), as well as science-fiction films such as the *Star Wars* series (1977–83; 1999–2005) which, as George Lucas has acknowledged, were directly influenced by Campbell's writings (see Campbell, 2003: 186–7).

Since both Greek mythology and the *Arabian Nights* tales were central aspects of Campbell's work, it is no surprise that the four films at the centre of this chapter closely relate to his archetype, although they are constructed with a much-simplified formula (see Table 1.1). Thus, Harryhausen's heroes start out in the (seemingly) ordinary world and undertake journeys to mysterious and magical worlds that are set in motion by father figures. The heroes face dangerous and magical adversaries and trials that they overcome with super-natural or divine aid: in *Jason* and *Titans*, the Greek divinities – Hera, Thetis, Zeus – play important roles, either helping or hindering the hero, whereas Sinbad must rely on his own wits and courage to defeat the magical world. In the end, they are rewarded with great gifts and, of course, the love of the heroines they encounter.

Harryhausen's films rely on tried-and-true elements, and familiar motifs recur over the span of twenty-three years. All four involve oracles that foretell the future. All include supernatural creatures which collapse and shatter, often by

Table 1.1 Elements of Campbell's archetype in Harryhausen's films

	Film			
Archetype	*7th Voyage of Sinbad*	*Jason and the Argonauts*	*Golden Voyage of Sinbad*	*Clash of the Titans*
Hero	Sinbad	Jason	Sinbad	Perseus
Heroine	Parisa	Medea	Margiana	Andromeda
Father figure	Caliph of Bagdad	Pelias	Grand Vizier of Marabia	Zeus
Adversary	Aeëtes	Sokurah	Calibos	Koura
Destination	Island of Colossa	City of Colchis	Lost continent of Lemuria	City of Joppa
Reward	Magic Lamp	Golden Fleece	Fountain of Destiny	City of Joppa

being thrust off a cliff. Two of the films contain battles between underground monsters. Ships' figureheads twice come to life, and the ship voyage itself is a central part of three of the films, culminating in isolated, magical lands. Two of the heroes set out to avenge a destroyed city. The films display prominent cities with exotic markets and elaborate feasts that include nubile female dancers. The list could go on.

The principal driving element of the films is Harryhausen's special effects, around which the plot and characters are constructed, sometimes in complete contravention of the integrity of the original myth. In the films, the moral and/or psychological lessons – an important part of Campbell's myth – take a secondary role to visual spectacle. The adventure is less a conduit for learning a larger life lesson than a convenient travelogue in which to portray Harryhausen's magical creations. The viewer cares less for Jason's or Sinbad's quest than for the battle scenes with Harpies and the Cyclops, and the clash between good and evil becomes almost irrelevant, except as entertainment. The ultimate goal – the Magic Lamp, the Golden Fleece, the Fountain of Destiny – is often reduced to Hitchcock's 'MacGuffin', a plot device which motivates the characters but about which the viewers care little. Likewise, even the characters themselves are often superfluous: we are unconcerned that the skeleton army or the Cyclops dispatches most of the hero's cohorts; indeed, their deaths are a necessary component to the spectacle.

Nor is the issue of historical or cultural authenticity as it relates to the original myths paramount in the film-makers' – including the composers' – intentions, and this too takes a back seat to spectacle. The Greek myths are altered and combined, with characters and plotlines freely modified or altogether invented.

The *Sinbad* films are even more removed from the original stories: very little of the plot of *7th Voyage* is based on the original seventh voyage, but draws instead on the previous six, as well as from other *Arabian Nights* tales and Greek, Indian and Persian mythology.[3] Any element that might fit the visual spectacle is fair game. Eschewing authenticity is par for the course in most American films of any genre, particularly those made before the 1960s. These are not documentaries, and the film-maker's goal is not to educate but to entertain, eliciting responses based more on emotion than on intellect.

Orientalism and the exotic Other

A major trope in fantasy films is the depiction of the exotic Other, which has long been part of colonial and post-colonial European discourse. The hero's journey is that much more dangerous if it takes place in mysterious, unfamiliar locations, where he will confront characters that are not part of his – and thus the audience's – worldview. The Other is a physical threat not only to the main protagonists but also to the moral construct with which the viewer is asked to identify.

Whereas Campbell's monomyth is purported to be universal, the exotic Other is very much a European cultural and aesthetic construct. Relevant to the discussion of these films is Orientalism, the view – examined at length by Edward Said (1978) in his book of that title – that since the eighteenth century Europeans have misrepresented Eastern and Arabic cultures as different, dangerous and inferior. Literary theorist Bart Moore-Gilbert, whose work is discussed in Christiansen (2008: 186), adequately summarizes Orientalist attitudes:

> *The East is characteristically produced in Orientalist discourse as – variously – voiceless, sensual, female, despotic, irrational and backward. By contrast, the West is represented as masculine, democratic, rational, moral, dynamic and progressive.* (Moore-Gilbert, 1997: 39)

The east is further perceived as decadent, luxurious, enticing, intoxicating; the west is ordered, civilized, virtuous. American film-makers inherited this view of the exotic Orient from nineteenth-century writers, philosophers, artists and composers, and the Harryhausen films are no exception, reflecting an Orientalist discourse that remained prevalent throughout the 1970s. All four films are replete with essential oriental signifiers: exotic markets, dark villains, nubile maidens, gongs announcing important figures. In *Jason* and *Titans*, the narrative retains the east versus west, European versus oriental dichotomy, as the Greeks – the quintessential Europeans – battle foes who are either oriental or supernatural, despite the fact that in the original myths all the players were part of the same, fairly homogeneous Greek world. *Jason's* exotic location is the city of Colchis, a (Greek) colony on the eastern shore of the Black Sea (now in the Republic of Georgia). In *Titans*, the Other is found in the city of Joppa, the ancient Phoenician city on the Mediterranean (now Jaffa, in Israel.) Both cities are portrayed as dangerous non-Greek cultures through costumes, sets and music.

In the *Sinbad* films, the depiction of the exotic Other is more complex, as all the protagonists are purportedly oriental. Sinbad begins his journeys in cities (Bagdad, as it is spelled in the film, and the fictitious Marabia) that are exotic to the viewer but familiar to the characters. The east/west dichotomy is suggested by making the mysterious island destinations even more exotic, relying on visual and musical effects that provide a stark contrast with Sinbad's points of departure. The islands are not part of the 'known' Orient and display various disparate cultures incongruently thrown together. The vagueness of the settings allowed the film-makers to throw in whatever exoticism was most convenient to the narrative. Thus, in *7th Voyage*, the fictional island of Colossa seems to belong more to Polynesia than to Middle Eastern culture and is populated by a Cyclops from Greek mythology, a dragon from medieval Europe and a Roc from the *Arabian Nights* tales. In *Golden Voyage*, Sinbad travels to Lemuria, never a locale in any ancient mythology but rather a lost continent hypothesized by nineteenth-century biologists, located somewhere between India and Africa. Its hotchpotch of cultures is also evident: the Vizier of Marabia wears a Greek mask; the centaur and griffin are derived from Greek mythology; the goddess Kali is drawn from Hindu epics; the homunculus is a product of European medieval alchemy; the priest of the Lemurian green men represents the Indian elephant-god Ganesha; and the Fountain of Destiny in the bowels of Lemuria gushes inexplicably in the centre of a Mesolithic Stonehenge-like monument.

Another powerful signifier of Orientalism is the exotic feminine: in Europe's (and later, Hollywood's) version of the Orient, the exotic and the erotic are conflated. Sex – or, more precisely, libertine attitudes towards sex – were thought to be an integral part of eastern cultures, despite the fact that Islamic mores were often far more restrictive than those of either Victorian society or the Hollywood Production Code. Campbell acknowledged that mythological heroes are almost always male, and the Harryhausen films follow suit, with female heroines often relegated to the role of lovers or dutiful brides-to-be. Though they sometimes play small roles in advancing the hero's quest – the diminutive Parisa enters the lamp and befriends the genie; Medea drugs the guards and releases the Argonauts – the heroines are mostly passive love interest. Moreover, they are usually portrayed as part of the Other, to be either saved or conquered, shown the error of their ways and 'civilized', presumably under the supervision of their rescuers. Andromeda, Medea, Parisa and Margiana, despite their exotic origins, quickly side with the heroes who come to rescue/marry them and are thus brought into the comfort zone of civilization. They are 'released' from the exoticism that was holding them hostage and presumably will lose their dangerous eroticism as they are wedded to the heroes.

In addition to exotic locations and heroines, the other element that signifies unfamiliarity and thus danger is the villain, invariably a member of the Other but not necessarily a denizen of foreign lands, sometimes instead appearing within the hero's world. In the nineteenth century, European Others were most often portrayed as either Gypsies, as in Bizet's *Carmen*, or Jews, as in Wagner's *Ring* cycle, where the Nibelung dwarves were subtly identified as Jews to knowing audiences. Derek Scott notes that "the Jew as Other is evident in the nineteenth century (for example in Sullivan's *Ivanhoe*) and the twentieth (for example, in Jerry Bock's music to the Broadway musical *Fiddler on the Roof*, 1964)" (Scott, 1998: 330). The identification of Jews as Others – rarely benevolent and often anti-Semitic – was also inherited by twentieth-century film-makers, who subtly (and sometimes not so subtly) portrayed them as villains, including in fantasy and science-fiction films. Thus, in the *Star Trek* franchise, the alien Ferengis are stereotypically portrayed as short, distasteful, money-grubbing traders with big noses and peculiar names, all signifiers inherited from centuries of European anti-Semitism.

Harryhausen's villains exude characteristics long associated with the oriental Other. In *Jason*, the villain – and the personification of the Other – is King Aeëtes, who mythologically is as Greek as Jason but whose distant kingdom permits him to be portrayed as a mysterious character whose attire, temple and retinue suggest a mixture of Jewish, Zoroastrian and Mongolian culture. Aeëtes' threat is amplified by his command of the supernatural: he harnesses the power of the Hydra to summon the army of skeletons, a display of magic heretofore reserved for the gods. In challenging the power – and thus the authority – of the Greek deities, Aeëtes becomes an even greater threat to the Greek cultural hegemony with which the audience has come to identify. In both *Sinbad* films, the villain/Other is a mysterious magician whose dangerousness is also accentuated by his supernatural powers. In *7th Voyage*, it is Sokurah the magician, whose bald head, black robe and menacing stare exude unsubtle violence and brutality. His transforming of Parisa's handmaid into a cobra vaguely suggests a connection with Indian culture. *Golden Voyage*, filmed sixteen years after *7th Voyage*, essentially recycles the same villain, even assigning him a similar name (Koura). By 1981, in *Titans*, cultural sensitivity precluded the portrayal of the villain as belonging to an ethnic minority, so the film-makers made Calibos a different order of being altogether – though one can speculate as to the insinuations of his physical characteristics.

Another signifier of Otherness is the use of accents. Pursuing a similar line of inquiry, Derek Scott has remarked that in the 1934 film *Chu Chin Chow*, the accents "are 1930s received English (for example, 'dazzled' is pronounced 'dezzled'), with the exception of the leader of the thieves, Abu Hassan (whose accent suggests simply 'foreign villain')" (*ibid.*: 325)· The same dynamic works itself into *Jason* and *Titans*, where the heroes (cast with American actors) and the gods in Olympus (cast with British actors) are meant to evoke recognition from the audience. Conversely, King Aeëtes' inflections are amorphously foreign, and Sokurah's accent appears to be a mixture of Yiddish and Russian – thus, to 1950s audiences, dangerous.[4] By 1974, however, the foreign accents in *Golden Voyage* are no longer just the property of the villain but are assigned to all players. This not-so-successful attempt at a more 'authentic' depiction of the characters is somewhat jarring for the viewer, pointing to the previous effectiveness of the accent as a narrative signifier.

Said's work has been challenged by numerous scholars, including, for example, Matthew Head, who posits alternative interpretations of Orientalist literature as, among others, "a mask for critique of European Society" (Head, 2003, cited in Christiansen, 2008: 190). While a very good case can be – and has been – made for this interpretation, it rarely applies to the films of Harryhausen, who was less concerned with making critical social or political commentary than with showing spectacular entertainment. Over the course of the twenty-three years that separate *7th Voyage* (1958) and *Titans* (1981), there is scarcely any noticeable progression in terms of socio-political commentary. Such progress has been readily identified in other genres, notably including Westerns – *High Noon* (Fred Zinneman, 1952), *A Man Called Horse* (Elliot Silverstein, 1970), *Dances with Wolves* (Kevin Costner, 1990);[5] political dramas – John Frankenheimer's *The Manchurian Candidate* (1962) and *Seven Days in May* (1964); and even science fiction, for example, in the *Star Trek* franchise (1966–2009) and *Star Wars* films (1977–2005). Yet it is hard to identify in Harryhausen's fantasy films any influence of or commentary (either from the left or the right) on contemporary issues, say, the Civil Rights movement or shifting Cold War attitudes. To paraphrase Sigmund Freud: sometimes an evil one-eyed monster is just an evil one-eyed monster.

Orientalism in film music

Attempting to portray exoticism in music has been a major component of western composition since at least the eighteenth century and was a pronounced facet of Romanticism. Derek Scott persuasively identifies distinct Orientalist depictions in nineteenth-century western music, including Turkish, Hungarian, Gypsy, Arabic, Spanish, North African, Indian, Chinese and Japanese music, each with its own cultural signifiers. Scott summarizes these musical elements as follows:

> *whole tones; aeolian, dorian, but especially the phrygian mode; augmented seconds and fourths (especially with lydian or phrygian inflections); arabesques and ornamented lines; elaborate 'ah!' melismas for voice; sliding or sinuous chromaticism ... trills and dissonant grace notes; rapid scale passages ... a melody that suddenly shifts to notes of shorter value; abrupt juxtapositions of romantic, lyrical tunes and busy energetic passages; repetitive rhythms ... and repetitive, small-compass melodies; ostinati; ad libitum sections (colla parte, senza tempo, etc.); use of triplets in duple time; complex or irregular rhythms; parallel movement in fourths, fifths, and octaves (especially in the woodwinds); bare fifths; drones and pedal points; 'magic' or 'mystic' chords (possessing uncertainty of duration and/or harmonic direction); harp arpeggios and glissandi ... double reeds (oboe and especially cor anglais); percussion (especially tambourine, triangles, cymbals, and gong); and emphatic rhythmic figures on unpitched percussion (such as tom-toms, tambourine, and triangle).* (1998: 327)

But Scott also wonders, as elements of Orientalism became cultural codes to European audiences, whether "it is necessary to know *anything* about Eastern musical practices; for the most part, it seems that only a knowledge of Orientalist signifiers is required" (*ibid.*: 309). Later in the same article, he notes that these devices

> *can be applied indiscriminately as markers of cultural difference ... Whether or not any of* [them] *exist in any Eastern ethnic practices is almost irrelevant. As Said* [1978: 177] *explains, "In a system of knowledge about the Orient, the Orient is less a place than a topos, a set of references."* (*ibid.*: 327)

When the nineteenth-century symphonic tradition was inherited by Hollywood film composers, these cultural codes became engrained in American film-goers as well, though the subtle ethnic and cultural distinctions identified by Scott were often lost in the process. Hollywood depictions of Spain, North Africa and the Middle East were generally achieved with castanets, tambourines and pseudo-Arabic modes with lowered or raised second scale degrees. Beyond these geographical areas, musical representations often morphed into a steady, menacing drumbeat, with an accent on the downbeat and falling minor thirds on brass instruments. This motif became the preferred signifier of a generic threat by any exotic Other, used to depict such dissimilar cultures as Native Americans in Westerns, Africans in *Tarzan* movies, Aztecs and Incas in historical dramas, and even Indian Ocean islanders in *King Kong*. Writing about this process as it applied to depictions of Native Americans in classic Westerns, Claudia Gorbman writes: "Hollywood cinema as a rule does not worry about authenticity – one chanting voice with drums is just as good as another"

(2001: 185). Herrmann, Rózsa and Rosenthal, well aware of the inherited Orientalist tradition, often availed themselves of well-established signifiers to portray the exotic. Just as Harryhausen and Schneer were unconcerned with authentic renderings of the Greek myths and Arabian tales, so too were the composers for the most part not particularly worried about authentic musical depictions.

But it was not just a question of ignorance or lack of research: authenticity was deliberately eschewed by composers as being counterproductive to the film-makers' purpose. Roy Prendergast succinctly summarizes the issue:

> The 'Chinese' music written for a studio film of the 1930s and '40s is not, of course, authentic Chinese music but rather represents our popular Occidental notions of what Chinese music is like. The Western listener simply does not understand the symbols of authentic Oriental music as he does those of Western music; therefore, Oriental music would have little dramatic effect for him. (1992: 214; quoted in Scott, 1998: 326)

Scott further refines the point: "Oriental music is not a poor imitation of another cultural practice: its purpose is not to imitate but to represent" (*ibid.*).

What was important for Hollywood film composers, then, was to portray the emotional responses elicited by exotic locations, villains, heroines and so on, without necessarily having recourse to the actual musical aspects of those cultures, aspects which were mostly unknown to American film audiences before the 1970s. Herrmann, Rosenthal and Rózsa provided what Harryhausen and Schneer demanded of them: music which unequivocally elicits from the viewer the 'correct' emotional response to the scene – the response the producers wished to convey. Far removed from any serious question of authenticity, the pseudo-oriental scales and orchestrations, for better or for worse, provide the viewer – long accustomed to such devices – with the knowledge that these locations are exotic and dangerous parts of the world of the Other.

The 7th Voyage of Sinbad

When Bernard Herrmann was hired to write the music for *The 7th Voyage of Sinbad*, he had already scored several films with exotic subjects, including *Anna and the King of Siam* (John Cromwell, 1946), *5 Fingers* (Joseph L. Mankiewicz, 1952), *King of the Khyber Rifles* (Henry King, 1953) and *The Man Who Knew Too Much* (Alfred Hitchcock, 1955). In early 1958, he had finished the scores for Hitchcock's *Vertigo* and Raoul Walsh's *The Naked and the Dead*, and in the spring of that year he began the score for *7th Voyage*.

Throughout his career, Herrmann famously eschewed broad sweeping melodies, complex counterpoint and traditional harmony, preferring instead short repeating figures, motives and simple triads moving in sequence or altogether static. He was especially concerned with focusing the listener's awareness through rich tone colour and unusual orchestral combinations, to convey psychological complexity through basic emotional responses rather than intellectual comprehension. His score for *7th Voyage* relies on atypical instrumentation, often emphasizing the woodwinds, especially oboe, contra-bassoon and cor anglais. Herrmann's biographer Steven C. Smith notes that the composer, along with many other Hollywood musicians, was inspired by Rimsky-Korsakov's *Scheherazade* (1888), but then adds:

> Herrmann's score is much more: its derivations are formal, its specific material unmistakably Herrmann's own. Orchestral timbre is used to create both mood and sense of scale, a world in which evil is characterized by low, 'heavy' instruments and in which heroism and beauty are depicted through light or traditionally balanced textures. (1991: 223–4)

Herrmann's own views of the score for *7th Voyage* are revealing:

> I worked with a conventional sized orchestra ... augmented by a large percussion section. The music I composed had to reflect a purity and simplicity that could be easily assimilated to the nature of the fantasy being viewed. By character-izing the various creatures with unusual instrument combinations ... and by composing motifs for all the major characters and actions, I feel I was able to envelop the entire movie in a shroud of mystical innocence. (ibid.: 223)

Herrmann found that fantasy film allowed him to take certain liberties and go in certain directions that other genres did not permit. Graham Bruce notes:

> Deprived generally of occasions for scoring truly comic films, Herrmann found in [Harryhausen's films] an opportunity for some tongue-in-cheek musical effects which display his virtuosity in scoring and his delight in matching bizarre instrumentation to equally extreme narrative situations. (1985: 109)

As one might expect, the composer was at his best during climactic moments of the film – those which presented Harryhausen's spectacular visual effects. Thus, the cobra dance is accompanied by intertwining, snakelike figures in piccolos, flutes and clarinets, accompanied by slow descending woodwinds and interrupted by strident chords in trumpets, horns, cymbals, triangle and tambourine, elevating the already fantastical dance to another level of wonder (see Figure 1.1). To portray the shrinking of Parisa, Herrmann uses one of his favourite devices, whose effectiveness often conceals its simplicity: a single note (in low woodwinds) slowly falling by half-steps, while another (in strings and vibraphone) rises, also by half-steps, the two notes inexorably pulling away from each other, symbolizing Parisa's inescapable separation from normality.[6]

Figure 1.1 Author transcription of 'Cobra Dance' from *The 7th Voyage of Sinbad*, composed by Bernard Herrmann[7]

The visual and musical tension is at its highest when Sinbad battles supernatural creatures. The lumbering but threatening Cyclops is portrayed musically with low brass, timpani and cymbals. During the subsequent fight, loud brass figures and pounding percussion, timpani, chimes and gong elevate the one-eyed, horned creature to imposing stature and accentuate the overwhelming odds that Sinbad must overcome. The high point of the film, both visually and musically, is Sinbad's duel with the skeleton. Not surprisingly, Herrmann portrayed it with two prominent xylophones, an instrument whose association with human bones had already become a cliché in innumerable musical works – notably in Saint-Saëns's '*Danse macabre*' (1874)

– and would continue as one in dozens of films and cartoons.[8] Herrmann adds to the xylophones his trademark low woodwinds and brass, as well as various rattling wood blocks and castanets.

Smith summarizes the composer's approach to scoring these confrontations:

> Herrmann gives Harryhausen's creatures a sense of gigantic scale through the density of his orchestration: the earth-shaking timpani rolls, cymbal crashes, and grunting brass of the Cyclops; the thumping timpani and bass crawl of the dragon. Elsewhere Herrmann uses strange instrumental juxtapositions for droll effect, as in the cobra woman's dance, which pits shrieking piccolos, brass, and glockenspiel against the seductiveness of low descending woodwinds, or the hatching of the giant birds, a chirping wind and bells figure that grows to encompass low brass and harp as the creatures emerge. (1991: 224)[9]

Graham Bruce's take on these portrayals is slightly different:

> The musical portraits of the fantastic creatures ... illustrate his capacity for creating humor and whimsy in music, an opportunity denied him elsewhere ... More obviously, these monsters in music enable Herrmann's interest in unusual instrumental combinations to be exploited to the full in appropriate response to fantastic narrative situations. (1985: 111)

But the action sequences, impressive as they are, tell only part of the story. Herrmann is also adept at evoking an eerie atmosphere in scenes in which characters enter magical places, a device that both Rózsa and Rosenthal would later imitate. In 7th Voyage, the first sighting of Colossa is accompanied by mysterious but static octave figures in harps, with slow meandering chords first in the low woodwinds, then in the brass. Later in the film, Parisa's entrance into the lamp is accompanied by an ostinato of falling arpeggios played by shimmering bells, celesta and triangles with a low woodwind meandering theme, almost like a quiet music box. Herrmann would reuse this magical entrance in Jason, as Jason is taken to Mount Olympus. The later cue is faster but otherwise almost identical, with the shimmering bells now accompanying harp arpeggios and the meandering theme in the horn. Both scenes convey a sense of mystery and awe, illustrating the wonder of the locations and the power of their inhabitants.

In spite of his preference for short motivic material and tone colours, Herrmann nevertheless did occasionally use traditional themes, melodies and harmony in his scores. One of the most prominent in 7th Voyage is the theme for Princess Parisa, a sinuous melody heard repeatedly in the strings, whose unusual modal characteristics suggest the mysteries of the Orient. Female characters in Harryhausen's films are often portrayed with 'oriental' modes, whose lowered or raised second degree of the scale came almost universally to imply generic oriental culture and particularly its exotic feminine aspects. The connection between the exotic and the erotic is so pointed that in *Titans* the scale appears just as the enticing women of Joppa appear on the screen. Another signifier of female exoticism is the use of tambourines and (especially) castanets, the quintessential Spanish percussion instrument, with little connection to Greek mythology. The use of castanets evolved from the nineteenth-century portrayal of Spanish gypsies to represent danger and sexuality in any European culture outside the mainstream. Both instruments have come to represent the exotic feminine, and it is no accident that Medea, Margiana and Andromeda are all associated – as mythological Carmens – with these instruments.

Herrmann uses many of the signifiers discussed above to evoke other aspects of exoticism: Bagdad is announced with a short fanfare, then portrayed by an ostinato of falling half-steps, around which meanders an undulating theme, first in the woodwinds, then in the strings, with exotic percussion throughout the scene. The 'Sultan's Feast' cue is a reprise of the Overture, with energetic and insistent dissonant grace notes, followed by falling modal figures in the strings and the obligatory triangles and other percussion. Herrmann also liked to suggest Indonesian music in his depiction of the Orient, and he did so on many occasions, for example, in *Anna and the King of Siam* and *King of the Khyber Rifles*, neither of which was actually set in Indonesia. In *7th Voyage*, Herrmann evokes a gamelan when Sinbad's crew encounters the Roc egg. The cue

> opens with a five-octave descent through the [Javanese pelog] scale, followed by flourishes which are a common gesture in that score. The orchestration is important here too: a celesta, two harps, two glockenspiels and two triangles are combined with hard-muted trumpets and stopped horns to capture the coarse metallic sound of the melodic instruments in the Javanese gamelan, recordings of which Herrmann listened to extensively when scoring Anna and the King of Siam.[10]

7th Voyage brilliantly depicts Sinbad's courage and his ability to defeat supernatural foes and win the love of Parisa. Yet there is an element of heroism missing from Herrmann's score. There is no real heroic theme: the overture is more evocative of the mysteries of the Orient, while the battle climaxes reflect more a sense of relief than of overcoming great odds. That lacuna would be remedied in the next epic film on which Herrmann and Harryhausen collaborated.

Jason and the Argonauts

Herrmann's penchant for unusual orchestral colour continued in *Journey to the Center of the Earth* (Henry Levin, 1959), which the composer scored without any string instruments except the harp. "I wanted to create an atmosphere", recalled the composer, "with absolutely no human contact and I eliminated all strings as a way of doing it" (Bruce, 1985: 105). A year later, Herrmann went to the other extreme with *Psycho*, which was scored entirely for strings, becoming a film-music milestone. For *Jason*, Herrmann reprised his stringless experiment. He assembled an enormous wind and percussion orchestra, which tripled or quadrupled the woodwind and brass alongside ten timpani and twenty-six other percussion instruments.[11] Once again, the only strings were the harps, ostensibly because ancient Greece had no bowed instruments. The result was an orchestral colour that mimicked the spectacular images, providing a heroic dimension to the film and creating, as Steven C. Smith puts it, "a militaristic sheen and feeling of power" (1991: 225).

It is significant that Herrmann made an exception for the harp, an instrument long associated with both the fantastic and antiquity. All three composers use the harp liberally in the Harryhausen films, to imitate or evoke the Greek lyre, to depict the gods of the ancient world – as in the numerous appearances and disappearances of Hera – or to accentuate the supernatural, as when Medea's flower potion magically cures Jason's wound, or conversely when Jason revives Medea with the Golden Fleece. Derek Scott, referring to *Scheherazade*, asserts that "Rimsky-Korsakov changes the harp's connotation of a mythical past to one of oriental exoticism" (Scott, 1998: 327). In *7th Voyage* and *Jason*, Herrmann repeatedly combines this exoticism with the wonder elicited by the film's magical elements.

If the score in *7th Voyage* had failed to evoke Sinbad's heroism clearly, the overture in *Jason* leaves no doubt as to the epic qualities of the title character:

> *Jason's title overture ... is the score's most distinctive sequence: a heroic, stirring battle march, Wagnerian in its militaristic grandeur and chorus-like brass voices. Its theme dominates Herrmann's score, the most monochromatic and self-derivative of his work for Harryhausen.* (Smith, 1991: 225)

The overture theme, with its distinctive arpeggiated major triad, bright trumpet fanfares and loud percussion, is closely associated with both Jason and his ship, the Argo. Its larger-than-life quality recurs throughout the film, for example, during the first sighting and subsequent departure of the Argo, and when it is rebuilt after being destroyed by Talos.

But heroism is not limited to Jason, and other epic moments occur which do not include the opening battle march, including prominently the various brass fanfares at the Olympic games, Hermes' ascent to Mount Olympus and Medea's rescue from the sea. Nor is Jason the only character who has a motif: the goddess Hera is repeatedly revealed by a quiet falling and rising figure in clarinets, while Medea is frequently portrayed by a furtive love theme, first in the woodwinds, then in the brass. Medea becomes even more mysterious when she performs an exotic syncopated temple dance, which Herrmann scores with prominent harps and tambourines.

Despite Jason's heightened heroic quality and Medea's exoticism, it is the confrontations between Jason's crew and supernatural creatures that remain the film's highlights, both visually and musically. The attack by the statue Talos is accompanied by a slow, terrifying brass and timpani march that culminates in the destruction of the Argo. Graham Bruce likens Talos' march to that of the robot Gort in another film scored by Herrmann, *The Day the Earth Stood Still* (Robert Wise, 1951), where "instead of the low woodwinds that join the loud brass [in *Jason*], we find in this earlier cue the electronic instruments that link Gort to the world of outer space" (Bruce, 1985: 105).

The other-worldly menace evoked by Herrmann in the earlier film is effectively reprised in *Jason*, with respect not only to Talos but to other mythological creatures as well. The Harpies are portrayed with pecking woodwinds and wild flurries in the harps – a musical pun perhaps. When Jason's crew attempts to capture the creatures, Herrmann reverts to a harmonically static but insistent triplet figure in the clarinets (later brass), with falling figures in the low woodwinds. Herrmann imbues the scene with supernatural terror, relieved only when everything shifts suddenly to the major – with crashing cymbals – as the Harpies are captured.

The skeleton duel in *7th Voyage* was so successful that five years later Harryhausen reprised it in *Jason*'s climactic battle, in which Jason and his cohorts fight an army of skeletons in perhaps the most famous stop-motion animation scene in film history. The living skeleton thus jumps from *Arabian Nights* tale to Greek myth, though it is native to neither. Herrmann introduces *Jason*'s skeleton army with the *Dies Irae* chant (another long-time signifier of the supernatural) in the low brass, then reverts to the rattling xylophone cliché, though it is now combined with wood blocks and castanets and integrated into an orchestral texture which does justice to the spectacular visuals. The passage is the dazzling 'Scherzo Macabre', which was borrowed (but re-orchestrated) from Herrmann's own *Nocturne and Scherzo* (1935).[12] Herrmann's choice of the word 'macabre' in the title is another intertextual reference to Saint-Saëns's 'Danse macabre', with its equally prominent use of xylophones and programmatic dancing skeletons. His choice of the word 'scherzo' suggests that the passage is far from dark and brooding, instead displaying elements of humour and light. Douglass Fake's liner notes are worth reproducing here:

> With a blood-curdling shriek the skeletons attack. Ray Harryhausen's effects and Bernard Herrmann's virtuoso scherzo come together in a highlight of their respective careers. Scored for brass, woodwinds and percussion, with particular color from xylophone, piano, tambourines and harps, the music works both as accompaniment to the on-screen action and as an example of music in the

foreground. A ferocious pace propels the scene forward and jagged, animated figures accent the movements of the skeletons sword-fighting the Argonauts. It's literally a 'tour de force' for the musicians. Adding to the challenge is unusually difficult scoring for trumpets and in particular, French horns. Just about every technique is called upon from the brass, including open and stopped playing, muted glissandos and flutter-tongued passages. For over three minutes the music becomes one giant musical monster of motion, color, spectacle, and most of all, power. The fight does finally come to an end. As the skeletons are defeated and the Argonauts leap to safety, Herrmann brings the orchestra to a piercing high trumpet cry and the music slashes dramatically to a close.[13]

As in *7th Voyage*, Herrmann also shines when he scores the depiction of magical entrances that reflect either wonder and awe, as when Jason appears at Mount Olympus, or imminent danger and eerie dread, as when he first beholds the Golden Fleece, with shimmering vibraphones and harp glissandos. For the entrance of Hercules and Hylas to the chamber of the gods, Herrmann reverts to a device he used effectively five years earlier in 'Carlotta's Portrait' from *Vertigo*: a static but insistent octave figure in the harps, under which a pair of flutes (later clarinets) in thirds slowly descend a chromatic scale, conveying in both films the foreboding of unknown things to come.

Herrmann's portrayal of a Greek dance during the feast is one of the few attempts to provide musical authenticity. The music emerges diegetically from six instrumentalists on screen: harp, two drums, hanging bells struck with mallets and two double-reed Greek auloi, accompanying sensuous maidens who perform a Greek dance of doubtful authenticity.[14] This dance is contrasted to the one later at Colchis, where both the music and the dancing are far more exotic and 'oriental'. Another diegetic moment is when Hermes plays on a lyre a tune reminiscent of the pastoral English folk song 'Greensleeves', which then becomes a motif for Mount Olympus.

One of the signifiers pertaining to departing ships in period film is the trumpet fanfare accompanied by a slow drumbeat, the latter played by or representing the on-board drummer who marks the rhythm for the oarsmen. This device was used effectively as a plot point by Rózsa in *Ben-Hur* (William Wyler, 1959), where the ship's drummer diegetically accelerates the beat (accompanied by an off-screen, non-diegetic brass choir) in order to test Ben-Hur's endurance. Herrmann once again uses the device in *Jason*, though his timpani do not always coincide with the strokes of the Argo's on-screen drummer. The signifying value conveyed by the slow drumbeat was so engrained for audiences in the 1960s and 1970s that even sailing ships that did not have oars were portrayed with the device, including Sinbad's ship in *Golden Voyage*. By 1981, the slow drumbeat did not even have to represent a ship, but merely the beginning of a journey, as in *Titans* when Perseus and his party initiate their inland quest on horses.

An important emotional (if not narrative) point in *Jason* is when Hercules, having failed to find Hylas, leaves the Argonauts and continues his adventures alone. Herrmann decided to score this scene with one of the most ancient surviving pieces of music, the 'Stasimon Chorus', composed in the fifth century BC for Euripides' drama *Orestes* (408 BC), quite possibly by the playwright himself.[15] Though there is no direct connection between the myths of Orestes and Jason, Herrmann may have been swayed by the fact that the singers of Euripides' chorus are women from the city of Argos (though the Argonauts' ship, the Argo, was named after its builder, not the city).[16] In any event, the chorus begs for protection and emotional release for Orestes, who has recently killed his mother Clytemnestra. The text of the chorus is as follows:

> You wild goddesses who dart across the skies seeking vengeance for murder, we implore you to free Agamemnon's son from his raging fury. We grieve for this boy. Happiness is brief among mortals. Sorrow and anguish sweep down on it like a swift gust of wind on a sloop, and it sinks under the tossing seas.
> (Burkholder and Palisca, 2006: 5)

In the film, Herrmann omits the words and the chorus is rendered instrumentally, but the invocation to the gods is clear: a plea for Hercules to be released from the trauma of having caused the death of Hylas – the imploration to the gods is a narrative motif that pervades both *Jason* and *Titans*. In ancient Greek tragedy, a stasimon did not describe action but rather was a stationary piece that conveyed and accentuated a static mood. Herrmann picks up on the device to comment on the action: the unusually slow rhythm emphasizes Hercules' anguish and distress; the sinuous and disjointed melody conveys an other-worldly character, far removed from not only European common practice but also the contemporary film-music culture (from which Herrmann often disassociated himself). The torment of Orestes/Hercules is perfectly illustrated by the falling chromatic figure of Euripides' chorus, which fits perfectly into Herrmann's motif-driven language. Herrmann thus accesses not only the ancient musical material but its emotional aesthetic as well. The juxtaposition of ancient music with Herrmann's modern idiom is, stylistically, neither inconsistent nor disjointed.[17]

The Golden Voyage of Sinbad

The Hungarian composer Miklós Rózsa was a veteran of fantasy films, having scored two of the most prominent and successful early entries in the genre, *The Thief of Bagdad* (Michael Powell *et al.*, 1940) and *Rudyard Kipling's Jungle Book* (Zoltan Korda, 1942), as well as a number of biblical epics (*Ben-Hur; King* of *Kings*, Nicholas Ray, 1961; *Sodom and Gomorrah*, Robert Aldrich, 1962) and other films that took place in antiquity (*Quo Vadis?* 1951; *Julius Caesar*, Joseph L. Mankiewicz, 1953) or in north Africa (*The Four Feathers*, Zoltan Korda, 1939; *Song of Scheherazade*, Walter Reisch, 1947). Thirty-four years after *The Thief of Bagdad*, Rózsa was called upon to score very similar characters and locales for *Golden Voyage* – both films, for example, contain the Indian-looking temple of Kali, the goddess herself and the mysterious green men who attend her. By 1974, however, his depiction of the exotic had changed, though he still relied on many of the enduring cultural codes and Orientalist signifiers.

Rózsa makes full use of the film's geographical hotchpotch to display various musical cultures. Lemuria is initially portrayed musically with an Arabic/oriental string melody, complemented by obligatory triangle and tambourines. Yet visually Lemuria shows many characteristics of Hinduism and for viewers paying attention, Rózsa's music provides a marked cultural disconnect. His use of exotic signifiers, however, is appropriate in light of what was coming: to evoke 'Hinduness' at this point would undermine Kali's 'authentic' dance a few minutes later. Before Kali's appearance, Harryhausen and Rózsa introduce yet another element of Otherness, but one which is primal and uncivilized: the green men. They are represented musically neither by the Arabic/oriental music of Sinbad's world nor by the Indian/Hindu sounds of Kali's supernatural realm but rather by the 'primitive' and 'barbaric' signifiers of the day: steady drumbeats and rattle sticks, played diegetically by the green men themselves. Later, the green men play a shofar-like ram's horn to summon the centaur.

Having travelled, both visually and aurally, from the 'oriental' world to the 'primitive' world, we now reach the magical world of Lemuria, where the six-armed Hindu goddess Kali stands guard. When Kali comes alive, the 'barbaric' drumming of the green men is replaced by 'authentic' Indian instrumentation: sitar, tabla, tambura and manjira cymbals. The historical complexity of this music signals a shift to a higher order of being, represented by Kali and her elaborate dance. By 1974, contemporary western audiences would have had no problem identifying the sounds of Indian classical music, which had gained popularity with the emergence in the West of Indian musicians such as Ravi Shankar and its embracing by the Beatles. Yet Rózsa's attempt to dispel the old cultural codes by relying on the audience's familiarity with this music was risky, and he did so at his own peril. In spite of its purported authenticity, the Indian passage is somewhat jarring within the context of the film, awkwardly bringing attention to itself in the midst of the brass and percussion sounds that had hitherto been associated with the fantasy genre.

Rózsa attempts to bring in some authenticity at other points in the film, including a short passage on the ship in which Haroun diegetically plays an 'oriental' tune on what he calls a lute. Recalling Herrmann's use of the Javanese pelog scale in *7th Voyage*, Rózsa employs it to depict the death of Koura in the Fountain of Destiny and the appearance of the Untold Riches. That Rózsa essentially duplicates Herrmann's instrumentation – highlighted by a shimmering celesta – suggests the allusion is neither unconscious nor accidental.

The influence of Herrmann's earlier scores is also evident when Sinbad first sees the homunculus flying overhead, which Rózsa depicts with a rising harp figure, recalling Jason's ascension to Mount Olympus. Rózsa also mimics Herrmann's evocation of eerie atmosphere for moments when characters enter magical places: as the Fountain of Destiny is first revealed, shimmering brass and string figures, accompanied by the ubiquitous xylophone, recall Herrmann's first depiction of the Golden Fleece eleven years earlier. The connection between human bones and xylophones is still present in *Golden Voyage*, as the bone-laden lair of the centaur is portrayed aurally with the instrument. Rózsa, however, takes it one step further. His depiction of Sinbad's battle with Kali – considered by many the film's centrepiece – also includes the xylophone. Seven years later, Rosenthal again used the xylophone, albeit more subtly, to depict the clash between Perseus and Calibos, suggesting that the instrument had metamorphosized from depicting only skeletons to representing any battle between the hero and a supernatural humanoid creature.

Clash of the Titans

Laurence Rosenthal's previous forays into exoticism and fantasy film included *The Island of Dr. Moreau* (Don Taylor, 1977) and *Meetings with Remarkable Men* (Peter Brook, 1979). But the biggest influence on his score for *Titans* was neither of those films, nor the works of Herrmann or Rózsa, but rather the composer who would come to dominate film composition for the next several decades: John Williams. Few composers in Hollywood escaped Williams's influence, whose scores for *Jaws* (Steven Spielberg, 1975), *Star Wars* (George Lucas, 1977), *Superman* (Richard Donner, 1978) and *The Empire Strikes Back* (Irvin Kershner, 1980) pervaded popular culture. *Titans*' aural similarities to Williams's scores is less surprising when one considers that during this period the two composers shared the same orchestrator, Herbert Spencer, who is partially credited with contributing to Williams's distinct sound.

Rosenthal's score is far more Romantic than those of Rózsa and Herrmann. He uses a full orchestra and his themes are melodically lavish and filled with triumphant brass fanfares, as opposed to the atmospheric, motif-driven material of the earlier composers. Thus, *Titans*' Mount Olympus is portrayed with lush chords in the strings and glorious brass flourishes, a clear contrast to *Jason*'s Mount Olympus, which, as noted, was imbued with a sense of static awe and mystery. The two main themes of *Titans* are more conventional than those of its predecessors: the Heroic/Perseus theme, first heard in the opening, is a triumphant fanfare, usually played in the brass with prominent triangles, and is distinctly reminiscent of the Rebel Fanfare from *Star Wars*. The other important theme is the Love/Andromeda theme, a slow, romantic melody that is subtly 'orientalized' by a neighbouring note on the flat second-scale degree (see Figure1.2). When Perseus gazes on the sleeping Andromeda, only a segment of this theme is first heard in the woodwinds, signalling that at this point the love is one-sided. Later, during their engagement, the love theme reappears in its entirety in lush strings. It also appears prominently at the end of the film, when Perseus and Andromeda consummate their marriage and are immortalized in the stars.

Figure 1.2 Author transcription of 'Love/Andromeda Theme' from *Clash of the Titans*, composed by Laurence Rosenthal

A favourite device of Rosenthal's is to withhold music when the supernatural appears, only to bring it in after the action reaches a climax. Thus, the first attack of the Kraken contains no music, which then enters dramatically to showcase the devastation of the city of Argos. The initial taming of Pegasus is silent but once the horse is tamed, Perseus' heroic theme re-enters, first in the brass, then in the strings. Similarly, no music is initially heard during confrontations between Perseus and supernatural characters but enters when the hero is gaining the upper hand (with tension-filled themes) and is ultimately victorious (with triumphant themes and fanfares). In two prominent battles – with the two-headed dog Dioskilos and again with the giant scorpions – Perseus initially (and silently) loses his magic sword, only to recover it as the heroic theme reappears in brass and percussion. The exception comes in the final confrontation with the Kraken, which is scored throughout, intertwining dark threatening chords with the heroic theme.

Yet, despite his contemporary style, Rosenthal was also influenced to a certain degree by Herrmann's and Rózsa's earlier scores and, for brief moments, the music reverts back to the atmospheric tone colour of the earlier composers. Thus, when Perseus discovers the divine weapons, and especially every time he puts on or takes off the magic helmet, Rosenthal reprises Herrmann and Rózsa's shimmering harp and percussion effects.[18] Calibos' transformation is portrayed with indefinite and dissonant high string harmonics, along with scattered percussion, prominently including a cabasa that evokes the rattlesnake-like danger of the creature seen only through shadow. The first sighting of the mechanical owl Bubo is a clear allusion to the first sighting of the homunculus flying overhead in *Golden Voyage* and to portray it Rosenthal once again reverts to the shimmering harp effect that, as noted earlier, Rózsa had borrowed from Herrmann. In another instance, the mysterious crossing of the river Styx recalls the earlier composers' 'magical place' atmosphere, here recreated with string harmonics and tremolos, timpani and trombones. The eerie atmosphere is further developed with harp figures as Perseus arrives at the Isle of the Dead, and again as he confronts Medusa, now with an even greater sense of dread: to the tremolo string harmonics are added dissonant brass flourishes and ethereal gongs and bells. Ultimately, though, the more conventional victorious brass fanfare reasserts itself as Perseus emerges from the temple with Medusa's head, striking the familiar pose from Cellini's famous statue.

As Rózsa had done in *Golden Voyage*, Rosenthal relies on cultural codes from completely disparate cultures and eras, juxtaposing anachronistic elements for the sake of the narrative. Thus, during the brief engagement scene between Perseus and Andromeda, a dancer entertains the court accompanied by an unseen but presumably diegetic ensemble of flute, triangle, castanets and a lyre-like harp, playing a melody in 6/8 time. Yet, in contrast to *Jason*'s feast scene (meant to recall antiquity) or Medea's dance (meant to suggest oriental exoticism), both the music and the dance in *Titans* are more evocative of medieval courtly dances. Other musical cues also indicate Rosenthal's reliance on cultural signifiers: as Perseus is magically taken to Joppa, a soft, high flute plays an 'oriental' scale. The exotic market at Joppa is portrayed by a bouncy theme with woodwinds and the obligatory tambourines, before switching to a darker and more 'oriental' theme in the lower strings when the seductive women appear. As in *Golden Voyage*, the shofar is again portrayed as an Otherness signifier, played by Calibos to summon the goddess Thetis and by Perseus to summon Charon the boatman. Yet when alpenhorns are used to summon the Kraken towards the end of the film, one would be hard-pressed to infer from them any commentary on the Otherness of Alpine cultures.

Rosenthal has less overall music than his predecessors. His score is imbued with a sense of innocence and wonder, different from the dark passages or ironic humour of Rózsa and Herrmann. Ultimately, he was influenced not only by John Williams's aural characteristics, but also by the sense of optimism found in *Star Wars* and *Superman*, a sense of optimism not found in the previous generation of fantasy film, but also absent from the next generation, for example, in Howard Shore's *The Lord of the Rings* scores.

Conclusion

Earlier in this essay I argued that Harryhausen's films were not particularly concerned with depicting political or social change. Yet one can detect in the music of Harryhausen's composers a progression that indicates just such a shift in musical and social commentary. While *7th Voyage* and *Jason* were clearly still imbued with traditional Hollywood cultural codes (particularly those relating to Otherness and exoticism), the scores of *Golden Voyage* and *Titans* begin to reveal a different attitude towards those representations. As noted, Miklós Rózsa had scored some of the earliest fantasy films, including *The Thief of Bagdad* in 1940, and as such was responsible for defining many of the musical depictions of exotic cultures. Yet by the time he scored *Golden Voyage* in 1974, Rózsa was looking beyond some of the Hollywood cultural codes he had helped create. It is perhaps here that we see for the first time a transitional milestone: Rózsa's attempt at a more 'authentic' score, including notably his use of Indian music and instruments to depict an Indian deity, signals a necessary break with the stubborn codes of Hollywood's Golden Age.

These codes would not be abandoned altogether (as we saw in Rosenthal's score for *Titans*), but henceforth the exotic Other and all its implications would generally entail a greater level of research and a more objective understanding of non-western cultures on the part of composers and directors. The scores of historical dramas such as *Gladiator* (2000) – with composer Hans Zimmer's depiction of North African culture – and fantasy films such as the *Lord of the Rings* trilogy (Peter Jackson, 2001–3) – in which Howard Shore infuses the Hobbits' Shire with unmistakable Irish elements – attest to this shift. Taken together, these films chart a sense of change in fantasy narratives and their scoring in a socio-cultural sense, particularly in their relationship to Otherness and exoticism.

Notes

1. Herrmann also scored two other Harryhausen films: *The Three Worlds of Gulliver* (1960) and *Mysterious Island* (1961).
2. Christopher Husted, liner notes for Bernard Herrmann (1998), *The 7th Voyage of Sinbad*, performed by the Royal Scottish Orchestra, conducted by John Debney, Varèse Sarabande VSD-5961 [CD].
3. The finding of the Roc egg by Sinbad's crew (and their subsequent consumption of the Roc chick) is a key narrative element in the fifth voyage. The Cyclops cooking the crew member on a spit, as well as Sinbad blinding him, is taken from the third voyage, though originally the creature was not a Cyclops.
4. Sokurah was portrayed by the British but Indian-born actor Torin Thatcher, who specialized in villain roles.

5. See C. Gorbman (2001) for an analysis of the changing cultural and political attitudes of so-called liberal Westerns such as *Dances with Wolves*, which attempted to portray Native Americans in both a more authentic and less offensive light.

6. Two years later in *Psycho* (Alfred Hitchcock, 1960), Herrmann famously used the same device – though with the notes pulling together rather than apart – in the scene where Lila Crane slowly approaches Norman Bates's gothic house.

7. This transcription is taken from Herrmann's manuscript score, held in the Bernard Herrmann Papers, 1927–1977 (PA Mss 3), in the Special Collections of the University of California at Santa Barbara.

8. See, for example, the animated short *The Skeleton Dance* (Walt Disney, 1929), in which a skeleton actually becomes a xylophone, diegetically playing Carl Stallings's arrangement of Edvard Grieg's 'March of the Trolls' from *Peer Gynt* (1875).

9. Smith is slightly mistaken regarding the orchestration of the cobra woman's dance, which, as seen in Figure 1.1, contains no glockenspiel.

10. Husted, liner notes for Herrmann (1998), *The 7th Voyage of Sinbad*.

11. Douglass Fake, liner notes for Bernard Herrmann (1999), *Jason and the Argonauts*, performed by the Sinfonia of London, conducted by Bruce Broughton, Intrada MAF-7083 [CD].

12. Herrmann often borrowed materials from his own previous scores, radio shows and concert works and neither *7th Voyage* nor *Jason* was an exception. Thus, *Jason* borrows from *5 Fingers*, *Beneath the 12-Mile Reef* (Robert D. Webb, 1953), *The Kentuckian* (Burt Lancaster, 1955) and *Mysterious Island* (Cy Enfield, 1961). Herrmann's self-borrowings are explored in depth in Wrobel (2003).

13. Fake, liner notes for Herrmann (1999), *Jason and the Argonauts*.

14. The music is actually played by flutes, clarinets, percussion, castanets and harp.

15. The other Greek piece that routinely appears in music history survey courses is the so-called 'Epitaph of Seikilos' from the first century AD, which was used by Rózsa as Nero's first song in *Quo Vadis?* (Mervyn LeRoy, 1951). Rózsa had done extensive historical research for *Quo Vadis?* down to the design of Roman instruments. Herrmann was undoubtedly aware of this precedent.

16. Eighteen years after *Jason*, Harryhausen would portray – and destroy – the city of Argos in *Clash of the Titans*.

17. Rózsa's similar juxtaposition in *Quo Vadis?* was criticized for just such an inconsistency by critic Lawrence Mortin. (See Prendergast, 1992: 128.)

18. At these points, Rosenthal also engages in some 'catching' (or mickey-mousing), using string glissandi to accentuate Perseus' invisible steps in the sand.

References

Bruce, G. (1985), *Bernard Herrmann: Film Music and Narrative*, Ann Arbor, MI: UMI Research Press.

Burkholder, J. P., and Palisca, C. V. (2006), *Norton Anthology of Western Music. Volume 1: Ancient to Baroque*, 5th edn, New York & London: W. W. Norton.

Campbell, J. (2003), *The Hero's Journey: Joseph Campbell on His Life and Work*, 3rd edn, Novato, CA: New World Library.

Campbell, J. (2008), *The Hero with a Thousand Faces*, Novato, CA: New World Library.

Christiansen, P. (2008), 'Turk in the Mirror: Orientalism in Haydn's String Quartet in D Minor, Op. 76, No. 2 ("Fifths")', *19th Century Music*, 31 (3), 179–92.

Gorbman, C. (2001), 'Drums along the L.A. River: Scoring the Indian', in J. Walker (ed.), *Westerns: Films Through History*, New York: Routledge, pp. 177–96.

Head, M. (2003), 'Musicology on Safari: Orientalism and the Spectre of Postcolonial Theory', *Music Analysis*, 22 (1–2), 211–30.

Moore-Gilbert, B. (1997), *Postcolonial Theory: Contexts, Practices, Politics*, London: Verso.

Prendergast, R. M. (1992), *Film Music: A Neglected Art*, 2nd edn, New York: Norton.

Said, E. W. (1978), *Orientalism: Western Conceptions of the Orient*, London: Routledge & Kegan Paul.

Scott, D. B. (1998), 'Orientalism and Musical Style', *Musical Quarterly*, 82 (2), 309–35.

Smith, S. C. (1991), *A Heart at Fire's Center: The Life and Music of Bernard Herrmann*, Berkeley and Los Angeles: University of California Press.

Wardell, D. (1976), 'Music to Commit Murder By', *Soho Weekly News*, 9 September.

Wrobel, W. (2003), 'Self Borrowing in the Music of Bernard Herrmann', *Journal of Film Music*, 1 (2/3), 249–71.

2   Numinous Ambience
Spirituality, Dreamtimes and Fantastic Aboriginality

Philip Hayward

Australian film-makers have represented Aborigines (and Torres Strait Islanders) on screen since the earliest days of the medium, initially in short ethnographic/travel films and subsequently in feature-length productions. Notable examples of the latter include Charles Chauvel's *Uncivilised* (1936) and *Jedda* (1955), Australian cinema 'revival' films such as *Walkabout* (Nick Roeg, 1971) and *Storm Boy* (Henri Safran, 1976), and recent features such as *Yolngu Boy* (Stephen Johnson, 2001), *Rabbit-Proof Fence* (Phillip Noyce, 2002)[1] and *Ten Canoes* (Rolf de Heer, 2006).[2] As might be expected, these films are imbued with ideologies that mirror the social-political zeitgeist of the periods in which they were produced and the variously affirmative and/or dissenting agendas and imaginations of their authors. In this manner, like any representation, the films reveal as much about the imagination of Australia's colonizers as they do of actual Aboriginal cultures and communities and the manner in which they inhabit the spaces of the Australian continent.[3] (Australian) Aboriginality has also registered an occasional presence in Hollywood and global cinema, where it has been posed as an ultimate Other to the rational and increasingly technologized west in films such as *The Right Stuff* (Philip Kaufman, 1983), *Where the Green Ants Dream* (Werner Herzog, 1985) and *Until the End of the World* (Wim Wenders, 1991).

Central to the image of Aboriginality as pre-modern Other is an interpretation of Aboriginal concepts of spirituality and attachment to nature. The latter concepts are, of course, highly complex: 'nature' being a concept of the flora and fauna of the living world as a coherent system within a broader geo-material one; and 'spirituality' being a broad catch-all term for the imagination of and engagement with a transcendent reality and power. Perhaps the best-known aspect of Aboriginal spirituality is that of its Dreamtime. This term refers to Aboriginal mythologies of creation and the earliest period of human life, when interaction with powerful entities shaped landscape, the biomass and human destiny. The concept first appeared in the work of the late-nineteenth-century anthropologists Gillen and Spencer and reflected their engagement with the Central Australian Arrente people and their common belief that the remote past was [an] *alcheringa* – a state that they understood and translated as "dreamtimes, in which their mythic ancestors lived" (Dean, 1996: 12). Current perceptions of this state as a core pan-Aboriginal concept appear to derive largely from the research of the Anglican clergyman and anthropologist A. P. Elkin, particularly as asserted in his 1969 article 'Elements of Australian Aboriginal Philosophy'. As critics such as Dean have identified, while Elkin's particular characterization of the Dreamtime may have accurately represented the cosmology of the Northern Territory Murinbata clan (at least at the time he researched them), there are a wider variety of inflections and perceptions of historical consciousness across different Australian Aboriginal societies than Elkin's work suggests. Drawing on a range of sources, Dean has identified a set of spiritual perceptions core to traditional Aboriginal societies:

> There is no sharp distinction between the sacred and secular, since the spirit world and human world interpenetrate. All aspects of the Aboriginal environment are affected by the power of spirits. The very land itself is a kind of 'church'; it is a kind of theophany where the land contains the essence of the Ancestors, and is the work of the Ancestors. The whole land is a religious sanctuary, with special regions throughout it which have acquired special sacred status. The Aborigines regard themselves, whether as individuals, groups, categories, sexes or genetic stock, to be in mystic communion, via the sacred spaces, with certain totemic beings ... They are intimately connected with their whole environment which is pervaded by the supernatural, the result being that their experience of the whole environment is charged with numinous ambience. (1996: 2)

Within this context, Dean identifies common Dreamtime beliefs as expressive of immutable values, an aspect that Yanyuwa clan[4] member Harvey Mussolini has expressed in the following terms:

> Dreaming is a really big thing for Aboriginal people. In our language, Yanuwa, we call the Dreaming Yijan. The Dreamings made our Law or narnu-Yuwa. This Law is the way we live, or rules. This Law is our ceremonies, our songs, our stories; all of these things came from the Dreaming. One thing that I can tell you though is that our Law is not like European Law which is always changing – new government, new laws; but our Law cannot change, we did not make it. The Law was made by the Dreamings many, many years ago and given to our ancestors and they gave it to us. (quoted in Hardison, 2005: 6)

A number of aspects of Aboriginal cosmology have been co-opted into western New Age beliefs, where they have been misrepresented and de-localized as a resource for transnational cultures. As Grossinger has expressed it, a perception developed in some New Age circles in the 1980s that Aborigines:

are not only 'dreaming' their olden legend-time: they are dreaming all of nature. They are maintaining the sacred hearths for all of us ... Their Dream Time is a universal human experience that has become totally unconscious and vestigial in the rest of humanity. (1986: 117)

As subsequent sections of this chapter discuss, this constitutes a significant appropriation of indigenous beliefs for western ends.

In mainstream cinema, uses of music and sound have been particularly prominent as signifiers of difference in films that have attempted to represent mystic and, indeed, paranormal Aboriginality[5] and its relation to (very specific white interpretations of) the Dreamtime. The role of music in cinematic representations of Aborigines was first characterized by Kibby and Neuenfeldt (1998) in a chapter that remains a seminal reference point for the field. As the authors demonstrate, the didjeridu,[6] an instrument traditionally confined to Aboriginal groups in the far north of Australia, has become a ubiquitous aural marker of Aboriginality (or simply of the Australian bush itself), either through its actual use or through the imitation of aspects of its timbre and pitch by other instruments (deployed primarily to produce drones and rumbles). Indeed, as the editors of a volume addressing the various musical and cultural applications of the didjeridu assert, it constitutes "a distinctive instrument, icon and sound; ... a nexus of social relationships; [and] a way of engaging with wider theoretical issues such as appropriation, globalisation and commodification" (Hayward and Neuenfeldt, 1997: 9).[7] Along with the didjeridu, Aboriginal songs, often accompanied by clap-sticks, provide further obvious aural markers of exotic Aboriginality that composers and sound designers can draw on or directly sample into their mixes.

This chapter commences with a discussion of the representation of mystic Aboriginality in two prominent American fiction texts that exploit the archetypal New Age perception discussed above, and then rewinds chronologically to a film only referred to briefly by Kibby and Neuenfeldt, Peter Weir's 1977 feature *The Last Wave*. Due to the fantastic nature of its scenario, the film has often been overlooked by critics concerned to address Australian cinema's engagement with issues of Aboriginal rights, living circumstances and politics. Despite this, the film merits attention as a rich audiovisual fantasy of Aboriginal Otherness marked by an unease about settler history and its relationship to the deep histories and Dreamtimes of the continent, a relationship in which Aboriginal spiritual Otherness provides an apocalyptic conclusion to white settler alienation rather than a pathway to spiritual rapture.

American imagination

The first significant Hollywood representation of Australian Aboriginal culture occurred in 1983 in Philip Kaufman's feature *The Right Stuff*. Adapted from Tom

Wolfe's 1979 publication with the same title, the film relates the development of manned space flight by the US National Aeronautics and Space Administration (NASA), focusing on the character and achievements of its pilots. Kaufman's screenplay and direction emphasize a spiritual – and often mystical – aspect to the narrative that is far more understated in Wolfe's original book. Suitably in this regard, the film begins with a piece of modern folklore, that there is a demon who lives on the sound barrier, intent on keeping humans at bay. After a prologue that shows this demon being (figuratively) conquered by test pilot Chuck Yeager (played by Sam Shepard) as he breaks the sound barrier in a suborbital test-plane, the film commences its main narrative about the early astronaut programme. The film scooped honours for its soundtrack at the 1984 Academy awards, securing Best Music and Original Score awards for composer Bill Conti and his collaborators, and Best Sound Effects Editing and Best Sound for its audio personnel. But while Conti's orchestral score (performed by the London Symphony Orchestra)[8] accompanied many of the film's most dramatic flight scenes, one of its most effective sequences combines more subtle underscore and sound elements specific to its scenario.

The scene in question involves NASA trainee astronaut 'Gordo' Cooper (Dennis Quaid) travelling to a satellite tracking station in the Australian outback at Muchea, north of Perth, to communicate with astronaut John Glenn (Ed Harris) as he passes over on his – and the Americans' – first manned orbit of the planet.[9] The representation of this real-life event begins with Cooper driving up to the station with an Australian colleague (played by Anthony Wallis). The Australian nature of the scene is flagged through the two duetting on a chorus of the iconic Australian bush ballad 'Waltzing Matilda', which Cooper cheekily confides to his driver he thought was written by early US country music icon Hank Williams.[10] Outside the small building Cooper encounters a group of Aborigines and converses with a young man (played by Aboriginal performer David Gulpilil) who asks Cooper what he is doing there. After hearing of the American orbiting the planet he asks, "You fellas do that too?" and identifies a tribal elder sitting by a rock as both capable of astral navigation and able to help the astronauts. This interaction is complemented in the soundtrack by a brief didjeridu sample followed by an unsettling electronic didjeridu-like motif as the sun sets. These tones continue as the scene cuts to the rocket launch pad at Cape Canaveral, giving a sense of foreboding. After the countdown and take-off, the score provides more triumphant, almost processional orchestral passages, underscoring the achievement of orbital flight and the impressive vistas Glenn witnesses. As Glenn's capsule orbits into night, the scene cuts back to Muchea, where the Aborigines' campfire crackles loudly. Glenn then talks to Cooper on the radio as he crosses the West Australian coast and flies on again into dawn, heralded by a rousing horn motif. At this point the mood switches: cutting back to the quiet business of mission control, a loud bleeping signal alerts the ground crew that there is a problem with the capsule's heat shield. The mission controllers have no clear answer to the problem and tension immediately rises, accompanied by an unsettling drone at the rear of the mix.

The narrative then cuts back to the campfire, which is now roaring. Gulpilil's character begins dancing, accompanied by a short rhythmic didjeridu motif and clap-sticks (the former soon morphing into an orchestral tone), and a Yolngu chant suggesting an incantation, with animal-like cries adding atmospheric intensity. The camera shows bright embers flying up from the fire into the night sky. Cutting to the capsule, Glenn – who is, as yet, unaware of his technical problems – sees a cloud of embers encircling his craft and responds with glee, describing them as like fireflies and wondering whether they can be alive. A series of further cuts between the capsule and campfire emphasize the connection between the Aboriginal dance and song, the embers from their fire, and the sparkling cloud that enmeshes the spaceship. As the film moves on to show Glenn's fiery re-entry and subsequent tickertape parade through Manhattan, the sense of spiritual aid, of an unspoken magical gift from the pre-Modern to the rocket age, further adds to the film's mythic celebration of America's grand enterprise – or, as Grossinger has less ambivalently embellished it, having "travelled by rocket back into the Dream Time, and, in the absence of his heat shield, [Glenn] is protected by Aboriginal shamans sitting before their fires" (1986: 116–17). Just as the term 'shamans' is inappropriate to Aboriginal culture, so is the performance. Gulpilil's dance and the chant are Yolngu clan properties and the didjeridu is a traditional instrument of Yolngu and adjacent clans from northern 'Top End' Australia – lands and cultures far from the traditional lands of the Noongar clan of Australia's south-west coast where the action takes place.

Although there is no evidence of a direct link between the texts, a second significant American mythologizing of Aboriginal mysticism – based on similar misrepresentations – followed in 1990 in the form of Marlo Morgan's book *Mutant Message Down Under*, a work that purported to recount the author's meeting with nomadic central Australian Aborigines.[11] Accompanying them on a three-month-long trek, she learns skills of telepathy and transformation, becomes acquainted with stories from the deep Dreamtime, attends didjeridu performances and – in a spirit of reciprocity – teaches the group the popular US spoke-line dance 'Cotton-eyed Joe', waltzing and square dancing.[12] Her experience transforms her perceptions and she returns to western culture with an important 'mutant' message for the spiritual health of mankind. Her fanciful observations on the particular powers of the didjeridu in a chapter entitled 'Medicine and Music' are, as Neuenfeldt (1998: 90) identifies, riddled with "inaccuracies and inanities" which have the overall effect of producing a "hyper-spectacularisation and hyper-spiritualisation of Aboriginal culture" that overwhelms the "genocide and ethnocide experienced by many Aboriginal people in the past" and "denies diminished life chances" in the present in favour of a fantastic exoticism.

First self-published in 1990 as a supposedly authentic narrative and promoted by the author on lecture tours across the USA in the early 1990s, the book gained Morgan a cult following and in 1994 it was republished by Harper-Collins, with a substantial advance to its author. The high-profile publicity attached to this republication rekindled accusations of its fictitiousness. These culminated in the Dumbartung Aboriginal Organisation publishing a comprehensive refutation in 1995. Key to their critique was the manner in which Morgan provides a garbled mishmash of New Age North American First Nations beliefs and secondarily sourced information about Aboriginal culture that mixes traditional 'Top End' (Northern Territory) references – such as the didjeridu being performed as a traditional instrument – with very different central Australian Aboriginal customs that do not, for instance, include use of the instrument.

News of Morgan selling the film rights of her book to United Artists for just under two million dollars in 1995 prompted a delegation of senior Aboriginal elders to visit Hollywood to protest against the projected film and to continue their denunciation of the book. In a statement issued as part of a series of press releases referred to as the *Bounuh Wongee* ('message stick') series, Dumbartung Aboriginal Corporation leader Robert Eggington called Morgan's book a "New Age Masquerade of Imperialism" and identified it as imbued with a more deep-seated attempt to constrain, desecrate and exploit indigenous culture, arguing that

> *whilst Governments and their instrumentalities, such as tourism commissions promote Aboriginal culture overseas to attract international tourist and business dollars. Our people suffer from the denigration of loss of culture and spiritual growth and identity.*[13]

Eggington goes on to castigate Morgan's book as a "New-age infringement into indigenous spirituality and cultures" that "creates the belief that all people through evolutionary change have a rightful claim of ownership to the knowledge and sacredness of indigenous cultures" and identifies his critique as part of "the world's indigenous peoples' struggle against spiritual colonisation".[14]

Eggington's delegation met with United Artists representatives, staged a successful media conference, and participated in a meeting arranged by actor and social activist Steven Seagal. During this, a phone conference was held with Morgan in which she apologized, retracted her account and undertook to publish and acknowledge the same. While the publicity resulted in United

Artists withdrawing its production plans, Morgan subsequently reneged on her promises and continued touring to promote her book amid growing publicity, with the film project being acquired by Next Wave Films. Although developed by Barbara Boyle and Michael Taylor and scripted by Gerald DiPego in 1997, the project never went into production.[15] As a fantasy of Aboriginal spirituality in which a white westerner is introduced to powerful indigenous powers and prophecies, Morgan's book invites comparison with the earlier fictional text that this chapter now turns to analyse, with particular regard to its use of sound and music, Peter Weir's *The Last Wave* (1977).

One of the salient points about the historical vignette provided above is that the space of recent Australian cinema is one in which wilder imaginations of Aboriginality have been largely absent, as Australian settler society belatedly attempts to redress past injustices and misrepresentations. *The Last Wave* is significant since its imagination of Aboriginal mythology and connections to mystic prophetic powers emanate from a moment of Australian cinema (and social) history when attitudes towards Aboriginal history and rights were in transition. Like Morgan's book, the film also attracted criticism and protest from Aboriginal rights groups during its production on the grounds of its misrepresentation of an embattled section of the Australian community who had only succeeded in being granted citizenship by a national referendum in 1967, and who were still subject to considerable institutional and informal racism and harassment. Unlike Morgan's book, the controversy aroused by the film was less sustained and acute, reflecting its nature as an entirely fictional work; its employment of Aboriginal actors and a cultural consultant (Lance Bennett, of the Aboriginal Cultural Foundation); and – it must be said – the less-organized and less well-facilitated Aboriginal activist network that existed at the time of its production. Such a film would be unlikely to be made in contemporary Australia and *The Last Wave* thus represents a period in which 'politically correct' sensibilities were still in their infancy – and is all the more revealing for that.

The Last Wave

The Last Wave was written and directed by the then-emerging film-maker Peter Weir and followed his first feature, the cult hit *The Cars That Ate Paris* (1974) and the more widely popular *Picnic at Hanging Rock* (1975). These films presented two very different representations of non-urban Australia, its Otherness and inhospitableness to urban white settler culture. *The Cars That Ate Paris* is an exercise in what has been termed 'Outback Gothic', presenting non-urban Australia as a place of threat, manifest in its landscapes and the uncivil population that inhabits it. The 'Paris' in question, a small country town, is dominated by wreckers[16] who cause car crashes in order to plunder the vehicles and their contents, often killing their (urban) drivers and passengers in the process. The threat here is of white settler society 'gone feral' and the discordant hurdy-gurdy waltz that welcomes the film's chief protagonist to town and the harsh growling tones of revved-up custom cars underline the menace of their drivers and the town's general support culture.[17] *Picnic at Hanging Rock,* by contrast, offers a more mystical, unseen threat – that of the film's central location, the monolithic 'Hanging Rock' that the genteel senior high school girls visit on a summer picnic, only to disappear, vanishing into a brooding, ancient materiality. The film's soundtrack is significantly different from that of its predecessor, blending deep, almost inaudible tones to signify menace with prominent environmental atmos, well-known classical pieces that signify the girls' cultured background and atmospheric pan flute melodies that evoke a seductive, mystical Otherness appropriate to the often trance-like nature of the film.[18]

In précis, *The Last Wave*'s plot involves a lawyer named David Burton (played by Richard Chamberlain) who represents a group of Aborigines he suspects of having murdered a member of their clan as part of a traditional law punishment. During this engagement he experiences increasingly vivid premonitions in dreams and begins to associate these with his real-life involvement in the case. Bizarre meteorological events convince him that traumatic events are about to unfold. After realizing that he is implicated within a spiritual narrative created in the distant Dreamtime – and, indeed, anointed as the agent of a divine power he can barely imagine[19] – he finds himself in combat with the clan's 'shaman' deep underground. Although he emerges triumphant, he realizes that his victory is in vain as he sees a giant wave surging towards the city.

In interviews in the mid- and late 1980s Weir characterized *The Last Wave* as having being inspired by his interest in writers on mysticism such as Carl Jung and Carlos Castaneda and in the forgotten events, races and beliefs suggested by the writings of pseudo-historians Immanuel Velikovsky and Erich von Däniken. Reflecting the latter in particular, early sketches of the film's narrative included ancient Australian indigenes pulling rafts across the continent. The film represents a synthesis of these western pseudo-historical fantasies and an interest in actual Aboriginal culture that Weir has identified as kindled by his meeting with young Yolngu performer David Gulpilil (who also starred in *Walkabout* and appeared in *The Right Stuff*) in 1973. As he later recounted:

> *He made me realize that everything I had been taught in school about the Aborigines was total hogwash. Through long conversations with him, I realized the absurdity of the history books, which teach that the Aborigines were a kind of Stone Age people in the dawn of time, nomadic, without any culture*

of significant or enduring qualities, that they collapsed in contact with a more advanced, superior, and complex culture.

Talking with David, I realized the Aborigine culture was very much alive, if underground, so to speak. It was simply a different culture, and we had been looking at it with our own definition of culture. The Aborigines use the same word, culture, to mean something far richer than what we have come to mean by it. Here was a most interesting case where we had lost something since contact with the Aborigines - something they still had. They lost something too - the land and a lot of tribes.[20]

Weir and his co-writers Tony Morphett and Petru Popescu channelled these elements into a scenario that revolved around a fictional 'lost tribe' who had inhabited the location of present-day Sydney in the pre-colonial period. This fabrication of an Aboriginal identity was, in itself, a problematic project and was one that Weir negotiated with Aboriginal Groote Island elder Nandjiwarra Amagula, who played the character Charlie in the film and acted as a key adviser on the limits of viable cultural appropriation. As Weir later revealed, while Amagula "accepted the principle of recreating a lost Sydney tribe and their symbols, and tokens" that was key to the film's script, he unequivocally vetoed Weir's request to use any actual Aboriginal symbols, so that the director had to employ his art director Goran Warff to create a wholly fictional set of motifs, which Amagula approved (Rayner, 2003: 91).

Weir has described the plot and themes of *The Last Wave* as initially inspired by a sense of premonition he had upon finding an artefact in the ruins of an ancient city in Tunisia. After considering how an archetypal rational westerner might grapple with such an impulse, he discussed the conflict with Gulpilil and "gradually the forces began to come together" to develop the film's plot and script.[21] As Grossinger has succinctly summarized, the final product was

a movie in which charismatic Aboriginal actors ... bring their voodoo and interior visioning to the cities ... Here the Dreaming is portrayed not as decorative myth but a source of real energy, from beyond the known forces of science, with the capacity to act geologically and meteorologically and to return the land to its aboriginal state. (1986: 116)

Despite severe budgetary constraints, the film was favourably received by critics and received Australian Film Institute Awards for Best Achievement in Sound (awarded to the team of Don Connolly, Greg Bell and Phil Judd) and Cinematography (to Russell Boyd).[22] The film also garnered international recognition, receiving a special jury award at the Avoriaz Fantastic Film Festival in 1978 and being nominated as Best Fantasy feature at the 1980 Academy of Science Fiction, Fantasy and Horror Films annual awards.

Soundtrack elements

> *It seems to me we've lost touch with the fear of nature ... Tonight when we*
> *leave this building and there's a special kind of wind blowing* [and] *if that*
> *wind is howling with a voice like the voice of a person, a four-year-old child*
> *might say to us, "The wind's talking to us," and we'll say, "No it isn't, don't be*
> *silly. It's just howling around those wires"... It's just part of something we've*
> *lost touch with, another way of seeing the world.*[23]

Sound plays a central role in *The Last Wave*. Indeed, many key sequences of
the film are imbued with the "numinous ambience" Dean (1996: 2) describes
for Aboriginal perceptions of place. While Dean's use of the term emphasizes
the spiritual infusion of place and resultant holiness, in Weir's film sound –
particularly various sonic ambiences – embodies a related aspect of numinosity,
namely, a sense of awe that borders on terror or panic. The term is derived
from the Latin term *numen*, referring to the power of the divine that inhabits
places, material artefacts and, on occasion, human agents. This aspect is
communicated in the film through a meld of atmos tracks – derived from
natural sound sources – and sonic ambiences, low-dynamic sound passages
that infuse the aural space as unsettling, reverberant underscore and which
occasionally rise to prominence for dramatic impact.

The mysterious aspects key to the film's drama are established from the
outset in a subtle opening sequence that plays on disjunctures between the
screen images and the sound that accompanies them. The opening shot shows
a mature Aboriginal male painting a design on a rock face beneath an overhang
at sunset. The soundtrack accompanies this with a low-volume, indistinct sound
(wind? waves? both?) punctuated by occasional birdcalls. The camera closes
in on the artist and shows him to be using a paintbrush before moving on to
look at the images painted on the rock surface – a starlike design resting on
a turtle's back, a dolphin or whale, and (accompanied by bassier rumbles) a
mysterious symbol consisting of a cross inside concentric white circles. The
image of this symbol then cross-fades to that of a sun-drenched, outback
settlement under blue skies. Enigmatically, the bass rumbles continue over
the transition. Indeed, they become more recognizably the sounds of a storm
and increase in volume. The characters' behaviour soon establishes that this
sound is now a diegetic element, as individuals look to the sky, puzzled by
the incongruous juxtaposition of sound and image. Realizing that nature is
'out of joint', an older Aboriginal male gesticulates to the sky and hurries two
Aboriginal boys into a shelter. The image track then switches to a schoolyard,
where the children are also increasingly puzzled. One boy encapsulates the
enigma with the simple phrase "There's no clouds...' The rising sound of the
storm gives way to different noises, mixed loud on the soundtrack – the sound

of rain gushing down and delighted children whooping with glee as they dance in it. The teacher then calls the soaked children inside, expressing her puzzlement, stating "[It] never rains in November". After the excited children have been quietened down, a further sonic element intrudes in the form of a hard percussive drumming on the roof. As the teacher and children listen in alarm the source becomes clear as first one giant hailstone and then a flurry smash the classroom windows and litter the yard, their impact sounds mixing with the children's screams. Peering out anxiously at a hail-strewn landscape under a resolutely blue sky, the teacher's nervous expression is underscored with a sustained, eerie electronic tone that continues over another image transition, this time to an equally sunny Sydney cityscape. The disjuncture of storms from a clear sky is not only foreshadowed and emphasized by the soundtrack; the sounds that cross over the transitions of image and locale shift from an ambiguous diegetic role to diegetic realism and then away again, weaving a trail across the narrative, cued by the mysterious circled cross symbol seen at the beginning.

While the opening sequence is non-musical, the film's score often blends in with such sonic ambiences and supports its mysterious and spiritually imbued and brooding atmosphere. Indeed, one of the notable aspects of the film is the convergence of these elements. Despite this complementarity, sound mixer Phil Judd has emphasized that the final mixes were made without reference to the score, which was produced separately, and that the convergence of sound and music was a fortuitous outcome of the respective personnel's interpretation of Weir's overall creative brief. While highlighting that Weir "is one of the few Australian directors who is not 'cloth-eared' and who is able to use sound to tell a story" (personal communication to the author, October 2008), Judd has also noted the considerable interpretative freedom afforded to the sound crew. This was, in substantial part, born of necessity, as lack of access to library music required the crew to produce their own foley effects – such as producing the hailstorm noises described above by pelting a corrugated iron sheet with walnut shells – and to record the film's distinctive environmental sounds, such as frog noises. The film's subtle sound mix, made in mono, also caused problems when mixed down for transfer to optical film track due to the number of bass frequencies present, a problem that was exacerbated by the use of similar frequencies in the score (ibid.).

Suitably enough for a commercial film representing a spiritual fantasy, the composer, Charles Wain, was an experienced TV advertisement composer, who lived on an ashram as a devotee of the esoteric Hindu Sidda Yoga guru 'Baba' Muktananda.[24] Wain has stated that his inspiration was "the element of spirituality in both the concept of the film and in many of the locations". His score was a notable innovation for Australian cinema by virtue of being primarily composed and performed on an (analogue) synthesizer. The instrument was, at that time, relatively novel as a primary soundtrack provider; it had been pioneered in this context in 1971 by Walter Carlos for Stanley Kubrick's *A Clockwork Orange* and by Gil Mellés for Robert Wise's *The Andromeda Strain*, and was then used by subsequent composers, such as Matt Camison for Just Jaeckin's *Story of O* (1975). Wain has identified that the synthesizer was judged appropriate for the film because of what he described as the tendency for early- and mid-1970s synthesizer music of the style typified by German artists Tangerine Dream and Klaus Schulze to resemble "chant-like tribal music", presumably referring to their use of drones, slow modulations and gradual crescendos and diminuendos. These elements are strongly in evidence in the film's soundtrack and are also associated with the iconic cinematic sound of Aboriginality – the didjeridu. Wain has characterized the decision to use didjeridu sounds in the score as Weir's idea but his approach was to retain its signature sounds while infusing it as an ambient element rather than a foregrounded one. The didjeridu sounds were derived from tracks performed by David Gulpilil, which were subsequently slowed down to half-speed to "embellish" the instrument's "eeriness and to make it a much thicker and fatter sound without destroying its natural qualities".

The predominant sonic colouration of the film, as described above, is an affective one, a numinous ambience that creates a continuing sense of unease for its white protagonist and its audience. The only point in the narrative where western music predominates is a brief diegetic sequence, the significance of which is more cryptic and even arcane. This is all the more notable for its inscription within what is arguably the key scene of the film and the one where the processed didjeridu is most overtly associated with Aboriginal spiritual power. The sacred objects of the city's secret Aboriginal clan are located within what has now become an underground sewage plant, close to the sea. While visiting there at night, an uninitiated Aborigine, Billy Corman (Athol Compton), is confronted by the clan's mysterious shaman who tells him that his theft of sacred objects has been discovered and that he will die. Corman's terror is signalled by a brisk rhythmic tapping that carries over the edit into a very different scene, inside a Sydney pub. The edit reveals the rhythm to be tapped out on a bodhrán (a traditional Irish frame-drum) by a performer in a neo-traditional Irish music band as the introduction to an up-tempo reel. The link between the two scenes is made apparent by the image of Corman, drunk, with his head on the bar surface. The band (comprising a bodhrán, two fiddles, two guitars, a mandolin and accordion) play as a group of young Aboriginal men walk in from the rain, confront Corman and chase him outside. A melee ensues and the police arrive, with Corman running off down an alley. The image then returns to the pub interior, where the band is playing on, unconcerned. As the number concludes, the image cuts to a building site where Corman seeks refuge – enmeshed in a sound mix of thunder, rain noises and police sirens – and then stops, startled, as he hears a high vocable call (not dissimilar to a traditional Australian 'cooee' call, but without the final syllable). After a moment of silent stillness the sound of the didjeridu fills the soundspace, growling, with occasional guttural 'barks'. In the dark, tense space of the building site, with Corman seeking to elude his pursuers as their shadows loom large on a wall behind him, the didjeridu signals primal power and menace, an interpretation that is reinforced when Corman encounters clan elder Charlie, pointing a bone at him and murmuring an incantation. Clutching his heart, Corman staggers back and slowly sinks down, dead.

The incantation, vocable and didjeridu sounds clearly conform to the standard cultural and cinematic conventions of 'sounding Aboriginal' and obviously function within the narrative in this regard but the cameo performance of Irish music is cryptic and open to interpretation in one of several ways. It can be seen to represent one essence of European settler society, a form implicitly Other to Aboriginal marginality. Alternatively, read in terms of the historical subordination of Irish settlers to an Anglo-British colonial establishment, it can be seen to offer a point of connection to Aboriginality. Senses of connection are, however, undermined by the narrative. The Aborigines in the bar appear indifferent to the music and enter the space primarily to pursue their target. Similarly, the members of the band are unconcerned either by the (somewhat surprising) presence of Aborigines in a 'niche' music venue – particularly in a decade in which Aboriginal presence in mainstream metropolitan pubs was minimal – or by the brawl that occurs. There is no sense of any interracial solidarity. In narrative terms, particularly in such a complex, subtly plotted narrative, the scene is oddly ambivalent. Turning to the music, the lively, up-tempo ensemble playing can be seen as spirited (if not spiritual) and the players are clearly communing, in that they are 'locked into' their groove; but the aims and effects of their collective engagement are so radically different to the collective spiritual murder that takes place outside that comparisons are strained. Nevertheless, there is a significant point of connection that has, if anything, increased since the decade of the film's production, even if it requires unreasonably specialist knowledge to discern. As Graeme Smith (2001) has stated, there has been a particular syncretic engagement of Aboriginal music and Irish/Irish-derived Australian bush band music resulting from the use of the didjeridu as a drone instrument in modern neo-traditional Irish music ensembles in the 1980s and 1990s. Although primarily sonic, rather than political and/or spiritual, a point of connection exists. However cryptically, *The Last Wave* inscribes the (actual) beginning of this connection in the form of the featured band, led by Declan Affley.[25] A committed socialist and anti-authoritarian, Affley was a supporter of Aboriginal rights during the campaign for Aboriginal citizenship in the mid- to late 1960s and went on to teach fiddle and banjo at the Eora Aboriginal Cultural Centre in Sydney's Redfern district in the mid-1980s until his sudden death in 1985. With this information, the scene can be seen to have a greater sense of connection to the film's general themes, particularly with the benefit of hindsight, but it still functions on a markedly different level of textual operation than the film's overall sonic design.

The narrative has an extended climax, the drama of which is substantially generated by its soundtrack. When Burton returns home after losing the court case, his rational universe becomes fully unhinged as his house disintegrates around him. Standing in his hall he hears deep subterranean rumblings as the house sways violently and the power cuts out. A loud barking didjeridu enters the mix, seconds before a tree smashes loudly through the rear glass door. Rain pours down on the house, flooding the upper storey, and thunder rumbles and lightning cracks intensify the mix as open doors and windows slam frantically to and fro. Looking outside into the storm he sees Charlie beckoning him, holding the sacred stone in his outstretched hand. They drive to the sewage plant together and climb down into the lower chambers, where Charlie reveals his clan's sacred place and shows how the paintings explain the myth-narrative that Burton has been attempting to comprehend. As he interprets the images, a slow synthesizer melody underscores the gravity of the revelation; and when he deciphers the calendar painted on the wall, a low rumble alludes to the film's imminent conclusion. At this point a harsh didjeridu passage intrudes immediately before Burton sees the figure of the clan's shaman, bedecked in ceremonial body-paint, speaking in indigenous language, but clearly forbidding him to interfere with what he has found. A brief conflict ensues off-screen, during which Burton kills the shaman with the sacred triangular stone. As he flees the scene, dense, ominous tones of processed gurgling waters rumble on the soundtrack. The film proceeds to its conclusion: the Laws configured in the Dreamtime and the specific elements of the clan's 'Mulkurul' prophecy that bind Burton into the narrative are enacted in the form of an apocalypse – represented as a giant wave (the 'last wave' of the film's title) that looms over Burton as he kneels at the edge of the sea. Its sounds are massive and monstrous, comprising deep, bassy rumbles and watery churnings that signal imminent, inescapable and numinous doom.

Conclusion

The Last Wave provides its audience with a fantasy of Aboriginal spirituality and paranormal power that is radically Other to the metropolitan colonial west that the city of Sydney, 1970s Australian society and the film's white characters represent. The soundtrack is dominated by tones and textures that imbue the cityscape, landscape and Aboriginal underground sacred site with powers that reflect the clan's "mystic communion" with "totemic beings" and their intimate connection with a "whole environment ... pervaded by the supernatural" (Dean, 1996: 2). In this manner, the film and its soundtrack posit an Aboriginal spirituality that collapses the sacred/secular split of western cultures and instead offers a holistic model along the lines of the one that Bradley and Mackinlay identify in Yanyuwa culture, where "there is only one world, one environment, one country that is simultaneously material and spiritual" (2007: 77). Unfortunately for Burton and white Australia, this world is not theirs and their fate is in the hands of a Dreamtime prophecy that precedes them and which they are powerless to deflect. *The Last Wave*'s fantasy thereby reflects the deep anxieties of colonial culture, transported from faraway Europe. The rumbling, slowed-down didjeridu sounds, blended with Wain's synthesizer score and processed atmos tracks, underlie the entire film and allow little, if any, sonic 'light' into the *numen* that Burton uncovers. Unlike *The Right Stuff*, where the didjeridu propels spiritual assistance to an astronaut in space, no protection (or quarter) is given. Unlike that other national cinematic icon *Mad Max*, produced two years later, there is no suggestion of a *post*-Apocalyptic future for white Australia, with the soundtrack dwindling to a single, regular bleep – like the audio signal on a cardiac monitor – that cuts out before the credits conclude, leaving silence.

Acknowledgement

Thanks to Mark Evans and Elizabeth Mackinlay for their comments on previous drafts of this chapter. An earlier version of this chapter appeared in *Screen Sound: The Australasian Journal of Soundtrack Studies*, 1 (2010); online at http://www.screensoundjournal.org/issues/n1/04.%20SSJ%20n1%20Coyle-Editorial.pdf (accessed 24 December 2010).

Notes

1. See Kibby (2005) for an insightful discussion of sound and music in the film.
2. See Krausz (2003) for a detailed overview of Australian cinema's representation of Aboriginality.
3. There is also a growing body of work by indigenous film-makers that reflects rather differently on Australia, Aboriginal experiences and settler society, Ivan Sen's 2002 feature *Beneath Clouds* and Rachel Perkins's features *Radiance* (1998) and *One Night the Moon* (2001) being notable examples.
4. The Yanyuwa people inhabit the area to the south-west of the Gulf of Carpentaria.

5. See, for instance, Grossinger's statement that "cut off from the rest of the species for anywhere from 10,000 to 100,000 years, they have perhaps developed unique parapsychological (and paraphysical) abilities" (1986: 117).

6. The name of this instrument is spelled variously, including the previously more common 'didgeridoo'. The usage here reflects an Australian ethnomusicological convention established in the late 1990s.

7. The authors add that it also (and in their words "most importantly") comprises a "local and global product and process" in active development (*ibid.*).

8. The score derived substantial inspiration from Gustav Holst's *The Planets* (1914–16) and Tchaikovsky's Violin Concerto in D Major (1878).

9. This event occurred in May 1963.

10. Possibly a garbled reference, since Jimmie Rodgers recorded a hit version of the song in 1959.

11. This was initially published under the title *Walkabout Woman: Messenger for a Vanishing Tribe* but is best known by its subsequent title.

12. In a spoke-line dance, lines of dancers enact a collective motion akin to a horizontal turning wheel.

13. R. Eggington for the Dumbartung Aboriginal Corporation (1996) 'A Report on "Mutant Message Downunder"', *Bounuh Wongee*, 2 (online at http://www. dumbartung.org.au/report2.html; accessed 24 December 2010).

14. *Ibid.*

15. This was the same producer/writer team responsible for the 1996 feature film *Phenomenon*, directed by John Turteltaub, which has a similar mystical/New Age/ paranormal slant. A script for the Morgan film can be found in the online archive of the University of California's Haskell Wexler Collection of Scripts for Television and Motion Pictures, 1967–1996 (listed as Box 31). While the catalogue credits this as being written by Morgan, the fact there is no mention in any available online or print materials of Morgan having developed her own script suggests that this is DiPego's script. See catalogue reference at http://content.cdlib.org (accessed 1 October 2008).

16. Similar to the coastal ship-wrecking communities of the settler population's 'home country', the United Kingdom. See Bathurst (2005) for a survey.

17. For an illuminating contextual discussion of *The Cars That Ate Paris* see Simpson (2006).

18. The nai (Romanian pan flute) in the soundtrack is performed by Gheorghe Zamfir. For an overview of Peter Weir's oeuvre and its uses of sound and music, see Johnson and Poole (1998).

19. See Evans (2006: 100–5) for discussion of the Christian concept of anointment.

20. P. McGilligan (1986), 'Interview with Peter Weir' (http://www.peterweircave.com/ articles/article.html; accessed 24 December 2010).

21. J. M. Kass (1979), 'Peter Weir (Interview)' (http://www.peterweircave.com/articles/ articlei.html; accessed 24 December 2010).

22. The budgetary constraints included a minimal special-effects budget, so that the final apocalyptic wave sequence was sourced from the 1973 Australian surfing film *The Crystal Voyager* (David Elphick).

23. See note 21.
24. Unattributed, 'Who the Hell Are You?' *Metro*, 43 (Autumn 1978). All the quotations from Charles Wain in this paragraph come from this source. Confusingly, he is referred to there as 'Charles Wayne', while he is registered with the Australasian Performing Rights Association for his composer credit for *The Last Wave* under the name Wain Myers. In this chapter I use his film credit surname.
25. Affley was a British immigrant of Irish and Welsh ancestry who settled in Australia in 1959. He became renowned for his spirited performances of Irish 'rebel songs' in inner-city pubs and folk clubs in the 1960s and 1970s, and he formed one of the first Australian 'bush bands', The Wild Colonial Boys in 1969. In 1970 he began playing the traditional Uillean pipes, one of the first Australian performers on the instrument.

References

Bathurst, B. (2005), *The Wreckers*, London: HarperCollins.

Bradley, J., and Mackinlay, E. (2007), 'Singing the Land, Singing the Family: Song, Place and Spirituality amongst the Yanyuwa', in F. Richards (ed.), *The Soundscapes of Australia: Music, Place and Spirituality*, Aldershot: Ashgate.

Dean, C. (1996), *The Australian Aboriginal 'Dreamtime' (Its History, Cosmogenesis, Cosmology and Ontology)*, Geelong: Gamahucher Press.

Elkin, A. P. (1969), 'Elements of Australian Aboriginal Philosophy', *Oceania*, 11 (2), 85–98.

Evans, M. (2006), *Open up the Doors: Music in the Modern Church*, London: Equinox.

Grossinger, R. (1986), 'Aboriginal Elder Speaks in Ojai', in R. Grossinger (ed.), *Planetary Mysteries: Megaliths, Glaciers, the Face on Mars and Aboriginal Dreamtime*, New York: North Atlantic Books, pp. 107–22.

Hardison, P. (2006), 'Report on Traditional Knowledge Registers (TKRs) and Related Traditional Knowledge Databases (TKDBs) – Prepared for the Secretariat of the Convention on Biological Diversity', online at http://209.85.173.104/ search?q=cache:9uozoPu71P8J:www.biodiv.org/doc/meetings/tk/wg8j-04/ information/wg8j-04-inf-09-en.doc+Mussolini+Harvey+yanuwa&hl=en&ct=clnk&cd= 1&gl=au (accessed 1 October 2008).

Hayward, P., and Neuenfeldt, K. (1997), 'One Instrument, Many Voices', in K. Neuenfeldt (ed.), *The Didjeridu: From Arnhem Land to Internet*, Sydney: John Libbey & Co./Perfect Beat Publications, pp. 1–10.

Johnson, B., and Poole, G. (1998), 'Sound and Author/Auteurship: Music in the Films of Peter Weir', in R. Coyle (ed.), *Screen Scores: Studies in Contemporary Australian Film Music*, Sydney: Australian Film, Television and Radio School, pp. 124–40.

Kibby, M. (2005), 'Sounds of Australia in *Rabbit-Proof Fence*', in R. Coyle (ed.), *Reel Tracks: Australian Feature Film Music and Cultural Identities*, John Libbey and Co/Perfect Beat Publications, pp. 145–57.

Kibby, M., and Neuenfeldt, K. (1998), 'Sound. Cinema and Aboriginality', in R. Coyle (ed.), *Screen Scores: Studies in Contemporary Australian Film Music*, Sydney; Australian Film, Television and Radio School, pp. 66–77.

Krausz, P. (2003) 'Screening Indigenous Australia: An Overview of Indigenous Australia on Film', *Australian Screen Education Online*, 32 (Spring), 90–5 (online at http://search. informit.com.au/documentSummary;dn=820526615263733;res=IELHS; accessed 24 December 2010).

Morgan, M. (1990), *Walkabout Woman: Messenger for a Vanishing Tribe* [self-published under the MMI imprint].

Morgan, M. (1994), *Mutant Message Down Under* [reprint of *Walkabout Woman: Messenger for a Vanishing Tribe*], New York: HarperCollins.

Neuenfeldt, K. (ed.) (1997), *The Didjeridu: From Arnhem Land to Internet*, Sydney: John Libbey & Co./Perfect Beat Publications.

Neuenfeldt, K. (1998), 'The Convergence of the Didjeridu, Aboriginal Culture, Healing and Cultural Politics in New Age Discourse', *Social Analysis*, 42(2), 73–102.

Rayner, J. (2003), *The Films of Peter Weir*, 2nd edn, New York: Continuum.

Simpson, C. (2006), 'Antipodean Automobility and Crash: Treachery, Trespass and Transformation on Our Open Road', *Australian Humanities Review*, 39–40; online at http://www.australianhumanitiesreview.org/archive/Issue-September-2006/simpson. html (accessed 24 December 2010).

Smith, G. (2001), 'Celtic Australia: Bush Bands, Irish Music and the Nation', *Perfect Beat*, 5(2), 3–18.

3   Who Wants to Live Forever
Glam Rock, Queen and Fantasy Film

J. Drew Stephen

The release of *Flash Gordon* (Mike Hodges) in 1980 marked a striking departure in the musical conception of the fantasy-film hero. Whereas other space-travelling heroes of the era – Luke Skywalker, Superman, Captain Kirk – were depicted with high-culture brass and orchestra fanfares, Flash's music was rock music and it spoke directly and powerfully to a generation well versed in its gestures and language. Rock music and rock bands were hardly new to the realm of film in 1980, yet Queen's creative involvement and the prominence of their music in *Flash Gordon* and later in *Highlander* (Russell Mulcahy, 1986) was substantial and unusual. The band's ability to meet the demands of film must be credited to their fluency in the wide range of musical styles that fell under the umbrella of 'glam', from progressive and psychedelic rock to heavy metal and disco. In fact, glam, with its emphasis on theatricality and role-playing, was a perfect match for fantasy film. Queen's soundtracks in the 1980s were a logical outgrowth of their musical projects from the 1970s.

There is more music in *Flash Gordon* and *Highlander* than just the contributions of Queen and there are other fantasy films that draw extensively upon rock-music styles. Nevertheless, I single out Queen's music and these two films to demonstrate the ways the stylistic codes and cultural meanings of glam rock and heavy metal were applied dramatically and scenically to fantasy film in the 1980s. I begin with a short overview of glam rock to establish its generic conventions. I then look at the placement and function of the music in both films to demonstrate the ways in which the music, and particularly the musical style, supports and enhances the dramatic situations and characterizations. Ultimately, I establish a deeper understanding of the conventions and dramatic elements of glam rock and explore the ways that rock-music styles are used dramatically in the genre of fantasy film.

Queen and glam rock in the 1970s

Glam emerged in the 1970s through a remarkable shift in the way rock music was presented and performed. Authenticity and audience community – traits inherent in rock and roll since its inception in the 1950s – were seemingly cast aside by glam musicians who embraced theatricality and extravagance in order to distance and distinguish themselves from their audiences. Whereas rock and roll musicians in the 1950s and 1960s often appeared to sing about their personal experiences and express them musically in ways that established a direct connection between them and their working-class audiences, glam musicians assumed roles and, in many cases, addressed topics that were blatantly foreign to the average listener's experience. Still, by emphasizing the fantastic over the mundane, glam musicians found a theme with undeniable resonance. Audiences may not have identified directly with the androgynous looks, outlandish appearances and assumed roles of the performers but they responded eagerly to the songs and subject matter, which, in both cases, had a direct appeal that was absent in the lengthy meanderings of progressive rock and the virtuosic posturing of heavy metal. Strikingly diverse performers, ranging from David Bowie and the New York Dolls to Alice Cooper and KISS, were drawn together through:

> a highly theatrical mode of presentation ... [a] parade of inauthenticity that hardly appeared to sell out to commercial interests ... [a] proclaimed dissatisfaction with the excessive machismo prevalent in growing hard rock ... [and] an emphasis on short, well-constructed, hook-based songs.[1]

Even though Queen's role-playing and fantastic costumes did not result in the fully formed alternative personas of David Bowie and KISS or the macabre theatricality of Alice Cooper, there was a strong fantasy element in their approach that was rooted undeniably in the aesthetic of glam and manifest in the profound theatricality of the music. This is most apparent in the striking stylistic diversity used to convey the meaning of individual songs. Even a cursory survey of Queen's music from the 1970s and 1980s reveals a remarkably eclectic range of styles that includes heavy metal ('Stone Cold Crazy'), rockabilly ('Crazy Little Thing Called Love'), gospel ('Somebody To Love'), folk ('Year Of '39'), disco and funk ('Back Chat'), exoticism ('Mustapha'), pop ballads ('You're My Best Friend'), stadium anthems ('We Will Rock You'), classical music gestures ('Love Of My Life'), operatic melodrama ('Bohemian Rhapsody'), vaudeville ('Killer Queen'), camp nostalgia through old-fashioned references ('Seaside Rendezvous'), and psychedelic sonic experiments to convey overt sexuality ('Get Down, Make Love').

Queen's comfortable fluency across such a wide range of styles was possible because the band, as Freddie Mercury acknowledged, was comprised of "four writers that write very different songs".[2] Queen's diversity is also apparent in their recordings and performances. This extended to the flexibility and agility of the singing voices; the band's willingness to exploit the potential of studio recording techniques; Brian May's symphonic approach to the guitar, which allowed him to obtain a vast array of sounds from the instrument (the harp-like flourishes and 'cello-like melodic lines in 'Love Of My Life' are good examples); and above all the inherent theatricality of Freddie Mercury's approach to singing and performing. As a singer, Mercury was capable of a wide range of expression and made use of his abilities to emphasize the dramatic nature of the texts through an array of techniques ranging from overblown camp posturing, powerfully soulful outbursts and poignantly lyrical expressions that seemed to speak directly to his listeners. "Of all the more theatrical performers," observed David Bowie, "Freddie took it further than the rest. He took it over the edge" (quoted in Ressner, 1992: 13). Even though Queen's live shows were already loaded with special effects, they were made memorable through Mercury's wildly flamboyant appearance and performance. As Jeffrey Ressner notes,

> [Mercury] *was even more extreme when it came to his concert performances, appearing in leather storm-trooper outfits or women's clothes and taking an arch, gay-macho stance that both challenged and poked fun at the decidedly homophobic hard-rock world. (ibid.)*

Mercury's theatricality extended even to his role models – he cited Jimi Hendrix and Liza Minnelli as his main influences – and the choice of names for himself and for the band. For a personal surname, he adopted Mercury (replacing his birth name, Farrokh Bulsara) in reference to the mythological messenger of the gods. For the band, he came up with the name Queen, as he explained:

> *I'd had the idea of calling a group Queen for a long time. It was a very strong name, very universal and very immediate; it had a lot of visual potential and was open to all sorts of interpretations. I was certainly aware of the gay connotations, but that was just one facet of it. (ibid.)*

Although the individual songs demonstrate a wide range of styles, Queen forged a distinct and immediately recognizable sound that defined the band's approach throughout its career. "The one word that ... sums it all up, is *layered*", argues radio DJ and TV presenter Bob Harris. "It was a very layered sound, you know, layered guitars, layered voices ... lots of them, big production."[3] The key, according to guitarist Brian May, is that "the three voices that we had blended instantly and sounded very big", something he and Queen's drummer, Roger Taylor, elaborated on in interview:

> *Taylor:* [the voices] *interacted quite magically and we all had different qualities in our voices. I had a sort of high searing quality, Freddie had an incredibly*

powerful quality in most ranges, and Brian had a very nice quality in the lower range, and so the three made a very good combination. But what we would do is we would not take a single part each, we would all together sing every part.

May: So as soon as the three of us sang a line it already sounded quite big. You double track that it sounds very big, and then we would sing the next line, and the next line, and the next line ...

Taylor: So, you really were looking after both ends of the sort of spectrum there. In fact all ends. You were covering everything, so it came out particularly strong and that was really part of the Queen sound I think, the fact that the three of us sang every part.[4]

Ultimately, Queen's rich and muscular sound was built from exaggeration and this made it perfectly suited to the films with their own emphasis on exaggerated archetypes.

Narrative archetypes and the fantasy-film genre

The distinguishing essence of the fantasy genre, vis-à-vis its related genres of horror and science fiction, is that fantasy deals primarily with the presence of the magical or the marvellous in the familiar world and familiar situations. As Alec Worley points out in his book *Empires of the Imagination*, fantasy is "the supernatural left unexplained" (Worley, 2005: 10). "If a fantasy film ever elucidates its magic through scientific reasoning," he observes, "it ceases to be fantasy" (*ibid*.: 11). Moreover, "although fantasy often engenders a sense of departure from earthbound reality, it remains stubbornly anchored by a processing of life's challenges, redefining the world in a fresh and foreign language" (*ibid*.: 4).

Flash Gordon and *Highlander* are grounded in the conceit of the ordinary made extraordinary while also conforming to the narrative archetypes proposed by Vladimir Propp (1958),[5] Joseph Campbell (1949) and Northrop Frye (1957). Flash Gordon is clearly from the realm of everyday experience. As a professional quarterback for the New York Jets, he is unquestionably an exceptional athlete, yet this hardly provides him with the necessary skills to face and defeat the powerful extraterrestrial villain Ming the Merciless and his magical powers. Flash's call to adventure arises when he assumes control of an aeroplane after the pilots are rendered incapable by a severe storm inflicted on Earth by Ming. Flash lands the plane on the grounds of the laboratory of Dr Hans Zarkov, where he and fellow passenger Dale Arden are taken by Zarkov aboard his rocket ship and unwittingly launched into space. Upon arriving in the realm of the unfamiliar – the planet Mongo – Flash is separated from his companions and sentenced to death. The execution is carried out but Flash's death is temporary, as he is quickly resurrected through the agency of Ming's daughter, Princess Aura. Aura takes Flash to the forest moon Arboria. There, and later in Sky City, Flash undergoes several trials that ultimately earn him the trust and respect of the Arborians and the Hawkmen. Flash returns to Mingo City, where he rescues Dale, defeats Ming, brings peace to the kingdoms of Mongo and saves Earth from annihilation.

Highlander follows a similar narrative arc but presents the events non-linearly by interweaving flashbacks from the past into the plot as it unfolds in the present. Like Flash Gordon, Connor MacLeod sets out from the ordinary world. He is a typical sixteenth-century Scottish clansman, whose call to adventure occurs when he miraculously and inexplicably survives a mortal wound incurred in battle. Believing MacLeod's recovery to be the work of the devil, the clan banishes him from the community. Thus isolated, he encounters Ramirez, a helper figure and fellow immortal who provides MacLeod with training in swordsmanship and essential information about his nature and his quest. Ramirez is confronted and beheaded by the villain, the Kurgan. Without Ramirez, MacLeod is left to determine his own path and fend for himself. After several additional trials, MacLeod faces the Kurgan in the final confrontation and successfully overcomes him to claim the prize. This grants him extraordinary abilities, which bring about a transfiguration that allows for his reintegration into society on a new, higher plane.

In addition to demonstrating monomythic aspects of narrative archetypes, *Flash Gordon* and *Highlander* fit easily into the conventions of fantasy film. The space voyage of *Flash Gordon* resembles the quest voyages of classical and oriental mythology in which a hero travels to an unfamiliar realm to encounter strange beings and demonstrates unusual skills to overcome the exceptional challenges he faces.[6] MacLeod's apprenticeship with Ramirez mirrors almost exactly the mentorship relationship between Luke Skywalker and Obi-Wan Kenobi in *Star Wars: A New Hope* (George Lucas, 1977). The similarities extend even to the mentor's death at the hands of a villain who must later be challenged by the apprentice. The mentor's death, in both cases, establishes the severity of the challenge and creates a context in which the hero can demonstrate the extent to which he has surpassed not only his humble origins and initial expectations but his mentor's abilities as well.

As with many movies in the fantasy genre, *Flash Gordon* and *Highlander* engage the audience because they allow us to identify closely with their heroes. Both heroes embody traits that we recognize and struggle with ourselves, and we celebrate their triumphs because they are able to transcend the seemingly insurmountable challenges they face. Queen's music plays an important role in establishing this connection by grounding the heroes in the familiar musical language of rock and by writing music with a direct clarity of expression. Still, given that rock music was rare in fantasy film in 1980, there are few who could have anticipated the impact it would have.

Flash Gordon

When producer Dino de Laurentiis turned to the question of music for *Flash Gordon*, the possibility of hiring a rock band was certainly not an obvious choice. The members of Queen also had concerns and were reluctant to work against a deadline, but they quickly warmed to the idea after seeing footage from the finished film (Purvis, 2007: 54). Unlike the common practice at the time whereby rock bands contributed songs with only a superficial relationship to the storyline – Ray Parker Jr's 'Ghostbusters' for the film of the same name (Ivan Reitman, 1984) and Glenn Fry's 'The Heat Is On' for *Beverly Hills Cop* (Martin Brest, 1984) are two well-known examples – Queen would be working with the rough cut of the film to produce music that was connected closely to the dialogue and dramatic situations. "We wanted to do something that was a real soundtrack," explained May:

> It's a first in many ways, because a rock group hasn't done this type of thing before, or else it's been toned down and they've been asked to write pretty mushy background music, whereas we were given the license to do what we liked, as long as it complemented the picture. (ibid.)

The film's production team nevertheless retained a backup plan by contracting the established film composer Howard Blake to provide up to 90 minutes of music. The only concession to Queen was the stipulation that Blake include various guitar phrases and the song 'Flash' within his large-scale score for 80-piece orchestra.[7] In the end, much of Blake's brass-dominant orchestral score was discarded in favour of the heavily synthesized music of Queen. The final result is thus an eclectic mixture of traditional orchestral underscoring, bombastic rock music and hypnotic meanderings worthy of the psychedelic experiments of the early 1970s – and it works surprisingly well. By embracing both classical and rock music rather than focusing on just one or the other, the score achieves a boldly atmospheric sound that closely matches the film in a way that has rarely been equalled since. As Daniel Ross observes in his 2009 re-evaluation of the album, "What separates this work from other soundtrack recordings is its relative complexity compared with much popular music, and its relative simplicity and clarity of expression compared with most action film scores."[8] The composition of the score resulted from an unusually collaborative effort. As Brian May explains:

> At first we simply spent a week in the studio playing with our ideas. That is basically how the soundtrack came about ... After the first week we knew exactly

what parts of the film still needed something. We had nothing suitable for Ming, Flash's enemy. Freddie suddenly said, "Okay, I always get the dark stuff", went home, and returned the next day with a great Ming Theme.[9]

Regarding the other themes, May notes that:

John [Deacon] had the idea for a beautiful three-note melody, from which he created the Arboria Theme describing the atmosphere on the planet of the tree people. Roger [Taylor] wrote 'Escape From The Swamp', which is heard when Flash escapes from the swamp with all the beasts pursing him. Roger also wrote 'In The Death Cell' and Freddie wrote 'Vultan's Theme'.[10]

The collaborations also extend to Howard Blake, who worked with Brian May and Freddie Mercury on certain passages in the score. A notable moment involves Mercury's 'The Kiss (Aura Resurrects Flash)', which is reprised in an orchestral underscoring version as Aura and Flash travel to the planet Arboria. As Blake recalls, "I remember Freddie Mercury singing the idea of 'Ride To Arboria' in his high falsetto and I showed him how I could expand it into the orchestral section now on the film, with which he seemed very pleased".[11]

Given Queen's lack of previous experience composing for film, the band demonstrates a remarkably intuitive grasp of the genre. The biggest surprise is their willingness to eschew the traditional rock song – only two occur in the entire film and they are relegated to the main title and end credits – in favour of what, at times, is clearly an operatic approach that is fully appropriate to the fantastical nature of the film. Many of the themes – notably Ming's with its ominous synthesizer sound, angular chromaticism and frequent use of the interval of the augmented fourth – draw on so many clichés that they should sound ridiculous. Instead, they are perfectly at home within the already overblown camp posturing of the film. Anything less would have been inadequate. Indeed, by writing music that could meet the gaudy spectacle of the film on its own terms, Queen was able to deliver something that a traditional orchestration could not.

Despite writing in a style that was unusual for film, Queen's awareness of cinematic conventions can be seen in their frequent use of leitmotifs to delineate character and establish setting as well as to convey concepts such as love, death and resurrection. Following a common practice found in films since the 1930s, many of the thematic materials are reprised in transfigured versions to illustrate changing dramatic situations. The music associated with the kiss with which Aura resurrects Flash is heard first accompanied by Mercury's voice, rendered other-worldly by the high tessitura, the layering that creates a multi-voice texture and the slippery chromaticism of the melodic lines. When this music returns as Aura and Flash travel to Arboria, the shimmering vocalizations are replaced by orchestral sounds. Although the magic of the earlier setting is absent, the rich orchestration lends a romantic glow to the scene. The love theme, 'In The Space Capsule', undergoes a similarly subtle transformation. The theme appears first as an accompaniment to the rocket voyage that takes Flash, Dale and Zarkov from the familiar realm of earth into the unfamiliar realm of outer space. The high-range synthesizer chords that meander over a deep bass pedal evoke the vastness of space. As the rocket proceeds into space, a drumbeat propels it forward. Apart from the 'Flash' theme heard during the main titles, this is the first time Queen's music appears in the film and the change in sonority is striking. Unlike the patently conventional orchestral cues that have been heard thus far, the arpeggiated guitar chords that begin the love theme effectively transport the characters and the audience to an entirely different realm. The theme is reprised after Flash has been sentenced to death and is granted a chance to speak with Dale one last time. Again a drumbeat emerges – this time a military-style death march – but now it emanates from the on-screen drums of Ming's soldiers and serves to propel Flash toward his impending death.

The atmospheric, mostly synthesized, cues are extremely successful in evoking the fantastic elements of the film including unfamiliar settings (outer space and the planet of Arboria) as well as strange powers (the hypnotic powers of Ming's ring and the resurrective powers of Aura's kiss). But it is the moments of unadulterated rock that truly set the score apart from others of the time and realize rock's potential as a means of conveying power and potency. A revealing demonstration occurs in the football match scene. As Flash defies Ming's order to remove Dale he is initially overwhelmed by the guards. Once Zarkov throws Flash one of the football-sized green eggs, he quickly takes control of the situation. The music shifts from orchestral underscoring to a synthesizer and guitar-heavy rock groove that effectively matches Flash's athletic abilities and domination of his opponents. This is even more true of the music for 'Vultan's Theme', 'Attack Of The Hawk Men' and the 'Battle Theme', in which the full arsenal of Queen's rock idiom is unleashed. The synthesized bugle calls, the power chords on the guitar, the driving bass and the thunderous drumming all combine to convey the excitement of the battle and the force with which Flash and his new allies will overwhelm Ming's cohorts. Even the appearance of Wagner's familiar 'Bridal Chorus' from *Lohengrin* is given a metallic sheen in Brian May's multi-voiced guitar performance.

The final thirty minutes of the film present a sustained onslaught of rock ferocity culminating in the song 'The Hero', which serves as the music for the end credits. It is a rich celebration of distorted guitars, pounding drums and Freddie Mercury's voice, matching the film's triumphant conclusion and Flash's transcendent abilities.

Highlander

As in *Flash Gordon*, the compositional duties in *Highlander* were divided between an orchestral composer, in this case Michael Kamen, and Queen, with some collaboration between them. Here, however, the distinction between the two is much more clearly delineated, with Kamen providing most of the underscoring used to establish setting and reinforce dramatic situations and Queen providing songs for the main titles and end credits plus some source music and underscoring. As director Russell Mulcahy and producers Peter S. Davis and William N. Panzer relate in the DVD audio commentary, Queen had initially intended to contribute just a single song until they were shown early footage of the film. "What happened", notes Mulcahy, "is that they all then took different scenes that they fell in love with as their own ... and then they finally ended up saying, 'we want the whole thing'."[12] This led to the composition of six original songs in which Queen, having seen rough edits of the film, wrote music inspired directly by the action and dialogue of the film. A seventh pre-existing song, 'Hammer To Fall', was also used in the film.

Faced with this "abundance of Queen songs", Mulcahy used several as source music, noting that "we really didn't have too many places to put them". From the band's point of view, this was not always ideal and John Deacon in particular was unhappy with the positioning of his song, 'One Year Of Love', as background music in the bar where Brenda meets Nash for the first time. "It's the worst place you can stick a song," concedes Mulcahy, "because you know it is going to be played low." Despite its weak scenic placement, the song works well dramatically and musically. As a sentimental rock ballad with a soulful lead vocal and a sultry sax solo, it serves as a love theme for Brenda and Nash and helps to establish the romantic connection between them. When Nash later visits Brenda at her apartment, the song is heard again in an arrangement for solo piano.

'Gimme The Prize (Kurgan's Theme)' and 'Hammer To Fall' also occur diegetically yet manage to be heard more prominently than 'One Year Of Love' since the music, in both cases, does not compete with dialogue. The heavy metal style of the songs reinforces the overtly masculine and violently aggressive nature of the characters with whom they are associated. In the case of 'Hammer To Fall', the song defines an ex-marine – conveniently driving through the city with an arsenal of machine guns in his front seat – who witnesses the duel between the Kurgan and Kastigir and attempts to intervene. 'Gimme The Prize' portrays the Kurgan himself as he enters New York in anticipation of the Gathering, at which the final champion will be chosen, the last survivor of these immortals. The heavy bass, thunderous drumming, gritty lead vocal and raw distorted guitar sound of 'Gimme The Prize' provide a particularly apt accompaniment for the Kurgan who, even when he is first introduced as a sixteenth-century warrior, is associated with a distorted power chord on the guitar. Although Mulcahy admitted 'Gimme The Prize' was his least favourite of the Queen songs heard in the movie, he acknowledged that it was highly effective in capturing the "heavy metal attitude of the Kurgan".

'Don't Lose Your Head' was written to accompany an extended scene in which the Kurgan kidnaps Brenda and terrifies her by driving with maniacal recklessness through the city. The song's constantly driving drumbeat, syncopated bass line and rhythmic synthesizer jabs provide a perfect counterpoint for the Kurgan's disregard for authority and Brenda's shocked reactions. With its relentless rhythmic repetitiveness, it also helps to build audience tension. About two minutes into his rampage, the Kurgan taunts Brenda by growling out the lyrics to 'New York, New York'. The Kurgan's diegetic singing seeps into and then transforms the non-diegetic underscoring. With the drums continuing at the same driving pace, the tempo is reduced by half and Freddie Mercury takes over the singing to deliver a soaring rendition, complete with a haughty laugh after the final phrase. The song's triumphant optimism and associations with the glamorous side of the city run counter to the violent action and seedy imagery in this scene, yet the irony – both in the use of this song and Mercury's camp performance of it – captures powerfully the Kurgan's brutal insolence. According to Mulcahy, Mercury was at first adamantly against performing the song but finally relented. "We put Liza Minnelli on and showed it to him", recalls Mulcahy "and he fell in love with it."

While most of the Queen songs in *Highlander* are presented as stand-alone entities entirely separate from Michael Kamen's orchestral score, one song in particular, 'Who Wants To Live Forever', is a fully integrated collaboration.[13] The title phrase initially appeared in *Flash Gordon* as a remark by Prince Vultan. Here, it is given an entirely different meaning in its use as underscoring for a montage showing the gradual ageing and death of MacLeod's first wife, Heather. It also demonstrates Brian May's remarkable ability to capture in music the dramatic essence of a cinematic scene. According to Mulcahy, May watched the scene, wrote the lyrics and then worked with Kamen to complete the song.[14] In the film's audio commentary, Mulcahy points out:

> you will notice [in the film] that the song carries on and then at a certain point Michael Kamen takes over the melody of the song with a sweeping orchestra ... It was a perfect match of basically a modern rock and roll band, so to speak, blending with traditional orchestration.

The effectiveness of the song lies in the way it conveys the poignant conflict of the Highlander's situation – living forever when love must die – through tonal conventions that define the relationship between a minor key and its relative major. The verses begin in E minor and end on a D major chord, suggesting a triumphant rise to the relative major, G. Rather than completing this motion, the chorus evades the expected resolution on G by beginning instead on the subdominant chord, C major, and twice presenting a progression that includes the G major chord only as a passing sonority: IV–I$_6$–ii. This leads to a suspended D major chord, again suggesting the tonic of G, and an incomplete statement in the text. The question of who wants to live forever has been asked but instead of an answer there is only an empty vocalization as the D major chord resolves to A minor for the second verse as the cycle begins anew. In the second presentation of the chorus, the question is asked even more emphatically by being stated twice and supported by a rich orchestral build-up. Ultimately, the phrase proposes a negation rather than an affirmation: who wants to live forever ... when love must die? At this point the entire triumphant build-up collapses. The rich orchestral texture is stripped away, leaving Mercury's voice alone in naked anguish as the dominant chord on D resolves to a hollow-sounding E minor (Figure 3.1). The music recedes into the background so that the dialogue between MacLeod and Heather on her deathbed can be heard. Nevertheless, the cycle runs a third time without the singing voices. In the final chorus, the deceptive cadence on E minor occurs at the moment of Heather's death to achieve a very powerful realization of the text's sentiment. This is followed by an utterly tragic chain of descending minor

Figure 3.1 Author transcription of 'Who Wants To Live Forever' from *Highlander* (1986) by Brian May. Words and music by Brian May. © 1986 Queen Music Ltd. This arrangement © 2011 Queen Music Ltd. Reprinted by permission of Hal Leonard Corporation.

Figure 3.2 Analytical reduction of descending chain of minor triads related by chromatic mediant in 'Who Wants To Live Forever' from *Highlander* (1986) by Brian May

chords related by chromatic mediant (Figure 3.2). Although this progression is common in film scoring, it is unusual in rock music and thus has a stronger impact by being used in this medium.

Scoring the superhero

Although *Flash Gordon* and *Highlander* follow narrative archetypes and cinematic conventions of plot, both films make striking departures in the scoring of their heroes. This can be seen by contrasting the main titles of both movies with the template established by John Williams in the late 1970s and 1980s in his symphonic scores to the *Star Wars* (1977–83) and *Indiana Jones* (1981–89) trilogies and the *Superman* quartet (1978–87). As Janet Halfyard observes, these heroic themes are:

> *major key, up-tempo, and largely devoid of chromaticism that might undermine the stability of the tonal center, musical metaphors for the largely uncomplicated, optimistic, and energetic heroes to whom they belong.* (2004: 65)

She further identifies traits that, with only minor variations, are clearly audible across the three sets of titles by Williams. Since all three demonstrate similar structural characteristics, I focus on *Star Wars* as a representative example.

The main title to *Star Wars* is a major-key march in a martial style scored for full orchestra (Table 3.1). It begins with a fanfare introduction followed by bold statements of the principal melody in the brass punctuated by timpani and accompanied by a syncopated rhythmic ostinato from the low brass and strings. The theme consists of a triplet upbeat followed by a perfect fifth and a falling figure. After two statements of the theme, a contrasting section ensues with a lyrical theme expressed warmly and richly by the strings. The opening heroic theme returns for two final statements and leads directly into the action of the first scene. The phrasing consists of regular and predictable four-bar groupings with monotony avoided through the use of obvious one-bar extensions at the ends of the third and fourth sections. Overall, the heroic character of the themes results from "the harmonic stability created by the use of tonic–dominant intervals and the energetic character of their march rhythms" while "the sense of action and optimism that is central to their main characters" is due to "the punchy, confident, militaristic orchestration" (*ibid.*: 64).

Table 3.1 Structure of *Star Wars* main title

Introduction	A		B		A	
3	8		9		9	
	4	4	4	5	4	5
Brass fanfare	Heroic theme in trumpets accompanied by emphatic rhythmic figures in low brass and strings		Contrasting lyrical theme in strings		Return to heroic theme (now in horns) and rhythmically emphatic accompaniment	

The main titles of *Flash Gordon* and *Highlander* depart strikingly from this model both in instrumentation and in the choice and handling of musical materials. *Flash Gordon*'s main title cue, 'Flash's Theme' (Table 3.2), begins with an ominous pounding in the drums joined shortly by the bass and low octaves in the piano. The singing voices enter in the sixth bar to proclaim Flash's name with a dazzling explosion of harmony on the downbeat that is answered by a syncopated stab from the lowest note of the piano. The voices then re-enter to enumerate Flash's extraordinary qualities with a rhythmically awkward yet exciting rush of syllables that accelerate toward the end of the phrase. When the guitar finally enters, it lifts the tonality from A minor to D major. This modulation, the rapidly accelerating delivery of the text and the large ambitus (five octaves from the low piano note to the highest falsetto voice) all contribute towards the musical construction of Flash's heroic character (see Figure 3.3).

Table 3.2 Structure of 'Flash's Theme'

Introduction	A				B	A			C	A		
10	45				8	35			18	24		
	10	18	10	7		18	10	7		8	16	
Pounding rhythm in drums, joined later by bass, then piano	Four statements of the Flash motif				Ascending sequence and chromatic progression	Three statements of the Flash motif			Slower tempo and momentary relief from pounding rhythm	Final statements of the Flash motif		

Figure 3.3 Author transcription of 'Flash's Theme' from *Flash Gordon* (1980) by Brian May. Words and music by Brian May. © 1980 Queen Music Ltd and Wide Music Inc. This arrangement © 2011 Queen Music Ltd. and Wide Music Inc. Reprinted by permission of Hal Leonard Corporation.

After four statements of the Flash motif and its undulation between A minor and D major, an ascending sequence rises confidently from C to A to reinforce the assertions in the text that Flash stands for and will save all of us (Figure 3.4). A contrasting lyrical section slows down the tempo considerably and provides momentary relief from the relentless pounding rhythm of the outer sections as the text turns to Flash's ordinary qualities while promising nonetheless that he can never fail because of the purity of his heart. The rhythmic pulse returns for the final statements of the Flash theme and the number is brought to a close with ominous punches from the lowest notes of the piano.

The main title and opening scene of *Highlander* are scored with Queen's 'Princes Of The Universe' (Table 3.3). It begins with rich vocal harmonies achieved through layering and a harmonic progression comprised of major ninth chords in the bright key of D major (Figure 3.5). After the opening vocal phrase, guitar power chords and heavy drums emphasize each downbeat while a bell-like synthesizer projects a strong sense of optimism. The optimism is undermined at the mention of the world's darkest powers. The tonality drops ominously to B minor and the texture thins to power chords on the guitar, a primal drumbeat utilizing low sounds with an emphasis on beats two and

Figure 3.4 Author transcription of triumphantly rising sequence in 'Flash's Theme' from *Flash Gordon* (1980) by Brian May. Words and music by Brian May. © 1980 Queen Music Ltd and Wide Music Inc. This arrangement © 2011 Queen Music Ltd. and Wide Music Inc. Reprinted by permission of Hal Leonard Corporation.

four and the raw energy of Mercury's voice. After two verses, the guitars and voice recede to leave the drums alone for an additional eight bars, thus providing a transition to the opening scene of the movie, a professional wrestling match.[15] There is about one minute without underscoring before the music re-emerges in the form of virtuosic drum fills and searing guitar passages. This music supports brief scenes of audience members cheering the

Table 3.3 Structure of 'Princes Of The Universe'

Introduction		Verse		Verse		Fade to action		Guitar and drum solos	
9		7		9				15	
4	5	2	2+3	4	2+3	8	[1:00]	3	12
Rich vocal harmonies and distorted guitar in D major		Shift to B minor and bare texture with sustained distorted guitar chords, intense drumbeat, and the raw power of Mercury's voice				Drumbeat gradually fades as action takes over without underscoring		Wrestling scenes underscored by virtuosic drum and guitar solos	

Figure 3.5 Author transcription of major ninth chords in the opening of 'Princes Of The Universe' from *Highlander* (1986) by Freddie Mercury. Words and music by Freddie Mercury. © 1986 Queen Music Ltd. This arrangement © 2011 Queen Music Ltd. Reprinted by permission of Hal Leonard Corporation.

wrestlers with exaggerated enthusiasm intercut with violent images from the match and displays of bravura from the wrestlers.

The musical, dramatic and social significance of the *Flash Gordon* and *Highlander* main titles is best understood by considering them within the discursive parameters of heavy metal identified by Robert Walser (1993). Queen draws upon the gestures and conventions of heavy metal to convey power and potency in ways that differ strikingly and surprisingly from the classical conventions used by Williams and others to convey energy, action and optimism.

The most immediately apparent departure from the classical model is in the use of timbre, specifically the distorted vocal and instrumental timbres that are among the most important aural signs of heavy metal power. "Distortion", explains Queen producer Reinhold Mack, "gives that feeling of ultimate power. The more distortion you get, the more satisfying it is. There's something slightly superhuman, psychologically speaking, about the sustain, the nearly endless notes" (quoted in Gill, 1992: 86). Queen employs distorted guitar as a signifier of power at key points in both songs. In 'Flash's Theme', the guitar is absent from the A minor passages but its energized sound and maximum sustain in the D major passages suggest unquestionable confidence in Flash's abilities. Likewise, in 'Princes Of The Universe', the guitar is absent during the introductory *a cappella* passages but enters shortly thereafter to lend strength to the word 'princes' and subsequently provides aural reinforcement of the concepts of royalty, immortality and inevitable triumph. As the tonality drops to the minor mode for the verses, power chords convey the severity of the struggle that will ensue while simultaneously suggesting that the effort to overcome it will be of epic proportions.

As with instrumental distortion, vocal distortion is attained through excessive power. It results from exceeding the normal capacities of the vocal chords and thereby functions "as a sign of extreme power and intense expression by overflowing its channels and materializing the exceptional effort that produces it" (Walser, 1993: 42). This vocal delivery is apparent in the verses of 'Princes Of The Universe', where the power of Mercury's voice is enhanced by raucous shouts punctuating the text. Still, it is Queen's distinctive multiple-voice layering – and not the solo voice – that is used most effectively to convey power. Heard within the conventions of heavy metal, the rich multiple-voice expressions expand the aural space and draw the listener into a collective affirmation of control and dominance. In *Highlander*, this is attained in the close harmonies of the major ninth chords in the *a cappella* introduction to suggest royalty and immortality. In *Flash Gordon*, the vocal proclamations of Flash's name convey power through the remarkably wide ambitus (see Figure 3.3).

Another significant departure from the classical model is in the use of mode and harmony. Williams's main titles lie unambiguously in the major mode and use diatonic conventions and gestures to establish harmonic stability as a signifier of energy and optimism. Both Queen main titles, by contrast, emphasize the minor mode and include moments of harmonic instability. But rather than acting as agents of destabilization, the minor mode and instability are used to articulate power by presenting key areas as objects to be challenged and overcome. 'Flash's Theme', with its pulsing pedal on A and the reiterated Am–G–F progression, is highly characteristic of the Aeolian mode (natural minor), a mode found frequently in heavy metal, where it is used to produce a "patented quasi-classical, Gothic sound" (*ibid.*: 46). Coded discursively as "aggressive and defiant" (*ibid.*: 48), the Aeolian gloom on A is repeatedly transcended to reach the key of D major, with the root of the VI chord, F, rising triumphantly to F♯ to become the major third of the D major triad. The fluctuation between A and D thus stands symbolically as a metaphor for Flash's imminent triumph over adversity.

'Princes Of The Universe' displays even more ambiguity. The opening *a cappella* passage, although rich in timbre, lacks a clear tonal centre. This is due to the fact that the four major ninth chords from which it is comprised – D, E, G, C – do not occur naturally in any one mode or key (see Figure 3.5). The final two chords fall with rhythmic strength on successive downbeats emphasized by power chords in the guitar so that the root movement from G to C outlines a strong V–I progression that points toward a tonic of C. Nevertheless, the D sonority that opens the phrase lingers to vie for dominance, especially since the second phrase begins by simply returning to this pitch level as if nothing had happened. At the end of the second phrase, there is a drop from C to B minor (the relative minor of D). Although B is heard clearly as the tonic, the initial gesture is a bold step up to the second-scale degree, a *minor* chord on C♯ instead of the diminished chord that would occur naturally in the minor mode. Any chord on the second-scale degree would normally be unstable, but here the C♯ minor chord is treated as a point of arrival from which most of the text is delivered. Only at the end of the phrase does the harmonic motion continue to D before resolving back to B minor.

Rhythm is the most fundamental of all musical parameters and plays a crucial role in eliciting a physical response from the body. It is no surprise, then, that rhythm is central to both Williams's and Queen's main titles. Still, a comparison of the two reveals a striking difference of approach. For Williams, rhythmic potency is imposed through the metric regularity of the march-like martial style. The extensive use of syncopation in the accompaniment does not undermine the rhythmic profile but rather strengthens it by leading to the downbeat. Consequently it is metre – the grouping of beats into a consistently recurring pattern – rather than beat that ultimately provides the basis of the rhythmic framework. The metric organization is particularly apparent in the regularity of the four-bar phrases (see Table 3.1). Rare departures from the four-bar phrasing occur, but they are presented as logical extensions so that the regularity of the phrasing is never undermined and the rhythm unfolds with confident inevitability.

Although the Queen main titles – like Williams's – are in 4/4 time, their rhythmic frameworks are organized not by metre, but by pulse. Both 'Princes Of The Universe' and 'Flash's Theme' are driven by a simple pulse that emphasizes each beat and allows for inconsistent and asymmetrical phrasing without weakening the rhythmic integrity of the music. There is an adherence to four-bar phrasing (with a one-bar extension on the second phrase) in the *a cappella* passage that opens 'Princes Of The Universe' (see Table 3.3). As the verses begin, however, a rhythmic pulse asserts itself and allows for a robust sense of rhythm despite the asymmetrical two- and three-bar phrases that comprise this section. After the second verse, the guitars and voices recede into the background, leaving only the drums to supply the rhythmic pulse. The pulse then serves as a transition to the action and establishes a direct correspondence between a primal conception of rhythm and the energetic wrestling images that ensue.

In 'Flash's Theme', the rhythmic pulse – heard first in the drums and soon reinforced by the bass and low octaves in the piano – dominates immediately and underlies most of the rest of the song. The only moment of respite occurs in the slow section that, significantly, focuses on Flash's ordinary rather than his extraordinary qualities. The absence of pulse here thus serves to reinforce elsewhere the association between rhythmic pulse and extraordinary power. Overall, pulse, rather than phrasing, serves to articulate the control of time and energy by presenting rhythm as a monolithic and unrelenting phenomenon that supersedes the irregular phrasing of asymmetrical groupings, dropped bars at the ends of sections and, in at least one place, a dropped beat that may have occurred in the final editing process (see Table 3.2).[16] Robert Walser's evaluation of the affective meaning of a similar pulse in Van Halen's 'Running With The Devil' is equally apt when applied here. Like 'Running With The Devil',

'Flash's Theme' "celebrates power and offers to the listener an experience of that power; the pulse lets us feel what we might imagine extreme power feels like" (1993: 50).[17]

Conclusion

Queen's music in *Flash Gordon* and *Highlander* demonstrates the full range of possibilities for a rock-music film score: it consists of songs used for main titles and end credits; songs used for source music and scenic underscoring; and atmospheric numbers used to establish a sense of time, place and character. Queen's eloquent grasp of – and responses to – the demands of film music, and particularly of music in the fantasy-film genre, is apparent throughout both scores. The main titles convey heroic power, the end credits are exuberantly triumphant and the music in between conveys a sense of spectacle in the ways it evokes and supports depictions of strange places, extraordinary beings and epic battles. Most importantly, the music captures the essential elements of fantasy film by expressing them in a musical language that is easily understood by the rock-immersed viewers of the films. Consequently, the music succeeds through a directness of expression but also because it establishes the heroes as people to whom we can relate and with whom we can maintain a connection as they strive to accomplish great feats. Rock music, in both movies, is the sound of the ordinary made extraordinary.

With their music for both films, Queen established an important legacy by demonstrating that rock musicians could make a legitimate contribution to the fantasy-film genre. By writing music that was innovative, thoughtful, and, above all, intricately woven into the creative conception of both films, Queen set a precedent and an example for many artists who followed them, including Toto in *Dune* (David Lynch, 1984), David Bowie in *Labyrinth* (Jim Henson, 1986), David Byrne in *The Last Emperor* (Bernardo Bertolucci, 1987) and Peter Gabriel in *The Last Temptation of Christ* (Martin Scorsese, 1988).

Notes

1. A. F. Moore, 'Glam rock', in *Grove Music Online*, *Oxford Music Online* (online at http://www.oxfordmusiconline.com/subscriber/article/grove/music/46248; accessed 16 April 2010).
2. Quoted in *Classic Albums: Queen, Making of a Night at the Opera* (2006), directed by M. Longfellow, London: Eagle Rock Entertainment [DVD].
3. *Ibid.*
4. *Ibid.*
5. Propp was first published in Russian in 1928 and was first made available in an English translation in 1958.

6. The quest voyages of classical mythology provided the producers of fantasy film with rich material for cinematic treatment. See Chapter 1 in this volume, 'Fantasy and the Exotic Other: The Films of Ray Harryhausen'.

7. Blake's description of the details of his involvement in the film are outlined on his official website. As he notes, it was only during the dubbing sessions that he discovered that much of his score had been replaced by synthesized music. See 'Flash Gordon,' in Howard Blake official website (http://www.howardblake. com/music/Film-TV-Scores/524/FLASH-GORDON.htm; accessed 25 June 2010).

8. D. Ross (2009), 'Flash Gordon, Queen and the art of the rock OST', *The Quietus* (http://thequietus.com/articles/01561-flash-gordon-queen-and-the-art-of-the-rock-ost; accessed 29 June 2010).

9. The quotations are taken from an interview with Brian May published in the German magazine *Bravo* in 1980. The original article is available online at http://www.queen-headquarters.de/artikel_queen_auf_dem_weltraumtrip.htm (accessed 26 November 2009). An English translation is available online at http://www.brianmay.com/brian/briannews/briannewsjul07b.html (accessed 26 November 2009). Translations in this essay are the author's own.

10. *Ibid.*

11. 'Flash Gordon,' Howard Blake official website (see note 7).

12. This and all subsequent quoted comments by Mulcahy are taken from Russell Mulcahy, Peter S. Davis and William N. Panzer (2002), audio commentary on *Highlander,* directed by Russell Mulcahy, Troy, MI: Anchor Bay Entertainment [DVD].

13. The versions of the songs discussed here are the versions heard in the film and not the subsequent releases on the Queen studio album, *It's A Kind Of Magic* (1986). With 'Who Wants To Live Forever' and 'Princes Of The Universe' in particular, the versions differ significantly, mostly by expanding or adding rock gestures on the studio album to compensate for the absence of the visual component.

14. This statement is made in the audio commentary. It seems likely that May completed more than just the lyrics on his own. Queen biographers Jacky Gunn and Jim Jenkins describe the situation thus: "Driving home after seeing one particular episode Brian wrote a song he called 'Who Wants To Live Forever?' He sang and hummed the idea into a small portable tape recorder, arriving home with an almost complete song." See Gunn and Jenkins (1992: 194).

15. The original plan, as outlined in the screenplay, was to use a National Hockey League (NHL) hockey game as the backdrop, with the New York Rangers being defeated badly by the Edmonton Oilers. The climax was to be a brutal on-ice free-for-all with the stick-wielding players becoming the fifteenth-century Highlanders wielding broadswords. Ultimately, the members of the NHL were unwilling to permit NHL players to be used in the film, as they thought the scene portrayed hockey as a violent sport. In fact, this is exactly what attracted the production team to the sport and precisely how they planned to present it. See Mulcahy *et al.* (2002), audio commentary on *Highlander.*

16. This anomaly can be heard as a hiccup that is partly obscured by the timpani flourish at 00:00:33 on the soundtrack CD and at 00:01:39 on the DVD (NTSC version). Although clearly a disruption in the metric organization, the primacy of the rhythmic pulse renders it otherwise unnoticeable.

17. In fact, the similarities between 'Running With The Devil' and 'Flash's Theme' extend beyond their shared sense of pulse. Both songs feature prominently the characteristic Aeolian chord progression, VI–VII–I (albeit leading to a major tonic chord in 'Running With The Devil' and a minor one in 'Flash's Theme'), and both alternate between two strong key areas as a means of conveying power and transcendence.

References

Campbell, J. (1949), *The Hero with a Thousand Faces*, Princeton: Princeton University Press.

Frye, N. (1957), *Anatomy of Criticism: Four Essays*, Princeton: Princeton University Press.

Gill, C. (1992), 'Dialing for Distortion: Sound Advice from 10 Top Producers', *Guitar Player*, October, 86.

Gunn, J., and Jenkins, J. (1992), *Queen: As It Began*, New York: Hyperion.

Halfyard, J. K. (2004), *Danny Elfman's Batman: A Film Score Guide*, Lanham, MD: Scarecrow Press.

Moore, A. F., 'Glam rock', in *Grove Music Online*, *Oxford Music Online*, online at http://www.oxfordmusiconline.com/subscriber/article/grove/music/46248 (accessed 16 April 2010).

Propp, V. (1958), *Morphology of the Folktale*, trans. L. Scott, Bloomington: Indiana University Press.

Purvis, G. (2007), *Queen: Complete Works*, London: Reynolds & Hearn.

Ressner, J. (1992), 'Freddie Mercury: 1946–1991', *Rolling Stone*, 621 (January 9), 13–16.

Walser, R. (1993), *Running with the Devil: Power, Gender, and Madness in Heavy Metal Music*, Hanover, NH: Wesleyan University Press.

Worley, A. (2005), *Empires of the Imagination*, Jefferson, NC: McFarland.

4 Fantasy Meets Electronica
Legend *and the Music of Tangerine Dream*

Lee Barron

During the course of her historical and cultural exploration of the figure of the 'faery', Maureen Duffy poses this question: "What happens to the fairies in an age of reason? Do they disappear or simply go underground?" (1972: 195). One answer is that they frequently appear on cinema screens within a film genre dubbed 'fantasy', a genre that was present at the birth of cinema itself. As Steinbrunner and Goldblatt state, Georges Méliès's early cinema was firmly committed to fantasy, so much so that many of his early films were "spectacular flights of bizarre imagination, embracing every facet of the weird, the make-believe, the not-yet-happened", with films featuring "demons and ghosts, high adventures and impossible travels" (1972: 7). Fantasy would endure within cinema, from the magical and supernatural to the mythic and stories that border on science fiction. This chapter will focus upon fantasy film in the 1980s and one film in particular, directed by the British film-maker, Ridley Scott.

In the wake of his claustrophobic horror film *Alien* (1979) and the dystopic science-fiction epic *Blade Runner* (1982), Scott embarked upon a film that was set firmly within the tropes of traditional fantasy – *Legend* (1985). Eschewing the visceral, technological and philosophical qualities of his previous two films, Scott opted for a narrative set within an enchanted world and centrally built upon the dualisms of good and evil, light and dark. *Legend* is notable for a variety of reasons: the casting of the then little-known American actor Tom Cruise as the hero; the troubled shoot, with the striking set design of the enchanted forest destroyed during production when a fire broke out at Pinewood; and the re-editing of the film, with the subsequent release of two different versions for the US and European markets. It is this latter issue that is the subject and focus of this chapter. Because of negative test audience responses, not only was *Legend* substantially (and rather brutally) re-edited and its length cut, but the original score by the iconic film composer Jerry Goldsmith was replaced with a newly commissioned score – principally by German electronic band Tangerine Dream (with additional contributions by the British singers Jon Anderson and Bryan Ferry). Consequently, American and European audiences experienced the film with very different musical soundtracks, which inevitably established very different tonal and ambient qualities for the film's action and images.

This chapter will analyse *Legend* in relation to the later electronic music score, discussing the development and nature of electronic music and comparing it with Goldsmith's score, critically examining the effect that Tangerine Dream's music brings to a narrative firmly located within a fantasy setting. Although the film can be experienced as Scott intended it, with Goldsmith's orchestral and arguably more 'suitable' soundtrack – the US 'Ultimate Edition' DVD contains both versions – the alternative version enables *Legend* to be experienced via music as a collision between the worlds of traditional fantasy (pastoral settings, unicorns, demons) and of 'modernity' in the form of the technologically established, electronic and synthesizer-driven music of Tangerine Dream. Hence, *Legend*, a tale of dualism, is a tale of two narratives with two very different soundtracks.

Good vs. evil/strings vs. synthesizers

As Sammon states, Ridley Scott's intention, in partnership with scriptwriter William Hjortsberg, was to create a film that was firmly located within the fantasy idiom, a film that combined distinctive elements of classical European folk tales and Judeo-Christian myth with hints of Disney's *Fantasia* (1999: 77). Consequently, *Legend* was a film complete with a hero, the forest-dwelling Jack (Tom Cruise), a princess, Lili (Mia Sara), unicorns, elves, fairies and goblins and a villain, the Satanic Darkness (Tim Curry), set against the principal mythic *mise-en-scène*, an 'Enchanted Forest', itself juxtaposed with Darkness's lair. In terms of structure and form, *Legend* concerns a Manichean confrontation, literally in this case, between the forces of light and dark within an entirely imaginary and fantastical world, a world with no diegetic trappings of modernity in any form. The heart of the narrative concerns the death of one of the last two remaining unicorns, killed at Darkness's command by Blix (Alice Playten), a Goblin minion, because the death of the creature will initiate the coming of an unnatural winter. The slaying of the other, female, unicorn will establish a state of eternal night. Because the sun weakens him, Darkness has the creature captured and prepared for sacrifice so that, in blotting out the sun, he will reign supreme. Although initially sceptical of his abilities, Jack becomes a hero and confronts and destroys Darkness. In the process, he is reunited with his beloved Lili and the dead unicorn returns to life, consequently re-establishing the equilibrium of the world.

Legend is centrally a fantasy film with allusions to the themes and structures of fairy-tales, but also to the Ur fantasy text, J. R. R. Tolkien's *The Lord of the*

Rings (1954–5), the tale of an epic battle between good and evil, including the creation of a fantastical world containing the industrial horrors of the Satanic Sauron, juxtaposed with a pastoral idyll, pastoral in the sense of a decisive contrast to the urban (Gifford, 1999: 2). Moreover, like many great sagas before it, *The Lord of the Rings* is built upon the epic Quest (Curry, 1997: 143). Although not on the epic scale of Tolkien's novels, *Legend* is similarly set firmly within an enchanted universe. Like *The Lord of the Rings*, *Legend* – in the form of Jack, the forest-dweller – conveys an archetypal quality of Romance and the birth of the hero (Thomson, 1967: 45). *Legend* has discernible allusions to High Fantasy: it is an 'impossible world' that has little or no connection with realism; and like High Fantasy, the narrative of *Legend* is populated with a range of fantasy characters, such as ladies, villains, wizards, elves, dragons and trolls (Sullivan, 2001: 281). Therefore, as part of his (admittedly, rather truncated) quest, Jack encounters a host of magical creatures who assist him, notably the fairies, particularly the Puckish Gump (David Bennent) and Oona (Annabelle Lanyon), and the comedic elves Screwball (Billy Barty) and Brown Tom (Cork Hubbert); he must also battle monsters in the form of the swamp-dwelling Meg Mucklebones (Robert Picardo) and bestial guards, before finally confronting Darkness to save Lili, the female unicorn and the world.

In terms of the nature of the fantasy world *Legend* conjures up, its central *mise-en-scène*, the Enchanted Forest, is an evocative space, a pastoral idyll that is visually marked by the constant presence of floating blossom in the air. It is a place of nature and peace. This space is then contrasted with the domain of Darkness, a great tree that houses an opulent throne room, dungeons and fiery furnaces spewing forth flame – sort of a mini-Mount Doom. And it is here that *Legend* actively begins to toy with tone. Although ostensibly framed as a fairy-tale, it contains decisive moments of darkness and suggestions of violence, torture and cannibalism. However, darker themes are intimately (and appropriately) connected to the villain, Darkness, for it is this figure who steers the narrative away from the potentially fey.

The figure of Darkness created by Rob Bottin is a visual and design triumph, a hulking, red-skinned, bull-horned demon who espouses a distinctly modern philosophy, pursuing a nihilistic vision of eternal night but underscored with a satanic ideology that accords with Social Darwinism and the quasi-philosophical trappings of the infamous creator of The Church of Satan, Anton LaVey. Lavey's seventh Satanic Statement listed in his 1969 text, *The Satanic Bible*, is subtly echoed by Darkness when, after being called an animal by the captive Lili, he replies: "We are all animals, my lady. Most are too afraid to see it."[1] Of the efficacy of Darkness in the context of the film, Schreck critically notes that "surrounded by so much saccharine whimsy, [Tim] Curry's flamboyant performance provides the only sign of life in this too-sweet-for-its-own-good confection" (2001: 202–3). Alternatively, for the film critic Roger Ebert, *Legend* ultimately fails as a narrative because it is not sweet enough and in place of a consistent tone of lightness and "plucky cheerfulness", Darkness and his malevolent scheme are so effective that the film is ultimately "too dreary and gloomy for its own good".[2]

In a similar critical vein, the *Variety* review of *Legend* on its release, although not overly impressed with the film (bar its visual effects and set design), concluded that Jerry Goldsmith's score was one of his best (in Sammon, 1999: 140). This is praise indeed for the composer of a number of very successful films that includes *The Planet of the Apes* (Franklin J. Schaffner, 1968), *Papillon* (Franklin J. Schaffner, 1973), *The Omen* (Richard Donner, 1976), *Coma* (Michael Crichton, 1978) and *First Blood* (Ted Kotcheff, 1982). Thus, the music effectively transcended the film. As an effective, evocative and successful score, Goldsmith's music ably reflects the central components of traditional film music. For Brown, film music acts as "wallpaper soporific" and "as a cogenerator of narrative affect that skews the viewer/listener towards a culturally determined reading of the characters and situations" (1994: 32). Furthermore, as Donnelly states, film music acts as a "medium of manipulation", a means by which film-makers can evoke "emotional responses within the audience" (2005: 6). Donnelly cites the composer Aaron Copland's categorization of the functions of film music: soundtracks create atmosphere, highlight the psychological states of characters, provide neutral background filler, build a sense of continuity, sustain tension and establish a sense of closure (Donnelly, 2005: 10). All of these components

Table 4.1 Track listing from the soundtrack album of Goldsmith's music for *Legend*[3]

Track title	Duration (min)
Main title/Goblins	5.48
My True Love's Eyes/Cottage	5.07
Unicorns	7.56
Living River/Bumps And Hollows/Freeze	7.24
Faeries/Riddle	4.56
Sing The Wee	1.11
Forgive Me	5.16
Faeries Dance	1.55
Armour	2.20
Oona/Jewels	6.44
Dress Waltz	2.50
Darkness Fails	7.31
The Ring	6.32
Reunited	5.19

are arguably discernible within Goldsmith's score for *Legend*. It is a rousing, sweeping score that establishes motifs that musically convey the fantastical images they accompany, and the heroic and romantic themes that lie at the heart of what is ostensibly a fairy-tale narrative.

Goldsmith's score is rendered on the official soundtrack album release as fourteen discrete compositions (shown in Table 4.1). At the start of the film, with his 'Main Title/Goblins' cue accompanying the titles, the links between imagery and music are immediately established, as the opening shots of the film stress the pastoral setting with images of a forest and forest creatures (birds, a small bear). The music consists of strings with subtle brass accents. However, the appearance of Blix and Darkness undercuts the pastoral images, and the music becomes suitably darker, characterized by ominous male choral voices. The pastoral motif returns with the introduction of Princess Lili, whose first appearance shows her singing a folk song on her way to Nell's (Tina Martin) cottage. Her subsequent meeting with Jack is underscored by distinctly romantic orchestral notes, with the addition of flutes and airy male choral voices.

Thus far, the music within this version of *Legend* is entirely conventional. It is a traditionally composed score for a fantasy narrative set within a never-never-land, a pastoral, pre-industrial world of magic and enchantment. The score has an appropriately opulent and sweeping quality; but there are divergences from the orchestral form. For instance, the introduction of the unicorns – the mythical creatures at the heart of the narrative – is granted a more experimental theme in that their musical accompaniment consists of a choral motif, strings and hints of synthesized sounds, while recordings of whale song overlying the music lend a distinctly 'New Age' quality to the soundtrack. The effect is to stress the magic of the creatures, their representation of all that is good in the universe and their status as the antithesis of Darkness. Thus, although it is a traditional score, Goldsmith does provide unexpected motifs and complexities.

Furthermore, Goldsmith's music is particularly effective during the film's key set pieces, one of which is the 'temptation' scene, a point in the narrative at which Darkness attempts to seduce the captive Lili to the ways of evil and persuade her to remain with him as his consort. Prior to Darkness's impressive visual emergence from within a mirror, Lili is captivated by a shadowy, dancing figure, which is actually a magically animated black dress that then impresses itself upon her body in preparation for Darkness. The music in this sequence takes the form of a waltz – the CD cue is entitled 'Dress Waltz' – the tempo rising and falling in synchronization with the dancing figures. A further noteworthy musical moment is the finale of the film, signifying the defeat of evil, the return of the sun, the revival of the slain male unicorn and the resurrection of the Princess. This takes the form of the rousing orchestral cue entitled 'Reunited', which is characterized by soaring male and female choral voices and cascading violins and strings, perfectly establishing the appropriately happy ending to the fairy-tale and the coming together of Lili with her 'prince', Jack, for the subsequent 'happy ever after'.

Goldsmith's score is emotive, dramatic and sweeping. Moreover, its use of choral arrangements and classical orchestration, with some nods to electronic sounds and effects, constitutes a seamless interweaving of sound and image to convey an array of fantastical pastoral and mythic settings. Nonetheless, Goldsmith's orchestral score for the US version of *Legend* was rejected by the studio in favour of a soundtrack by Tangerine Dream. The rationale was that a "more 'accessible' sound was needed to attract the youth audience" (Kermode, 1995: 19) and that Goldsmith's music was too sentimental and traditional (Sammon, 1999: 83). What the studio wanted was 'New Age' music, and Tangerine Dream, with its synthesizer-laden sound, was perceived to be the ideal band to provide this. Whereas film-score music originally functioned to set the mood, convey character emotion or heighten the drama of a film, by the 1980s film music had firmly shifted from the screen to become a product in its own right. As Kermode states:

> In recent years there has been a notable trend toward the youth promotion of often unremarkable films via rock and pop music tie-ins. Although this is nothing new, the 80s saw a previously unparalleled explosion of the 'pop promotion' gimmick with often artistically bankrupt results, thanks largely to the rise of music video as a primary marketing tool ... By the time Tony Scott's Top Gun (1986) passed into movie lore as the quintessential pop-promo 'feature', the 80s had already become the decade of the 'pop soundtrack'. (1995: 17)

Tangerine Dream did not mirror the populist, radio-friendly, video-producing songs of *Top Gun* (Tony Scott, 1986) – principally illustrated by Berlin's global hit 'Take My Breath Away' – but it was ostensibly a more 'modern' sound, as befitted an electronically based band. Of course, if a wider appeal was the studio's rationale for replacing Goldsmith's music, then it was arguably short-sighted on its part, since the timbre of the electronica that Tangerine Dream provided was of a very different order from the bouncy, light rock of *Top Gun* or the earnest balladeering of Joe Cocker and Jennifer Warnes for the soundtrack of *An Officer and a Gentleman* (Taylor Hackford, 1982). Tangerine Dream had its fans but it still appears as an eccentric choice given the nature of the film it was commissioned to score. Electronic music was more readily utilized within cinema for science fiction than for fantasy. As Donnelly (2003: 133–4) argues, from films such as *The Day the Earth Stood Still* (Robert Wise, 1951) to *The Thing* (John Carpenter, 1982) and *The Terminator* (James Cameron, 1984), science fiction habitually used electronic instruments and for sound reasons, because synthesizers would frequently be "exploited in sci-fi and futuristic genres to create an other-worldly effect" (Kalinak in Donnelly, 2003: 134). Indeed, science-fiction cinema was closely linked with the early development of electronic instruments, from the Theremin (invented in the 1920s and soon a staple within 'weird' science fiction) to early synthesizers and nascent electronic composers such as Louis and Bebe Barron, who composed an electronic score for *Forbidden Planet* (Fred M. Wilcox, 1955), and Stanislav Kreichi, who used an early ANS synthesizer when composing for the 1961 art-film project *Into Space* (see Kreichi, 1995). As a result, in stark contrast to Goldsmith's score, Tangerine Dream's music accords not with traditional composition but with an explicitly twentieth-century technological art form – electronic music.

The history of electronic music, for many historians of the form, begins in 1906 in Holyoke, Massachusetts, when Thaddeus Cahill exhibited his 'Dynamophone' or 'Telharmonium', the first instrument to create music by an electrical process. Electronic music became a recognizable genre in 1948 with Pierre Schaeffer's concert of his compositions created from existing sound recordings. This new form of music, *musique concrète*, was created by processes of "subjecting natural, pre-recorded sounds to any number of recording techniques, like speed changes, playing the sounds backwards or tape reversal, and overdubbing" (Ernst, 1977: 3). Elektronische Musik, pure electronic music, was established in Germany in the early 1950s, differing from *musique concrète* in the way that it utilized electronic sound generators and modifiers rather than manipulating natural sounds. Composers such as Karlheinz Stockhausen led the way and the evolution of purely electronic music intensified when, in 1955, RCA demonstrated the Olson-Belar Sound Synthesizer (Schwartz, 1973: 62). The synthesizer represented a "multi-function machine, possessing sound generators, modifiers, and mixers" (Ernst, 1977: 49) and rapidly led to a series of synthesizer-only recordings such as Vladimir Ussachevsky's *Wireless Fantasy* (1960) and Milton Babbit's *Composition for Synthesizer* (1961). However, as Schwartz (1973: 62) argues, the important development for the genre was that of smaller, voltage-controlled synthesizers, principally the commercially marketed Buchla (invented by Donald Buchla) and the Moog (invented by Robert Moog), instruments which rapidly found their way into popular music.

Although the Grateful Dead and Frank Zappa and the Mothers of Invention had toyed with early electronic techniques, it was in the 1970s that an array of artists fully utilized electronic instrumentation and effects. Alongside Lou Reed's use of distortion on his 1975 album *Metal Machine Music* and Brian Eno's 1975 album *Discreet Music*, synthesizers were employed by a host of rock/progressive rock artists and bands such as The Tubes, Todd Rundgren, King Crimson, Yes, Rick Wakeman, Patrick Moraz, Keith Emerson, Jean-Michel Jarre, Vangelis, Kraftwerk and Gary Numan. But while many of these artists and bands used synthesizers in conjunction with traditional instrumentation (guitars, bass, drums), the early 1970s saw the rise of bands that were fully, if not exclusively, founded upon the use of electronic instruments and the synthesizer in particular. In identifying Germany as the true birthplace of electronic music, it is fitting that Ernst identifies Edgar Froese and his band Tangerine Dream as one of the foremost exponents of synthesizer-driven music (1977: 204). Formed in 1967 and rising to prominence in the early 1970s, Tangerine Dream gained popularity initially as part of the West German Krautrock collective of bands that also included Can, Popol Vuh, Cluster, Harmonia, Ash Ra Tempel and Neu! (Albiez, 2003: 358). In terms of sound, Griffiths describes Tangerine Dream as:

> essentially an ensemble of keyboard players using synthesizers and other electronic instruments; guitars and percussion have a relatively limited part. Often they make use of sequencers to maintain simple ostinatos, these representing fragments creating a foundation for rich, consonant textures. (1979: 64)

Releasing albums from 1970 to the present, Tangerine Dream's key recordings include *Phaedra* (1974), *Rubycon* (1975), *Ricochet* (1975), *Stratosfear* (1976), *Cyclone* (1978) and *Hyperborea* (1983). If *Phaedra*, *Stratosfear* and *Cyclone* are taken as key illustrations of the Tangerine Dream sound, they consist mainly of extended instrumental pieces – tracks running to twenty minutes in length – with the occasional use of computerized, modulated voices or Yes/Pink Floyd-like singing. Compositions frequently bear quasi-mystical or portentous titles such as 'Mysterious Semblance At The Stand Of Nightmares', 'Movements Of A Visionary', 'The Big Sleep In Search Of Hades' and 'Rising Runner Missed By Endless Sender'. The music is often slow and consists of rising oscillations, multi-layered electronic chimes, simulated choral voice-effects and synthesized, modulated melodies. Although with differing personnel and the use of better musical technologies over the years, the band has remained within this ambient, electronic musical form throughout its career. Moreover, besides its prolific album output, the band has also periodically provided soundtracks for a number of films including *Sorcerer* (William Friedkin, 1977), *Thief* (Michael Mann, 1981), *The Keep* (Michael Mann, 1983), *Risky Business* (Paul Brickman, 1983), *Near Dark* (Kathryn Bigelow, 1987) and *Miracle Mile* (Steve De Jarnatt, 1988). Sometimes described as New Age, the members of Tangerine Dream have also been characterized as composers and performers of 'space' music (Holm-Hudson, 2005: 386), in reference to their futuristic electronic sound, machinic percussion and reputation as musical 'technotricians' (Lanza, 1991: 48). Thus, a band that carried with it the legacy of electronic music-making was brought in to replace Goldsmith's score for *Legend*, whose narrative was far removed from any of the trappings of the modern world and technology.

What is the effect of Tangerine Dream in place of Jerry Goldsmith? The answer is a radical one. As listed in the (now difficult to obtain) soundtrack album, Tangerine Dream's music consists of ten pieces of music composed by the band and a final track composed and performed by Bryan Ferry (see Table 4.2). The Tangerine Dream soundtrack, not surprisingly, transforms the tone of *Legend*. The US version of the film for which the band produced music was 89 minutes long, a substantially shorter narrative than either the director's cut, which ran to 114 minutes, or the European version, which was some 94 minutes long. The immediate narrative differences in the US version consist of an initial *Star Wars*-like rolling text that establishes the nature of the *Legend* universe and the threat posed by Darkness. Moreover, Darkness is visually introduced in the first minutes of the film – a narrative aspect withheld in the European version and director's cut until the final quarter – and Jack's first encounter with Gump is substantially cut. Furthermore, returning to Aaron Copland's categorization of the functions of film music, principally in creating atmosphere and highlighting the psychological states of characters, the difference between Tangerine Dream and Jerry Goldsmith is also readily apparent.

As the film begins, in place of subtle strings and rising orchestration, Tangerine Dream's 'Opening' consists instead of electronic ambience. Simulated bell sounds and pan pipes are underscored with a minimalist and synthesized ascending keyboard scale that is buttressed with low chords. Indeed, the use of lower and distinctly ominous bass chords becomes a leitmotif in the early part of the film. For example, while the introduction of Princess Lili is accompanied by a lilting piece (but not replicating the folky quality of Goldsmith's score), the scene within Nell's cottage is overdubbed with ominous electronic chords, as is Lili's first on-screen meeting with Jack. These sounds serve to alter the feel of the film, giving it a sense of foreboding that is slightly at odds with

Table 4.2 Track listing from the soundtrack album of Tangerine Dream's music for *Legend*[4]

Track title	Duration (min)
Opening	2.55
Cottage	3.23
Unicorn Theme	3.27
Goblins	3.03
Fairies	2.57
Loved By The Sun (Jon Anderson with Tangerine Dream)	5.57
Blue Room	3.24
The Dance	2.23
Darkness	3.05
The Kitchen/Unicorn Theme Reprise	4.49

the enchanted pastoral surroundings in which the characters are presented. This musical ambience continues in the scene in which Jack leads Lili to the unicorns. Here the musical mood changes to a distinctly upbeat sound to announce the first appearance of the two mythical animals, with an electric guitar-like keyboard melody accompanying their on-screen arrival. The scene is then further swathed in ambient electronica, which is intensified when Blix shoots a poisoned dart at the male unicorn. With the perpetration of this act of evil, the music transforms into industrial-like 'noise'. This tonal quality is similarly later repeated in Nell's cottage, where Lili takes refuge from the goblins in the wake of the slaying of the unicorn and the coming of the glacial darkness. Here, the music is distinctly discordant, with stabbing synthesized chords which almost evoke the musical anatomy of the horror film, harsh chords which culminate in an electronic screeching sound. Consequently, as established in the early segment of the narrative, the music is utterly different from Goldsmith's sweeping, string-driven sounds.

In place of orchestral instrumentation, the alternative version of *Legend* is instead dominated by electronic sounds, from the atonal horror-motifs of the goblin pursuit of Lili to the industrial percussive beats that attend Jack's search for her. However, there are more conventional melodies; for instance, the courtship of Lili by Darkness is accompanied by a distinctly eastern-sounding keyboard scale, appropriately supported by moody and atmospherically dark keyboard chords. Generally, the US version of *Legend* has a score that rises and falls in tempo, a soundscape of minimalist chords and electronic melodies, of staccato tones and machinic percussion. The tonal and structural differences are perfectly illustrated within the waltz scene; accordingly, the waltz scene of the US version of the film is no longer constructed from traditional classical music motifs, but is instead a technologically scored event.

The finale of the US film is different in two ways from the European version. The happy ending, the resurrection of Lili and of the male unicorn, and the reunited lovers running towards the sun, is accompanied by a piece of music entitled 'Loved By The Sun', and this song does indeed conjure a pastoral quality. Principally, this is because 'Loved By The Sun' is a song, not an instrumental or incidental piece. The music, composed and performed by Tangerine Dream, consists of a piano melody and rousing, rising synthesized notes with vocals provided by Jon Anderson. The presence of Anderson infuses both the scene and the music with a sense of enchantment otherwise arguably lacking in the stark electronica that characterizes the US version of the film. His high vocals provide a subtle counter to the electronic instrumentation: as lead vocalist with the UK progressive rock group Yes, Anderson was no stranger to songs with pastoral and mystical or New Age lyrical leanings, as illustrated on Yes's concept album *Tales From Topographic Oceans* (1973) and most clearly in

Anderson's fantasy-themed solo album, *Olias Of Sunhillow* (1976). The tone and feel of 'Loved By The Sun', with its ethereal keyboard themes and chimes and its ascending tones, represents a fitting musical ending for a film so firmly rooted within fantasy. The lyrics similarly reflect the narrative and its themes of magic and fantasy, containing words such as 'mystics', 'enchantment' and 'legends'. The Tangerine Dream/Jon Anderson collaboration is a piece of music that, even if rather sentimental, represents a suitably climactic point in the score in that it musically reinforces the narrative sense of closure and triumph achieved by the characters in the final scene – the defeat of Darkness and the return of light. However, one significant aspect is the superimposition of the face of Darkness over the reunited unicorns (not present in the director's cut/ Goldsmith-scored version), suggesting a possible return of evil and a future threat, thereby injecting a sour note into the happy ending.

As the credits begin, 'Loved By The Sun' fades into the film's final piece of music, a track not composed by Tangerine Dream. Rather (and with a sure nod to commercial film soundtracks and pop/rock fandom), the final music consists of a song entitled 'Is Your Love Strong Enough', composed and performed by former Roxy Music singer, Bryan Ferry. Although 'Loved By The Sun' is also a song, it is in keeping with the generic themes of the film: indeed, I would argue that it constitutes a moment of connection with Goldsmith's music, if not in form or structure, then at least in terms of filmic tone. On the other hand, 'Is Your Love Strong Enough' has no pretensions to mysticism, magic or fantasy, but is a modern, up-tempo, sophisticated pop song marked by brash keyboards, sliding bass, wailing guitar, blaring saxophone and, of course, Ferry's distinctive vocals. Thus, the US version of *Legend* with its Tangerine Dream soundtrack ends with a thoroughly 1980s tone that is a stark departure from Jerry Goldsmith's orchestral finale, as heard on the restored director's cut and on the European version.

Concluding the tale of two soundtracks: magic meets modernity

If, as Brown asserts, film music functions as a form of wallpaper to visual content, as a "co-generator of narrative affect" (1994: 32), then the two versions of *Legend* and their differing soundtracks potently illustrate the efficacy of such music. The use of an explicitly electronic soundtrack is singular for a film rooted within fantasy. Other notable fantasy films of the 1980s, such as *Dragon Slayer* (Matthew Robbins, 1981), *Clash of the Titans* (Desmond Davis, 1981), *Conan the Barbarian* (John Milius, 1982), *The Dark Crystal* (Jim Henson and Frank Oz, 1982), *Krull* (Peter Yates, 1983) and *Willow* (Ron Howard, 1988), employed traditional orchestral scores with music composed by Alex North,

Laurence Rosenthal, Basil Poledouris, Trevor Jones and James Horner. Jerry Goldsmith's score was in this tradition; but it is worth noting that commercial music could succeed within the fantasy genre. For instance, *The NeverEnding Story* (Wolfgang Petersen, 1984) successfully combined music composed by Klaus Doldinger and electro-composer Giorgio Moroder and even produced a hit single performed by Limahl, formerly of the UK pop group Kajagoogoo. Nevertheless, the outcome for *Legend* was neither so precise nor, arguably, as successful. Ridley Scott had utilized the electronic music of Vangelis to potent effect within *Blade Runner*, but the music of Tangerine Dream within *Legend* is arguably problematic due to its generic nature. Although impressive, the set pieces and locations of the *Legend* world are limited, notably to the Enchanted Forest and the Tree of Darkness, both of which are thoroughly other-worldly. As stated earlier, Darkness's domain has some visual similarities with Sauron's Mount Doom or Saruman's Isengard but none of their industrial nature. This means that music which bears a distinctly industrial and machinic quality is rather incongruous in the milieu of the film. This is particularly apparent in the earlier scenes of the film, the magical setting of the Enchanted Forest, complete with rustic cottage. Whereas Jerry Goldsmith's orchestral music fits these scenes perfectly, Tangerine Dream's electronic notes change the feel decisively both in this scene and throughout the film. As Ridley Scott states of the differences:

> *I felt awful about having to replace Jerry Goldsmith's music on the American version, because Jerry had given me exactly what I'd asked for ... and I still think Jerry's score for* Legend *was bloody good ... But somehow, during all the second-guessing that went on while we were re-editing the film, Jerry's music began to be perceived as being too sweet; frankly [Universal] got a little paranoid and thought Jerry's stuff too sentimental. I was persuaded to be insecure about Goldsmith's score as well. So Tangerine Dream was hired to rescore the film for America. But comparing the Goldsmith and Tangerine Dream scores is difficult, because we only had three weeks to do the Tangerine Dream one. And I think that what the Dream guys did in the time they had to do it in was pretty good. But was it as sophisticated as Jerry's music? No.* (Sammon, 1999: 83)

For Donnelly, "film and music have different floor plans of logic and aesthetics. Sometimes they converge. Sometimes they work off each other in a seamless manner. At other times, destructive feedback occurs" (2005: 12). In the case of *Legend*, this statement is valid in terms of perceptions of the differing films. In one sense, the use of futuristic electronica in a film set firmly within a fairy tale-inspired pastoral setting was bold, but it was motivated by commercial studio concerns rather than aesthetic choice and it does not readily fit the narrative. While the electronic music of Vangelis suitably underscored the science-fiction motifs of Scott's earlier *Blade Runner*, the use of synthesizers within a pastoral, fairy-tale film is jarring.

In terms of evaluating electronic music, Schwartz argues that it has frequently been dismissed as a mode of music that equates to "dehumanization" and the "final victory of the Machine over Man ... the triumph of Noise over Music" (1973: 3). At the same time, electronic music established new modes of instrumentation and new techniques for composing (*ibid.*: 8). Taken together, such appraisals can be discerned within the two distinct versions of *Legend*. With regard to narrative, the director's cut is the most cohesive and coherent telling of the tale. Underscored with Goldsmith's music, it is, bar some dialogue anachronisms, a story firmly rooted within the fairy story and the fantasy romance. In comparison, the shorter US version of *Legend* is more ruthlessly edited than its European counterpart, and such cuts are reflected in the music, which also, in places, rises and falls abruptly and is marked by banks of electronic sounds counterpointed with sharp keyboard strokes and discordant electronic sounds. Similarly, on the subsequent soundtrack albums, Goldsmith composed significantly more music, in terms of both number of pieces and their length, than did Tangerine Dream.

With the advent of DVD and the resulting vogue for director's cuts for the aficionado, Scott's original vision and Jerry Goldsmith's music have been remastered and re-presented to audiences. Although Goldsmith's music feels more appropriate to the nature of the film, while Tangerine Dream's electronic music – bar 'Loved By The Sun' – has a more sci-fi than fantasy feel, both are held in high regard by differing factions of fans, with the review forums of online shopping sites such as Amazon.com displaying written expressions of loyalty to either Goldsmith or Tangerine Dream. As one reviewer unequivocally states, "Tangerine Dream's music was listless and lame, laughably simplistic and devoid of any emotion. Jerry Goldsmith transforms the scene utterly: now it positively overflows with dark desire. What a difference the right score can make."[5] However, many of Amazon's US customers remembered the Tangerine Dream score from the film's theatrical and VHS release, felt surprised and even cheated to find they had bought a DVD with a different soundtrack and found the Goldsmith version too saccharine, preferring the edginess and darkness of what, to them, was the original score: "the score by Tangerine Dream is what MAKES the movie! I could have done without the director's cut. The score doesn't come close to capturing the spirit of the story or scenery; it sounds like a cartoon."[6] However, there are 'third-way' reviewers who offer a more conciliatory evaluation, suggesting that having both versions of the soundtrack clearly augments the experience of the film.[7]

Goldsmith's music, like that for many other fantasy films of the 1980s, provides more traditional and rich composition. The Tangerine Dream soundtrack is evocative but tends towards the ambient rather than the striking. Indeed, the score only truly attains a 'mystic' quality with the inclusion of Jon Anderson's vocals. The use of orchestration in more recent fantasy films, such as Howard Shore's multi-layered score for Peter Jackson's *The Lord of the Rings* trilogy (2001-3) and the scores for the *Harry Potter* film series (2001-11), emphasizes the musical expectation that fantasy seems to bring. One could argue that *Legend* represents an exercise in originality and that, although not Scott's initial choice, the use of electronic music, as evidenced within classic and contemporary science fiction, does effectively conjure the other-worldly.

The production story of *Legend* is itself a saga; and the most dramatic episode was played out in music – but critics of the orchestral soundtrack missed a crucial issue. Although a typical film soundtrack in many senses with its traditional instrumentation, Jerry Goldsmith's music did also utilize, amongst the strings, brass and soaring choral work, the defining instrument of electronic music – the synthesizer. Consequently, with or without re-edited versions, charges of sentiment and studio judgement, the enchanted fantasia of *Legend* was *always* destined to contain a touch of the machine. This was, after all, fantasy 'Ridley Scott-style', and so the dualisms between the industrial and the pastoral that have been referred to throughout this chapter find an apt musical expression and combination within *Legend*. It is there in Goldsmith's soundtrack to subtle effect, but it finds a far more stark articulation when Scott's fantasy-based visuals, plot and motifs are underscored by the electronic sounds composed by Tangerine Dream. Therefore, although Scott ultimately preferred Goldsmith's music, given the machinic quality of his earlier films *Alien* and *Blade Runner*, Tangerine Dream formed a musical continuum with such themes, even in a landscape dominated by fairies, princesses, demons and unicorns.

Notes

1. Cf. "Satan represents man as just another animal" (LaVey, 2005: 25).
2. R. Ebert, 'Legend', *Chicago-Sun Times*, 18 April 1986 (http://rogerebert.suntimes. com/apps/pbcs.dll/article?AID=/19860418/REVIEWS/604180302/1023; accessed 27 March 2009).
3. *Legend: Original Soundtrack Recording* (2002), performed by the National Philharmonic Orchestra and Chorus, conducted by Jerry Goldsmith, Silva America SSD 1138 [CD].
4. Tangerine Dream, *Legend* (1995), Varèse Sarabande, VSD 5645 [CD].
5. Movie Nut, 'What a difference...', *Amazon.com*, 22 October 2009 (http://www. amazon.com/Legend-Ultimate-Tom-Cruise/product-reviews/B000063UR2/ ref=cm_cr_pr_link_3?ie=UTF8&showViewpoints=0&pageNumber=3&sortBy=byS ubmissionDateDescending; accessed 2 August 2010).

6. Bob God, 'Tangerine Dream MAKES the movie!' *Amazon.com*, 26 February 2010 (http://www.amazon.com/Legend-Ultimate-Tom-Cruise/product-reviews/B000063UR2/ref=cm_cr_pr_link_3?ie=UTF8&showViewpoints=0&pageNumber=3&sortBy=bySubmissionDateDescending; accessed 31 December 2010).

7. See, for example, Totally Honest Reviewer, 'Wonderful fairy-tale – great DTS sound!', *Amazon.com*, 21 August 2006; Kala C. Tremitti, 'A classic of inner instincts', *Amazon.com*, 22 June 2006; Luis Carillo, 'one of the best of the 80's fantasy movies', *Amazon.com*, 21 June 2006; Michael Ensley,'Classic fantasy from the 80's', *Amazon.com*, 15 June 2006 (http://www.amazon.com/Legend-Ultimate-Tom-Cruise/product-reviews/B000063UR2/ref=cm_cr_pr_link_next_14?ie=UTF8&showViewpoints=0&pageNumber=14&sortBy=bySubmissionDateDescending; accessed 31 December 2010).

References

Albiez, S. (2003), 'Know History! John Lydon, Cultural Capital and the Prog/Punk Dialectic', *Popular Music*, 22(3), 357–74.

Brown, R. S. (1994), *Overtones and Undertones: Reading Film Music*, Berkeley: University of California Press.

Curry, P. (1997), *Defending Middle-Earth: Tolkien, Myth and Modernity*, London: HarperCollins.

Donnelly, K. J. (2003), 'Constructing the Future through the Music of the Past: The Software in Hardware', in I. Inglis (ed.), *Popular Music and Film*, London: Wallflower Press, pp. 131–48.

Donnelly, K. J. (2005), *The Spectre of Sound: Music in Film and Television*, London: BFI.

Duffy, M. (1972), *The Erotic World of Faery*, London: Hodder and Stoughton.

Ernst, D. (1977), *The Evolution of Electronic Music*, New York and London: Schirmer Books.

Gifford, T. (1999), *Pastoral*, London and New York: Routledge.

Griffiths, P. (1979), *A Guide to Electronic Music*, London: Thames and Hudson.

Holm-Hudson, K. (2005), ' "Come Sail Away" and the Commodification of "Prog Lite",' *American Music*, 23(3), 377–94.

Kermode, M. (1995), 'Twisting the Knife', in J. Romney and A. Wootton (eds), *Celluloid Jukebox: Popular Music and the Movies since the 1950s*, London: BFI.

Kreichi, S. (1995), 'The ANS Synthesizer: Composing on a Photoelectronic Instrument', *Leonardo*, 28(1), 59–62.

Lanza, J. (1991), 'The Sound of Cottage Cheese (Why Background Music Is the Real World Beat!)', *Performing Arts Journal*, 13(3), 42–53.

LaVey, A. (1969), *The Satanic Bible*, New York: Avon Books.

Sammon, P. M. (1999), *Ridley Scott: The Making of His Movies*, London: Orion Books.

Schreck, N. (2001), *The Satanic Screen: An Illustrated Guide to the Devil in Cinema*, London: Creation Books.

Schwartz, E. (1973), *Electronic Music: A Listener's Guide*, London: Secker & Warburg.

Steinbrunner, C., and Goldblatt, B. (1972), *Cinema of the Fantastic*, New York: Saturday Review Press.

Sullivan, C. W. (2001) 'Folklore and Fantastic Literature Author(s)', *Western Folklore*, 60(4), 279–96.

Thomson, G. H. (1967), '*The Lord of the Rings*: The Novel as Traditional Romance', *Wisconsin Studies in Contemporary Literature*, 8(1), 43–59.

5 Entering the Labyrinth
How Henson and Bowie Created a Musical Fantasy

Liz Giuffre

Nearly thirty years after its initial release, the fantasy film *Labyrinth* (Jim Henson, 1986) continues to gain audience attention and favour. This can be attributed in part to the opportunity for new audiences to engage with the film as it has been re-released in various home entertainment formats but also to the continued interest in the careers of *Labyrinth*'s core creative team: director Jim Henson (the mastermind behind *The Muppet Show* and *Sesame Street*) and musician/performer David Bowie. This chapter will argue that the film's continuing appeal centres on the collaboration between Henson and Bowie rather than simply on its content as a narrative and, most importantly, that this collaboration was essential in locating *Labyrinth* as a fantasy film. *Labyrinth* not only allowed Henson and Bowie to develop the career trajectories they had already initiated in other media, but their involvement in the film invited existing Bowie and Henson devotees to engage with the film as well. In a sense, *Labyrinth* is a film about Bowie and Henson rather than just about a young girl embarking on a journey in a fantasy world. The combination of Bowie's and Henson's distinct musical and visual skills ensured that *Labyrinth* was remarkable at the time of its release and it still is.

Fantasy film, the marvellous and the fantastic

Defining film genres is often a difficult and highly contested process but it is a way of enhancing our understanding of specific films and their impact. Tudor argues that "*genre* terms ... can be usefully employed in relation to a body of knowledge and theory about the social and psychological context of film" (Tudor, 2000: 98) and before examining *Labyrinth* in detail, I want first to provide the film with some context, briefly suggesting what might be gained by categorizing it in this way. Fantasy is a genre that encourages the breaking of conventions considered essential for other types of storytelling; while fantasy has often been stigmatized for that reason, this room for experimentation has also facilitated some bold creative collaboration. In addition, I suggest that fantasy can be defined in terms of how it facilitates a particular interaction between the audience and film-makers and, as I will show in the case of *Labyrinth*, the imaginative scope of fantasy allows for a distinctive level of interaction between creative artists and their bodies of work.

In her work *In Defence of Fantasy* (1984), Swinfen begins by citing J. R. R. Tolkien's definition of fantasy as "the Sub-creative Art ... [with] a quality of strangeness and wonder in the Expression" (Tolkien in Swinfen, 1984: 5). Specifically, Swinfen notes that fantasy is defined by the presence of "'the marvellous' .... anything outside the normal space-time continuum of the everyday world ... composed of what can never exist in the world of empirical evidence" (*ibid.*).[1] Swinfen argues that the marvellous is an essential ingredient in the interaction between fantasy and its audience, as it is through the marvellous that the author and audience enter into a shared understanding of the different worlds created for the fantasy text. In a recent collection of essays focused on fantasy film, Fowkes also describes the way fantasy engages its audience, and while she refrains from using 'marvellous', she begins by articulating a similar concept: "it is generally agreed that fantasies tell stories that would be impossible in the real world" (2010: 2). With specific reference to film genres, Fowkes notes that:

> assessments of the realism of a film often have little to do with actual reality but more to do with the specific conventions of realism and storytelling as we have come to know them through an accretion of Hollywood movies (ibid.: 4)

and that defining fantasy as a part of a 'real'/'unreal' binary is simplistic because, for example, "when Gene Kelly sings and dances in the rain, we don't complain that it's unrealistic – it's realistic in a musical" (*ibid.*). In defining fantasy film, then, Fowkes argues that films in this genre need to have "'fantastic' story elements that are integral to the film's story-world" (*ibid.*: 5). She argues that, although all films offer an escape from reality, fantasy film makes such escapism explicit in a distinctive way, and that while "viewers may not be consciously aware that they have escaped into an 'alternate universe' when watching an action movie (for example), ... [fantasy] makes it explicit in its *content*" (2010: 7).

This investigation of *Labyrinth* will draw on notions of both the marvellous and the fantastic. A key to the film's appeal is its ability to present the audience with content that is obviously escapist, which not only relinquishes the reality of everyday life but also subverts traditional expectations of popular-music artists and other forms of entertainment. To achieve this required the participation of artists – Henson and Bowie – who had, by the mid-1980s, established a body of work characterized by such unpredictable subversions.

In terms of the film's content, the fantasy narrative of *Labyrinth* follows the young protagonist Sarah (Jennifer Connolly), who unthinkingly commands the Goblin King Jareth (David Bowie) to relieve her of her babysitting duties by abducting her crying baby brother. After her wish is granted, Sarah must enter and solve a labyrinth in order to find the king again and rescue the baby. On the way she encounters a variety of the king's subjects who serve either to help or hinder her journey. Sarah's journey in *Labyrinth* is set up by the opening scenes in the film, where we watch a game in which she imagines herself playing with goblins and their king, a scenario which is then fleshed out as she enters the fantasy world we have seen her imagining. In this world she must conquer the labyrinth; assisted by the goblins and other creatures, she finally defies the king and returns home, where she makes peace with her life and responsibilities. In terms of the film's style and content, *Labyrinth* is distinctive in its depiction of a fantasy world, specifically the world of the labyrinth itself, as a place inhabited mostly by goblin creatures realized by puppets developed by Henson and his associates. The exception is Jareth, who appears human but is somehow able to command the goblins through song and other techniques of persuasion.

Featuring a musician – David Bowie – as an actor/performer, *Labyrinth* can also be located in a fantasy subgenre, that is, a musical fantasy film. Fowkes defines this subgenre with specific reference to *The Wizard of Oz* (Victor Fleming, 1939), a film which relies on "the strong affinity between musical and fantasy genres" (Fowkes, 2010: 24). As such, it is able to appeal to audiences who are interested in either music or fantasy or both. The continued appeal of *Labyrinth*, like the continued popularity of the 1939 version of *The Wizard of Oz*, can thus also be attributed to the film's status within this subgenre. Fowkes notes that while musical fantasies have been particularly popular in the Bollywood tradition (*ibid.*), in mainstream Hollywood there have been few other excursions into the genre, with the notable exception of *The Wizard of Oz* remake *The Wiz* (Sidney Lumet, 1978). The 1939 *Wizard of Oz* remains attractive to audiences as much for its showcasing of Judy Garland as a singer and performer as for the film's story and its depiction. As Salman Rushdie argues in his essay on *The Wizard of Oz* for the British Film Institute, "Garland singing 'Over The Rainbow' did something extraordinary: in that moment she gave the film its heart" (2006: 26). Although Bowie's overall performance in *Labyrinth* has not attained anything like the level of affection and acclaim of Garland's Dorothy, his musical performance was a key to the reception of *Labyrinth* at the time of its release and in subsequent years. Like *The Wizard of Oz*, *Labyrinth* is a musical fantasy that uses aspects of both genres to equal effect.[2]

The combination of Henson's and Bowie's previous creative trademarks was noted particularly by reviewers of *Labyrinth*. Although these highly distinctive artists would have been able to dominate a film individually, the musical fantasy genre enabled their idiosyncratic styles to work together effectively.[3] For example, in an opening-week review of *Labyrinth* for the *New York Times*, Nina Darnton (1986) used only a picture of Bowie in costume from *Labyrinth* to illustrate her piece and described the actor/musician as "perfectly cast ... [with] his songs add[ing] a driving, sensual appeal" to the film.[4] Other preview and early reviews of *Labyrinth* also focused on Bowie, with *Variety* magazine arguing that he appeared in the film as "a fish out of water ... contribut[ing] a few interesting, if out of place, songs" (Greenberg, 1986). Bowie's established reputation as a musician appears to have impeded the reviewer's appreciation of him as an actor. Notwithstanding these mixed reactions at the time of *Labyrinth*'s release, the emphasis on Bowie's appearance as both cast member and a contributor to the music soundtrack stresses the centrality of the combination of music and image to the film. Wojcik and Knight argue that "popular music becomes a key aural component of the mise-en-scène in genre films" (2001: 4) and indeed, the review's emphasis on how Bowie's music fits the film demonstrates the importance of music and image interaction. Fantasy films are far from the only genre to utilize popular music in this way, but by drawing on Bowie's existing popular-music persona with its own fantasy profile, and his acting and songwriting ability, Henson and Bowie were able to create *Labyrinth* as a fantasy film that constructed a distinctive relationship between music and puppet characters.[5]

When *The Muppet Show* met Ziggy Stardust: creating a scenario

By the time of *Labyrinth*'s release Henson had worked on three successful films – *The Muppet Movie* (James Frawley, 1979), *The Great Muppet Caper* (Jim Henson, 1982) and *The Dark Crystal* (Jim Henson and Frank Oz, 1982) – as well as leading the creative and artistic teams behind the popular and widely respected television shows *Sesame Street* (PBS, 1969–) and *The Muppet Show* (ATV, 1976–81). For Henson, *Labyrinth* was instrumental in the consolidation of a new (and what would become hugely influential) production company, Jim Henson's Creature Shop, as well as an opportunity to further explore approaches to fantasy film-making.[6] As Henson explained a few years after *Labyrinth*'s release, "I've always thought that fantasy should have the ability to go a good deal more abstract, more expressionistic, and anytime I see a film that does that, I think it's really terrific" (Henson in Unattributed, 1989: 20). Two decades later, Fowkes's assessment of Henson's contribution to fantasy film concludes that:

Jim Henson provided a refreshing foray into fantasy ... building on his signature puppetry from the popular television shows ... to make whimsical movies such as The Muppet Movie *(1979) and the more serious but notable* The Dark Crystal *(1982). (2010: 32)*

Both *The Dark Crystal* and *The Muppet Movie* create that sense of the marvellous that characterizes fantasy film, but it is important to note the differences between these films, particularly in terms of their relation to Henson's other work. As Henson explained just prior to the release of *The Muppet Movie*, he had been keen to make the film distinctly different from the Muppet television show: "On the television show we'd invite one guest into the world of the Muppets. In the movie, we are taking the Muppets out into the real world" (Henson in Parmiter, 2009: 129). This insistence on showing puppets on location rather than in a puppet-friendly studio is something that Henson had moved away from by the time he made *The Dark Crystal*; that fantasy film moved to a further stage in featuring puppets in a puppet world exclusively, with no live actors on screen at all. As Andrew Wright describes:

> The Dark Crystal *was a 'whole world' concept created in the tradition of epic fantasy adventures ... It* [sought] *to transport its viewer to an unfamiliar world where magic is all-powerful and humans have no place amongst the bizarre animatronic creatures. (2005: 259)*

Wright also notes that this tactic was not as commercially successful as Henson had hoped and that ultimately *The Dark Crystal*'s value "went beyond any box office receipts" (2005: 262).

In an interview shortly after *Labyrinth*'s release Henson said "one of the best things about *Labyrinth* is it enabled us to do something like the Muppets and slightly like *The Dark Crystal* – a nice middle ground" (Henson in Magid, 1986: 71). The return to combining live actors and puppets, a combination which Henson first used in his television shows, defined *Labyrinth*. This mixed style of presentation was possible because *Labyrinth* was one of the first fantasy films to capitalize on the technological developments in film-making that occurred in the 1980s. Its production required "literal[ly] tons of extra equipment" (Magid, 1986: 76) so it could be made to the standard the producers, directors (and audiences) were expecting. As Darnton (1986) noted at the time of *Labyrinth*'s release:

> *Mr. Henson uses the art of puppetry to create visual effects that until very recently were possible to attain only with animation ... Mr. Henson's creations have put him at the forefront of a development that expands the possibilities of imaginative fantasy that can be transferred to the screen.*

In addition to realizing his vision for the puppet characters, Henson also had a clear idea of what he wanted to achieve with the casting of the live actors in *Labyrinth*. His vision for the film was the collaboration between his puppets and live performers, and particularly between his creatures and a musician. As he explained in the documentary *Inside the Labyrinth* (Des Saunders, 1986):

> When I first started to write the film we had this evil Goblin King, and then somewhere, quite early on, we said 'what if he was a rock singer, a contemporary figure'? And we thought, who? Michael Jackson, Sting, David Bowie? And there are only a few people you would think of and he [Bowie] was immediately the one we wanted to do it. (Henson interview in *Inside the Labyrinth*)

Henson's desire to feature a contemporary musician in his film was far from unusual, with many directors in different genres also recruiting popular musicians to appear in their films as actors and performers.[7] However, Henson's very specific vision required a musician with an equally distinctive profile. Henson had previously used many popular musicians in his television work (in *Sesame Street* and *The Muppet Show* especially),[8] and he approached Bowie to be part of *Labyrinth* after seeing him perform his Serious Moonlight tour of America in 1983. Bowie, who during the 1970s preferred to consider himself a 'theatre artist' rather than merely a popular musician (Auslander, 2006: 109), described being taken with Henson's proposal and with the "potential of making that type of movie with humans and songs" (Bowie speaking on *Inside the Labyrinth*). Speaking about how he created the character, Bowie described his view that Jareth should be "very reluctant with the inheritance [as the Goblin King]; one gets the feeling he'd rather be down in Soho or somewhere like that" (*ibid.*). This imagined location of Jareth as a denizen of Soho – a district famous, if not notorious, for its secular music and down-to-earth nightlife – demonstrates the extent to which Bowie conceptualized the role in terms of his own popular-music background rather than in a realm of pure abstract fantasy.

Prior to *Labyrinth*, Bowie had already taken on a number of film acting roles including *The Man Who Fell to Earth* (Nicholas Roeg, 1976), *The Hunger* (Tony Scott, 1983) and *Merry Christmas, Mr. Lawrence* (Nagisa Ôshima, 1983). Bowie's visual appearance, especially in these last two films, was relatively sedate and understated, his pop persona disappearing behind the specific requirements of each film role: an undercover alien and a vampire in a contemporary city (in *The Man Who Fell to Earth* and *The Hunger*, respectively), and a soldier in World War II in *Merry Christmas, Mr. Lawrence*. His appearances in these films had not significantly reflected his various personae as a popular musician up to this time, which were characterized by flamboyant, colourful and often effeminate costumes and performance styles. What set Bowie's role in *Labyrinth* apart from his other film work was that it allowed him to demonstrate his ability as a musician, by performing his music on screen as well as providing a soundtrack, and to appear in a costume and character that resembled some of those he had developed in his musical career.

When *The Muppet Show* met Ziggy Stardust: drawing audiences

In an article on the marketing of a number of 1980s films including *Labyrinth*, Andrew Wright (2005) notes how important the specific combination of music and Henson's puppets was in attracting audiences. Specifically, he argued that "*Labyrinth*, in comparison [with *The Dark Crystal*] ... drew partly from the formula of the popular television programme, *The Muppet Show*, enhancing the audience's entertainment through lively musical numbers" (2005: 257). He went on to argue that:

> the relationship to The Muppet Show *is evident on a number of levels within* Labyrinth, *but primarily through the puppets and animatronic creations who, after the sombre inhabitants of* The Dark Crystal, *are an explosion of colour and character.* (ibid.: 268)

He goes on to identify the way that *Labyrinth* "mimics the performance criteria of its predecessor [television series by] encouraging dynamic interaction between humans and puppets" (*ibid.*: 269), and explores in particular the first time audiences are introduced to Bowie's character Jareth, at home in the Goblin City surrounded by his (puppet) goblin subjects. In this scene the actor and puppets combine to perform 'Magic Dance'. Wright describes this scene as "a lively musical number" (*ibid.*) but this musical performance is not merely ornamental. With this scene audiences are introduced to Jareth who, although human, is also fantastic because of his ability to command the non-human creatures.

Music plays a key part in establishing this fantasy role for two reasons. Firstly, Bowie's depiction of a singing and performing Jareth works – as in other musicals – as the exposition of a key moment in the narrative and, in this scene, to demonstrate the relationship between the goblins and their king. Bowie's Jareth is surrounded by puppet goblins on the floor and on various platforms around the walls as he sings and dances; he interacts with them by singing to and with them, with the chorus in particular acting as a call and response (as when Jareth asks what kind of magic spell should be used and selected goblins answer "slugs and snails and puppy dogs' tails"). The interaction through song serves to demonstrate the affinity between Jareth and the goblins as they collaborate over how to stop Sarah reaching the end of the labyrinth. Secondly, Bowie's appearance in *Labyrinth* also bears a strong stylistic resemblance to his early 1970s musical persona Ziggy Stardust, particularly Jareth's tight clothing and high boots.[9] Figures 5.1 and 5.2 show both characters in heavy eye make-up and long, 'rock', teased hair, even though sonically Bowie used each one to make quite different music. However, while performing 'Magic Dance', a song with a light pop sensibility, Jareth does not sound like Ziggy because, if nothing else, "Ziggy played guitar".[10] In contrast, the upbeat pop sound of 'Magic Dance' – with its 1980s production style and era-distinctive use of keyboards, synthesizers and drum machine – has since been compared to some of Bowie's other 1980s material, specifically his then-recent single 'Let's Dance' (1983).[11] Audiences, therefore, are presented with a dual representation of Bowie as musician and Bowie as actor. This tactic of deploying a popular musician's persona for an appearance in a Henson production was used repeatedly in *The Muppet Show*; it played to the audience's existing knowledge of the artist, while offering something new through the interaction with Henson's creations.[12] In the 'Magic Dance' scene in *Labyrinth*, the musical-fantasy film rewards audiences who have previous knowledge of Bowie's musical personae by recreating part of the Ziggy Stardust look, while providing something additional as his performance moves from the guitar-driven, often soul-inspired 1970s sound to more contemporary 1980s synth-driven pop.

Figure 5.1 David Bowie as Ziggy Stardust (1973)

Figure 5.2 David Bowie as Jareth (1986)

Music and puppetry in *Labyrinth*

Two high-profile fantasy films, Ridley Scott's *Legend* and Jim Henson's *Labyrinth*, were released within a few months of each other in December 1985 and June 1986 respectively.[13] As Ron Magid notes, the films invited comparison because their "subject matter sounds somewhat similar ... [and each film was] photographed by the same man [cinematographer Alex Thompson]" (Magid, 1986: 65). It was the collaboration between Bowie and Henson, or Jareth and the puppets, that ultimately served to set *Labyrinth* apart from its main fantasy-film competition at the time of release. Explaining the general difference between the two films, Thompson argues that in terms of tone, "*Labyrinth* is a lighter film; there's probably more humour in it and there's music and it's not meant to be taken seriously, whereas there are elements in *Legend* that are quite serious" (Thompson in Magid, 1986: 65).[14] Thompson's comment again foregrounds the importance of Henson (humour) and Bowie (music) in setting *Labyrinth* apart. Thompson continues:

> There's a number that Bowie does and there are about fifty goblins all in the shot at the same time ... Each goblin had at least one puppeteer, some of them had two, and the majority had three people operating them. The whole floor was strewn with people and we had to knock holes in the floor of the set where they could stick their hands up through ... that's why it took us so long to make this movie! (ibid.: 70)

Thompson does not specify which scene in the movie he is referring to here, with this generalization suggesting that the interaction between Bowie and the puppets was, in many ways, more compelling than *Labyrinth*'s story or other key elements. Thompson's focus on the logistical and technical difficulties of matching up the puppets with live actors underlines the patience both Henson and Bowie brought to the task, and therefore their own appreciation of the importance of that convergence.

Labyrinth works because of the way human action and puppetry can interact without challenging the audience's credulity. The fantasy genre enables this to work particularly because, as noted above, it is in the nature of that genre to encourage the suspension of disbelief far beyond what is usually acceptable in other genre films. *Labyrinth* invites audiences to accept the combination of live actors and puppets, including shared musical routines, as normal. Indeed, in the few sequences where live actors are interacting without the puppet creatures, notably the masquerade ball where Jareth attempts to seduce Sarah, there is a sense of some important narrative component being missing, an aberration, as if this is in fact the 'abnormal' world.

The masquerade ball is set in a fantasy frame within *Labyrinth*'s own fantasy world. After eating a piece of poisoned fruit, Sarah finds herself dressed in an elaborate (and somewhat cartoonish) ball gown surrounded by couples in strange, slightly goblin-like masks. Jareth soon appears in the frame and eventually moves through the crowd to dance with her. Bowie's voice is recognizable in the vocal for the song playing during this scene, the slow-paced 'As The World Falls Down'. Jareth, however, does not perform the song, but rather moves silently through the crowd until he meets Sarah. It is only after the two have been dancing for a short while that Jareth mouths one line of the song, "I'll be there for you as the world falls down", singing to Sarah directly as they continue to dance. This is markedly different from how music is presented elsewhere in the film, and it is the only place in the narrative where a song is presented without being overtly performed.

In his account of the masquerade scene, Wright makes no explicit mention of Bowie's (or Jareth's) disconnectedness from the music that plays throughout. While he does describe Bowie as "taking on the role of a fantasy Prince Charming ... not dissimilar to the flamboyant style of early 1980s New Romantics" (2005: 271), it is curious that there is no mention of Jareth's 'absent' performance as compared to the dominating explicitness of his performances in other staged musical scenes in the film. This disconnection makes the masquerade sequence seem more like a music video than the *Muppet Show*-like performance pieces in the film so far. Indeed, when 'As The World Falls Down' was released by Bowie as a single separate to its appearance in the film, the song's own video featured two different representations of him; one where he appears as Bowie the singer, performing on stage while styled as a 1950s teen idol (complete with the film set to black and white), and another where he appears as Bowie depicting Jareth, with sequences from the film intercut and shown in colour. Again, either audiences are encouraged to engage with one element (the song itself or its role as a marker of the film) or they are rewarded for recognizing both (the connection between the two worlds is the Henson puppet Hoggle, who appears in the colour clips from *Labyrinth* as well as on the black-and-white set with Bowie). This cross-marketing between the film and the music video, something that was achieved by creating a distinct relationship between Henson's puppets and Bowie's musical profile, was another tactic used to draw audiences to the film but it also functions particularly well as part of the fantasy film. Audiences are engaged through the invitation to consider Bowie as a fictional character as well as a real-life musician, with the apparent impossibilities of this dual representation (most obviously as we hear him singing while also delivering separate dialogue) typical of the fantasy film. We see a demonstration of the impossible, the real and the fantastic delivered simultaneously as Bowie the musician and Jareth the character sound together.[15]

Although *Labyrinth* received disappointing box-office figures on its original cinema release, it has since been repeatedly re-released in home-entertainment formats. A Collector's Box edition was released on DVD in 2004, as well as a Universal Media Disc version in 2005. *Labyrinth* was also part of a double home-entertainment DVD release with *The Dark Crystal* in 2000, with Sony Pictures developing a marketing subcategory of 'Henson Fantasy Films' specifically to accommodate the resale of these films to contemporary audiences.[16] In addition, Sony Pictures released an anniversary edition of *Labyrinth* on DVD in 2007 – although this did not specify what 'anniversary' it actually celebrated, an ambiguity maintained perhaps to make the film appear timeless, or at least to avoid drawing audience attention to its unusual release date.[17] Following these, a CD release of the soundtrack was issued in 2007 by Capitol/EMI, followed by a digital download version of the album. Full film versions of *Labyrinth* were made available to download via iTunes in March 2008, heavily promoted on the official Jim Henson website; and more recently *Labyrinth* and *Dark Crystal* have both been released on Blu-Ray.[18] There has also recently been a re-release of books associated with the film, including *The Goblin Companion: A Field Guide to Goblins* (Jones and Froud, 2003, originally developed in 1996 for the film's tenth anniversary) and *The Goblins of the Labyrinth: 20th Anniversary Edition* (Jones and Froud, 2006); in the same year manga publisher Tokyopop published a written sequel to the film, *Return to Labyrinth*.[19] The music videos of songs that had been made to accompany *Labyrinth*, 'Underground' and 'As The World Falls Down', were included on Bowie's DVD release *Best Of Bowie* (EMI, 2002), and a 12-inch talking Jareth plush doll was produced by Neca in 2007.

This rush of cross-market interest in re-releasing *Labyrinth* and its associated merchandise was not unusual in some respects, as in recent times production companies in a variety of media have explored ways of capitalizing on new formats of distribution for their products. However, *Labyrinth*'s releases have been driven not only by the desire of its copyright owners to maximize their assets, but also by the strong fanbase the film has maintained (and continued to expand) since its original release. As Wright discovered, "an Internet search uncovers many fan sites revealing that ... [not only does *Labyrinth*] have longevity, but that it now has a significant adult following" (2005: 271). In particular, he notes the development of the fan-organized 'Labyrinth of Jareth Masquerade', a ball that had been held annually in the USA for nearly a decade at the time of Wright's publication,[20] at which:

> participants at this gathering are encouraged to take inspiration from the film's mystical world of fairies, goblins and elves for their costumes, with the evening presided over by one guest who is dressed as Jareth, King of the Goblins. (ibid.)

Although Wright does not go into detail about how these fans have come to engage with the film, a more recent internet search indicates that sometimes they appear to have emerged through engagement with the various re-releases of the film itself, while individual Bowie and Henson/Muppet fansites also contain references to *Labyrinth* and its various re-releases.[21] As within the film itself, the interaction between Bowie and Henson's creative identities has continued to attract audiences to the film now, decades after its original release. Thus, it may be said that in terms of the growing audiences for the film, Henson and Bowie are *Labyrinth*'s real focal point, and that this is enabled by the fantasy genre in itself. Both Bowie's and Henson's fan bases had come to expect 'marvellous' and 'fantastic' scenarios from these artists. The connection in the case of Henson and his puppets is self-evident. For Bowie, during the period leading up to the making of the film, his career had been based – to an unusual extent among pop musicians – on the construction of fantastic personae and fantasy worlds.

In conclusion: solving the *Labyrinth*

Labyrinth has become an important part of the fantasy-film canon. The film's combination of two key creative talents, Henson and Bowie, helped to ensure that artistically the film was a type of fantasy that rewarded both audiences already familiar with one or both of these artists' previous works and those (particularly younger ones) who might still be new to film-going at all. Furthermore, as a musical fantasy, a rare crossover between the musical and fantasy genres, *Labyrinth* has continued to appeal to audiences interested in either genre and the output of these artists, with fans of Bowie's music coming to the film on that basis, just as fans of Henson's other legacies, his Muppet characters and television programmes, are also drawn to the film.

In seeking to account not only for the limited interest in *Labyrinth* on its first release but also for its growing cult status nearly thirty years on, identifying it as a musical fantasy film is a useful starting point. As such, the specific team of Henson and Bowie is of central importance, since they attracted pre-existing fans to the film in a way that transcended the appeal of a specific narrative, but also because each had already established a career through the creation of fantasy realms. Henson's was based on presenting puppetry on television and film, while Bowie's was based on his creation of musical personae, most notably Ziggy Stardust. When Bowie's and Henson's existing fantasy experiences were combined in *Labyrinth*, the result was a musical fantasy that drew audiences from a variety of standpoints, and continues to do so as the years pass.

Acknowledgement

The author would like to acknowledge the generous and swift attention that was given by Bruce Johnson in the preparation of this chapter.

Notes

1. Swinfen, writing specifically about fantasy fiction written post-1945, also argues that the marvellous is key to distinguishing fantasy from science fiction, which she argues deals with "what does not exist now, but might exist in the future" (1984: 5).
2. Although they are not the focus of this study, there are conspicuous parallels between *Labyrinth* and *The Wizard of Oz* in terms of narrative as well. For example, see Andrew Wright's analysis of the similarities between the characterization and journey of *Labyrinth*'s Sarah and *The Wizard of Oz*'s Dorothy (2005: 267; see also Arendt, 2002: 44).
3. *Labyrinth* also included work by some other well-established creative artists, notably George Lucas, who became the film's executive producer after his sudden success with the *Star Wars* franchise, and Terry Jones, known for his work with the Monty Python team, who wrote the screenplay. However, it was the combination of Henson and Bowie that attracted most attention.
4. What little reference there is to the new talent in the film – particularly the lead (and then very young actress) Jennifer Connelly – is brief and unflattering, with Darnton again using the established work of Henson and his company as a frame through which to view the newer elements of the film: "perhaps Mr Henson gave too much attention to his puppets and not enough to developing a compelling performance in his lead actress [Jennifer Connelly]" (Darnton: 1986).

5. For a non-genre-specific discussion of the use of popular music in films, see Wojcik and Knight (2001).

6. As reported in *Variety* in 1999 (nine years after Henson's death):

   The Creature Shop got its start in London in the mid-1980s because the late Jim Henson didn't want to disband the group he'd gathered together to make the movie "Labyrinth". The creative team that developed the advanced inner workings of the puppets in the film in 1983-4 eventually formed the core staff when the Creature Shop opened for business in August 1985. (Grove, 1999: 31)

7. For example, see Powrie's study (2003) of Bowie's and Sting's various film appearances. Other popular musicians had appeared in films, especially during the 1960s and 1970s (with 'Elvis films' becoming a genre in their own right), and prior to that popular recording artists such as Frank Sinatra appeared regularly as actors and performers, particularly in Hollywood musicals.

8. For a full list of the guests featured on each season of *The Muppet Show*, see Garlen and Graham (2009: 217–22).

9. Bowie first developed Ziggy for his concept album and the accompanying tour The Rise and Fall of Ziggy Stardust and the Spiders from Mars (1972), and the character has continued to be connected to him for the rest of his career, even though Ziggy Stardust was famously 'killed' soon after his creation. For details, see Auslander (2006: 113–14; 126–7).

10. This is the first line of Bowie's song 'Ziggy Stardust' from the album *The Rise And Fall Of Ziggy Stardust And The Spiders From Mars*.

11. In a biography of Bowie, David Buckley, who was clearly unimpressed with Bowie's contribution to *Labyrinth* generally, described 'Magic Dance' as "a 'Let's Dance' retread" (Buckley, 2001: 431).

12. For example, in the television show's second season (episode 14), Elton John appeared performing 'Crocodile Rock', in a costume covered in huge feathers, which made his body look inflated and furry like those of the Muppets (PBS, first broadcast 25 October 1977).

13. *Legend* was released first in the UK; the US release dates of the two films are even closer, with *Legend* released in April 1986.

14. Although both films used popular music in their soundtracks, the Tangerine Dream music used for the US release of *Legend* was, in fact, a last-minute replacement score. See Lee Barron's chapter in this volume for a full discussion.

15. The author wishes to thank Janet Halfyard for help in developing this final point.

16. The continued existence of this subcategory can be seen at www.sonypictures. com/homevideo/hensonfantasyfilms (accessed 20 January 2009).

17. Usually re-releases and reissues of films celebrate anniversaries in groups of five years, for example, a twentieth or twenty-fifth anniversary. Therefore, 2007, which was *Labyrinth*'s twenty-first anniversary, would be an unusual date for promotion.

18. See http://www.henson.com/press_releases/2008-3-3.pdf (accessed 20 August 2010).

19. See http://www.tokyopop.com/product/1712 (accessed 12 August 2010).
20. Further information about the ball can be found at http://www.labyrinthmasquerade.com/about.php (accessed 3 October 2011).
21. For example, see the Bowie website section on *Labyrinth*'s appearance on iTunes (http://www.crackedactor.com/2008/03/09/download-labyrinth; accessed 10 August 2010) and the Muppet site's section on *Labyrinth*'s release on Blu-Ray (http://www.muppetcentral.com/news/2009/081709.shtml; accessed 10 August 2010).

References

Arendt, E. (2002), *Braveheart and Broomsticks: Essays on Movies, Myths and Magic*, Commack, NY: Six Star Publishing.

Auslander, P. (2006), *Performing Glam Rock: Gender and Theatricality in Popular Music*, Ann Arbor: University of Michigan Press.

Buckley, D. (2001), *Strange Fascination: David Bowie: The Definitive Story*, London: Virgin Books.

Darnton, N. (1986), 'Screen: Jim Henson's "Labyrinth"', *New York Times*, 27 June 1986, p. C14.

Fowkes, K. A. (2010), *The Fantasy Film*, Oxford: Wiley-Blackwell.

Garlen, J. C., and Graham, A. M. (eds) (2009), *Kermit Culture: Critical Perspectives on Jim Henson's Muppets*, Jefferson, NC: McFarland & Co.

Greenberg, J. ['Jagr'] (1986), '*Labyrinth* (Review)', *Variety*, 25 June, p. 90.

Grove, C. (1999), 'Dream Weavers: Muppet House Remodels for CG Clients', *Variety*, 25 October, pp. 31–2.

Jones, T., and Froud, B. (2003), *The Goblin Companion: A Field Guide to Goblins*, London: Pavilion Books.

Jones, T., and Froud, B. (2006), *The Goblins of Labyrinth: 20th Anniversary Edition*, New York: Harry N. Abrams.

Magid, R. (1986), 'Goblin World Created for *Labyrinth*', *American Cinematographer*, 68(8), 71–81.

Novak, R. (1986), '*Labyrinth*', *People Weekly*, 26 (7 July), p. 10.

Parmiter, T. M. (2009), 'The American Journey Narrative in the Muppets Movies', in J. C. Garlen and A. M. Graham (eds), *Kermit Culture: Critical Perspectives on Jim Henson's Muppets*, Jefferson, NC: McFarland & Co, pp. 129–41.

Powrie, P. (2003), 'The Sting in the Tale', in I. Inglis (ed.), *Popular Music and Film*, London: Wallflower Press, pp. 39–59.

Rushdie, S. (2006), *The Wizard of Oz*, London: BFI.

Swinfen, A. (1984), *In Defence of Fantasy: A Study of the Genre in English and American Literature since 1945*, London: Routledge.

Thompson, K. (2003), 'Fantasy, Franchises, and Frodo Baggins: *The Lord of the Rings* and Modern Hollywood', *Velvet Light Trap*, 52, 45–63.

Tudor, A. (2000), 'Critical Method ... Genre', in J. Hollows, P. Hutchings and M. Jancovich (eds), *The Film Studies Reader*, London: Arnold, pp. 95–8.

Unattributed (1989), 'Jim Henson Dialogue on Film: Miss Piggy Went to Market and $150 Million Came Home', *American Film*, 15(2), 18–21.

Wojcik, P. R., and Knight, A. (2001), 'Overture', in P. Wojcik and A. Knight (eds), *Soundtrack Available: Essays on Film and Popular Music*, Durham, NC: Duke University Press, pp. 1–15.

Wright, A. (2005), 'Selling the Fantastic: The Marketing and Merchandising of the British Fairytale Film in the 1980s', *Journal of British Cinema and Television*, 2(2), 256–74.

Wright, R. (2003), 'Score vs. Song: Art, Commerce, and the H Factor in Film and Television Music', in I. Inglis (ed.), *Popular Music and Film, London: Wallflower Press*, pp. 8–21.

6 *Superman* as Mythic Narrative
Music, Romanticism and the 'Oneiric Climate'

Ben Winters

Fantasy film has maintained a lasting relationship with the products of German romanticism; indeed, one could make a case for arguing that many fantasy films are direct descendants of the mythic narratives so beloved by the nineteenth century – including the fairy-tales of the Brothers Grimm, the *Niebelunglied* and the prose and poetic *Eddas*. Aside from those films directly modelled on German sources – for example, *Snow White and the Seven Dwarfs* (David Hand, 1937) or *Die Niebelungen* (Fritz Lang, 1924) – an emphasis on nineteenth-century Germanic concerns with religious symbolism, origins and/or racial identity can also be seen in such popular films as Peter Jackson's recent *The Lord of the Rings* trilogy (2001–3), *The Dark Crystal* (Jim Henson and Frank Oz, 1982) and the *Harry Potter* series (Chris Columbus and others, 2001–11). Nor are fantasy films averse to reinforcing this connection with German romanticism in their use of music. With its extensive quotations from *Götterdämmerung*, *Parsifal* and *Tristan und Isolde*, John Boorman's interpretation of Arthurian legend, *Excalibur* (1981), seems to be actively filtered through Wagner's music dramas; while James Horner's score to *Willow* (Ron Howard, 1988) alludes overtly to the first movement of Schumann's Third Symphony. The debt of fantasy film to German romanticism is particularly clear, however, in the case of *Superman: The Movie* (Richard Donner, 1978), henceforth *Superman*, a film whose narrative and visual symbolism (not to mention its title), though ostensibly the very image of American twentieth-century self-identity, nonetheless appears to allude to nineteenth-century concerns. In its religious allegory, its concerns with origins and its overt nationalistic tendencies, *Superman* seems to assert its status as twentieth-century American myth in ways similar to Germanic intellectual and artistic output of the previous century; moreover, nowhere is this debt clearer than in John Williams's Oscar-nominated score.

In this chapter, then, I want to explore the origins of *Superman*'s mythic identity, tracing the religious concerns evident in the film back to Friedrich Schelling's and Friedrich Schlegel's call for a new mythology in the years around 1800. After briefly sketching some of the issues current throughout the nineteenth century, their twentieth-century legacy and their parallels with many of the narrative ideas in *Superman*, I will draw attention to the ways in which the opening of John Williams's score appears to allude to Brucknerian symphonic models of absolute music and, in so doing, partakes of these influential ideological currents. Finally, by invoking Umberto Eco's discussion of the comic book's temporally paradoxical 'oneiric climate', I address the continuing importance of Williams's *Superman* themes for the status of the film franchise as mythic narrative.

Superman as myth?

> This is no fantasy, no careless product of wild imagination.
> Jor-El in *Superman: The Movie*

The idea of discussing an obviously fictional character in terms of myth or mythology might seem specious at first glance: myths are surely stories about origins that a culture has once believed to be true, rather than the flights of fancy created by comic-book writers or Hollywood. Yet, we cannot escape the fact that the Superman story presented to us in the cinema bears striking resemblances to the archetypal myth identified by a number of theorists. The approach of Otto Rank (1884–1939), for example, outlines an archetype of the hero myth that shares a certain amount in common with the Superman story. Though Rank, in his analysis of hero myths from Moses, Oedipus and Dionysus to Siegfried, Lohengrin and Christ, is concerned with a psychoanalytical interpretation – and argues therefore that the ego of the child behaves like the hero of myth (Rank, 2004: 52) – his outlining of a standardized legend provides much of interest:

> The hero is the child of very distinguished parents, and usually the son of a king.
> His origin is preceded by difficulties, such as sexual abstinence, prolonged infertility, or secret intercourse of the parents due to external prohibition or obstacles. During or before the pregnancy, a prophecy, in the form of a dream or oracle, warns against his birth, usually threatening harm to the father.
> Therefore the newborn child, usually at the instigation of the father or his representative, is doomed to be killed or exposed. As a rule, he is surrendered to the water, in a box.
> He is then saved by animals, or by lowly people (herders), and suckled by a female animal or a lowly woman.
> After he has grown up, he finds his distinguished parents in a variety of ways. He takes revenge on his father, on the one hand, and is acknowledged, on the other, achieving greatness and fame. (ibid.: 47)

As told in the 1978 film, Superman (Kal-El) is the son of Kryptonian royalty (or at least very distinguished members of that society) and though no harm appears to be directed against him by his father, Jor-El, he is nonetheless surrendered to the water (outer space) in a box (starship) to escape the destruction of his home world, Krypton. He is saved by lowly people (the farmers Martha and Jonathan Kent on Earth) and raised as their own, with the name Clark Kent. After he has reached his eighteenth year, he discovers his distinguished parents in the crystals that have accompanied him on his voyage to Earth and achieves greatness and fame.

Much of this basic plot outline can also be found in the first part of Lord Raglan's heroic archetype which, in dealing with the hero's entire life, represents a less overtly psychoanalytical interpretation (Lord Raglan, 1936). Joseph Campbell's idea of the monomyth, expounded in his 1949 book *The Hero with a Thousand Faces*, likewise suggests much that maps onto the Superman story as it is told in the 1978 film. Campbell's 'separation–initiation–return' structure, wherein

> a hero ventures forth from the world of common day into a region of super-
> natural wonder: fabulous forces are there encountered and a decisive victory
> is won: the hero comes back from this mysterious adventure with the power
> to bestow boons on his fellow man (1993: 30)

might describe Clark Kent's journey of discovery to the Arctic. He encounters a region of supernatural wonder in his Fortress of Solitude, where the knowledge he needs to be able to harness his powers is granted – he achieves flight for the first time. He returns to the world of Metropolis, equipped to serve his fellow man as the ultimate crime-fighter and saviour of the planet. In another sense, Kal-El has also ventured forth from Krypton (the everyday of his infancy) into a region of supernatural wonder (deep space and planet Earth). His victories won there allow him, at least in some Superman stories and, to a degree, in *Superman Returns* (Bryan Singer, 2006), to return to his home planet – though as in stories such as 'Superman Returns to Krypton' (1949), an element of time travel is required in order to enable his return to a destroyed world.[1]

Although analysing the plot of a film in this basic way does not necessarily warrant us referring to *Superman* as myth – at least not in the sense that Robert A. Segal defines it, as a "story, which [is] held tenaciously by adherents" (2004: 5) – it certainly suggests that *Superman* could be considered as mythic narrative; that its story is founded on mythic archetypes. It appears likely, therefore, that an interpretative approach grounded in mythic discourse might reveal much. I begin my examination of *Superman* as mythic narrative, then, by considering the context provided by the nineteenth century's search for a new mythology, a context that will ultimately enable a more nuanced understanding of the film's score.

The new mythology

"For this reason, above all, their capacity for good, I have sent them you,
my only son."
Jor-El to Kal-El in *Superman*

The persistence of religious modes of thinking within the allegedly secular institutions of art, scholarship and literature is, as George S. Williamson argues, a particular feature of nineteenth-century intellectual history (2004: 295). Moreover, as he argues, the longing for myth with which it became associated was something that although not confined to Germany was nevertheless of fundamental importance to Germanic culture throughout the century and beyond. Thus, the revolutionary call by Schelling and Schlegel for a new mythology that would overturn or challenge the received wisdom of certain aspects of Protestantism was motivated, as Dieter Sturma puts it, by the need for "a mythology that [could] do for modernity what traditional mythology did for ancient cultures" (2000: 224). Growing out of the climate surrounding the French Revolution, this new mythology questioned many of the fundamental assumptions of Cartesian thought and Enlightenment rationality; furthermore, it led to an explosion of theological debate and a search for a national mythology in Germany.

In theological circles, for example, the historical truth of the Bible was challenged in such controversial texts as David Friedrich Strauss's 1835 book *Das Leben Jesu*, which disputed the divinity of Christ. At the same time, other theologians like Christian Hermann Weisse, in his *Die evangelische Geschichte, kritisch und philosophisch bearbeitet* (1838), attempted to reconcile the historical and mythical aspects of the gospels; while the search for a national mythology that would replace the Hebrew texts of the Old Testament also led to a renewed scholarly interest in the medieval *Niebelunglied*, the Nordic prose and poetry *Edda*s of the eighth to thirteenth centuries and the *Veda*s of ancient India. Thus, when Jacob Grimm published his *Deutsche Mythologie* (1835), insisting that the Nordic myths were closer to original Indo-Germanic sources than the Christian/Jewish myths from the Orient (G. S. Williamson, 2004: 109), the figure of Wotan, portrayed so vividly in Wagner's *Der Ring des Nibelungen*, was offered as the source of the earliest German religious activity. All that was popular in Christianity was traced to a Germanic source, while negative aspects were blamed on Catholic mysticism or foreign interlopers – including ultimately the Semitic races. Similarly, Max Müller's *Comparative Mythology* of 1856 saw ancient Vedic (Sanskrit) mythology lying at the root of western culture and, in particular, German national identity; it also provided a nature religion of equal cultural value to ancient Hebrew texts. Müller claimed that Germans were inherently Aryan – a term he applied to those who spoke original Indo-European – rather than Semitic and, as Ivan Strenski notes, "[his] belief in the special place of myth in Vedic religion was thus in effect part of a deeper theological and sociological idealism, linked with Aryanist cultural ideology" (1996: 62).[2]

A gradual polarization thus seemed to take place in attitudes towards organized religion. While the early Romantics were sceptical of Protestantism and were pantheistic in attitude, they nevertheless clung to many religious truths generated from within Christianity. As the century progressed, however, the myth discourse they had called for began to be used increasingly in opposition to Christian modernity, taken over by Feuerbachian humanism and given its most potent expression in Wagner's music dramas. Although Wagner's goal of creating a new post-Christian mythology, articulated in his Zurich writings, was ultimately abandoned when he fell under the spell of Schopenhauer (G. S. Williamson, 2004: 208),[3] it was his visions of the mythical characters of Parsifal, Wotan, Siegfried and Brünnhilde that carried currency in the late nineteenth century and helped reinforce anti-Semitic stereotypes that saw the Jews in contrast to the German peoples as a race lacking a mythology. Although changing markedly in character and political force over the century, then, the search for a new mythology appears to be a trope that characterizes the entire period, not merely the *Frühromantik* years around 1800.

Evidently there is much in *Superman* that draws on these nineteenth-century concerns, its title not withstanding (though Nietzsche's *übermensch* is literally worlds away from Kal-El's alien origins). Jor-El's invocation of John 3:16 ("For God so loved the world that he gave his only Son") draws attention to Superman's Christ-like mission to save the world and thus appears to challenge or to allegorize Christian gospel with American mythology. We, who "only need the light" to guide us, as Jor-El puts it, are sent Kal-El, the son of the father, in a Star-of-Bethlehem spaceship. Indeed, while the father ostensibly dies in the destruction of Krypton, he is preserved as spirit in the crystals sent along with his son, suggesting an almost Trinity-like equivalency of father, son and spirit ("The son becomes the father, and the father the son", as Jor-El tells his baby son in *Superman*). This seemingly sinfree all-American hero – "I never lie, Lois" as the character states in *Superman* – thus appears to embrace many aspects of Judaeo-Christian mythology.[4] He is raised by Earthly parents who are not Mary and Joseph but, in a barely disguised linguistic allusion, Martha and Jonathan, and though "forbidden to interfere with human history" by his 'heavenly' father, Jor-El, he is also told by his Earthly father, Jonathan Kent, that he is "here for a reason" and ultimately plays the part of saviour of mankind.

Aside from his allegorical resemblance to Christ – a feature that was emphasized even more overtly in *Superman Returns*, in which the character appears to die and is resurrected – Superman's exodus from Krypton's royalty as a baby and discovery by farmers Jonathan and Martha Kent also seems to offer us an inverted Moses tale. Indeed, Danny Fingeroth has argued that the Mosaic interpretation has more credibility when considering the mythology of Superman as a whole (2007: 44);[5] the films, by contrast, tend to emphasize the messianic metaphor. Fingeroth makes a powerful case for arguing that the character, which first appeared in its familiar form in *Action Comics* No. 1 in 1938, is part of the American Jewish response to the rise of fascism, as others have also recognized.[6] Superman can thus be seen as the first immigrant from the Old World and, as already noted, in post-war stories is able to travel back in time to visit Krypton, the Europe of the past which was forever lost to US immigrants fleeing Nazi tyranny. This search for origins, which was emphasized in *Superman Returns* with Clark's attempts to discover if anything is left of the 'old world', continues romanticism's preoccupation with establishing the theological and philological origins of German identity. Even the emphasis on the 'S' symbol seems to resonate with the philologist Georg Friedrich Creuzer's work, which tried to show the universality in the ancient world of a few key symbols.[7] Krypton and its symbology seem to echo German romanticism's search for the origins of its new mythology, while Superman himself appears to offer generations of Americans since the 1930s a new mythology that draws upon Judaeo-Christian symbols and metaphors as a way of redefining the origins of contemporary society. And crucially, perhaps, it wraps up this new mythology in an American flag: Superman is not for all nations; or, at least, he appears to stand specifically for the values of the United States. Using the new popular culture of the comic and later of Hollywood, Siegel and Schuster and the inheritors of their creation thus appear to have unconsciously followed many of the same thought currents as those nineteenth-century thinkers whose ideas appealed to the very forces of tyranny against which they were symbolically fighting. While, as G. S. Williamson argues, mythological thought did not create National Socialism or anti-Semitism, it did offer:

> in its Wagnerian or völkisch guise ... a way of thinking about art, religion, and the nation that was particularly suited to the political fantasies of Hitler and the racist policies of the Nazi state. (2004: 293)

Indeed, Frederic Wertham's diatribe against the comic-book industry in 1950s America notoriously interpreted Superman in such terms:

> Actually, Superman (with the big S on his uniform – we should, I suppose, be thankful it is not an S.S.) needs an endless stream of ever new submen, criminals and 'foreign-looking' people not only to justify his existence but even to make it possible ... it makes [children] submissive and receptive to

> *the blandishments of strong men who will solve all their social problems for*
> *them – by force.* (1955: 34)

I do not wish to suggest, however, that identifying a rather Germanic mythic source of parts of *Superman*'s narrative connects it with the appropriation of this strand of romanticism by twentieth-century fascist movements; rather, it is merely an acknowledgement of the continuing currency of these nineteenth-century ideas about religion, mythology and national identity.[8] Moreover, nowhere were these ideas more potent than in music; and so we turn to Anton Bruckner and John Williams.

Superman's titles: referencing the absolute?

Beginning with a short black-and-white narrative preamble, which emphasizes the comic-book origins of the character,[9] the title sequence of *Superman* is remarkable for the prominent role it assigns Williams's score. While music is often 'foregrounded' in films' title sequences, *Superman* devotes a good five minutes to a locked camera, flying text (designed by Denis Rich) and music; indeed, with the introduction and the first Krypton cue, we are presented with an unbroken stretch of music lasting over six minutes. This large slice of initial music is common to the three *Superman* films under discussion here (*Superman*, *Superman II* [Richard Lester, 1980] and *Superman Returns*), though admittedly each has its distractions that may prevent us listening to it with our full attention. *Superman* features some rather noisy competition in the form of the sound effects associated with Rich's flying text.[10] The title sequence of *Superman II*, in contrast, has quieter effects; but our engagement with the music may be hampered more by the much greater amount of visual information present, wherein the events of the previous film are recapped. Its similarly conceived flying text is also more dynamic in terms of pitch, roll and sideways movement than the largely static figurations of *Superman* – compare Figures 6.1 and 6.2. Though the title sequence in *Superman II* is only slightly longer than in *Superman*, the already somewhat repetitious structure detailed in Table 6.1 is unbalanced further through repetitions of sections C and E. *Superman Returns* is likewise visually more active than the original, and its flying titles (which are much closer in design to the original) take us swooping past planets, comets and clouds of interstellar gas in dizzying manner – see Figure 6.3. It also restores the more audible sound effects. Its version of Williams's *Superman* March, though – in excising the contrasting material of section B and jumping straight from section A to D – arguably suffers from similar problems to *Superman II*, with the balancing effect of the contrasting sections lost through either repetition or excision.

Figure 6.1 Flying text in *Superman*

Figure 6.2 Flying text in *Superman II*

Figure 6.3 Flying text in *Superman Returns*

Table 6.1 Structure of title sequence

Section	Description	Tonality
Prelude	Introduces falling fifth and other motivic kernels:	F minor ↓
	Ends with a timpani roll, and introduction of dotted compound duple rhythm as dominant preparation:	C major (V pedal)
A	C major. 8-bar phrase repeated with varied orchestration:	C major
B	Contrasting material. 8-bar phrase repeated with varied orchestration and a 6-bar extension that works by motivic diminution and repetition:	
C	8-bar phrase emphasizing falling fifth motif:	
D	10-bar arpeggiaic phrase ('Love' theme):	F major ↓
E	11-bar phrase emphasizing rising seventh:	B♭ major
A	Single phrase of 8 bars, with a 2-bar extension	B♭ major
C	Truncated version of 4 bars	F major
C	8-bar phrase	G major
Coda	Fragments motivically (dominant preparation for Planet Krypton cue in C major)	

In all three films, though (and with *Superman* in particular), the prominence afforded the music in these opening titles appears to advocate a deep and contemplative immersion in its sound world. Moreover, the score's language appears to allude generally to German symphonic music of the late nineteenth century. Yet, in what sense is this evident? As can be seen in Table 6.1, the structural principles in operation in *Superman*'s title sequence are mostly concerned with juxtaposing five different (if related) themes, with a few examples of repetition in the latter half of the cue, coupled with a broad move from C to G major – hardly processes that, at first glance, suggest the label 'symphonic' (the move to the dominant notwithstanding). Indeed, a sense of climax is achieved towards the end of the cue through the dramatic shift in tonality up a tone from F to G major, a strategy not unknown in the world of popular music.[11]

Although betraying no overtly structural symphonic attributes, aside from an initial presentation of themes with symphonic potential, the musical gestures and orchestration of this opening sequence are, nevertheless, symphony-like; moreover, they appear to allude specifically to the late-nineteenth-century symphonies of Anton Bruckner. Thus we might recognize, in its compound duple metre and motifs based on the interval of the perfect fifth, the scherzo of Bruckner's Fourth Symphony (see Figure 6.4); or in the arpeggiaic shape and submediant tendencies of the Love theme, also introduced here as contrasting material in the manner of a symphonic scherzo, the opening theme of his Seventh Symphony (see Figure 6.5). Though we may also point to other nineteenth-century models for these themes – the compound duple dotted rhythm evokes the Nibelung motif of Wagner's *Das Rheingold* while the harmonic and melodic attributes of the Love theme bear a striking resemblance to Richard Strauss's *Tod und Verklärung*, itself an irony given Lois's cheating of death in the film (see Figure 6.5) – Williams's treatment of the material also suggests Brucknerian process, if on a much smaller scale. Notably, the numerous repetitions of material and small-scale examples of *Steigerung* (intensification) – in the terminology of the Bruckner critic Ernst Kurth – point to *Superman*'s debt not to the architectural outward features of Bruckner's symphonic writing but rather to the idea of symphonic form "considered as a continuous process of transformation of initial motives throughout a work", as Stephen Parkany puts it (1988: 262). Kurth talked of Bruckner's symphonic language in terms of waves which intensified motivic kernels set out at the beginning of a work; after each wave reached its peak, it would dissipate quickly to be succeeded by the next greater wave, eventually to reach a climax, a factor which accounts for the frequent stop–starts in Bruckner's music which so many find unpalatable (see *ibid*.: 268). While perhaps nothing so formally directed exists on the large scale in Williams's score, nonetheless the small scale reveals similar structures. The introductory section of the opening titles, for example, introduces certain motivic kernels that, perhaps as a cipher indicating their ultimate source,[12] include the so-called 'Bruckner rhythm' (see Figure 6.6).[13] These are then worked out in the main body of the title sequence with a series of melodic sections that could be seen as developing in a manner similar to

a) Bruckner, Symphony No. 4, Scherzo, bars 103–104

b) *Superman*

Figure 6.4 Allusions to Bruckner's Fourth Symphony

a) Bruckner, Symphony No. 7, opening

b) Author transcription of Love theme from *Superman*, composed by John Williams

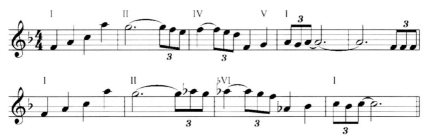

c) Richard Strauss, *Tod und Verklärung*, bars 430–31

Figure 6.5 Allusions to Bruckner's Seventh Symphony and Richard Strauss

Figure 6.6 The 'Bruckner rhythm' in the *Superman* prelude

Figure 6.7 *Steigerung* (intensification) in *Superman*

that which Kurth describes. Figure 6.7 shows how the Brucknerian repetition and intensification of melodic fragments occurs in section B. The first phrase (bars 1–2) is varied with the first iteration (bars 3–4) before being extended through sequential repetition (bars 5–8). Similarly, the pastoral theme that surrounds Superman in the rural idyll of his life in Smallville has clear roots in the character's more bombastic, heroic music, first heard in the titles.

Why, though, might we seek to emphasize Bruckner in a reading of the score? In what ways do the score's allusions to his music and formal processes enrich the idea of locating *Superman*'s narrative within the context of German romanticism? Alluding to Bruckner may, at first glance, seem odd in a film whose mythologizing impulses are connected with a philosophical movement that sought to challenge the received truths of Christianity; Bruckner's popular image, after all, is that of a devout Catholic who was known to shun discussion of weighty intellectual matters. And yet, there are a number of reasons why Bruckner's music, and the reception of it, illuminates the interpretation of *Superman* as 'new mythology'. Hermann Kretzschmar's hermeneutic reading of the Fourth Symphony, the so-called 'Romantic', is a case in point. In his 1898 work *Führer durch dem Konzertsaal*, Kretzschmar saw the Fourth very much as a 'forest symphony', in which an air of deep religiosity is nonetheless situated in pre-Christian contexts:

> *Bruckner, like the pagans of ancient Germany, performs his religious rituals in the forest ... His thoughts have gone back to those long-gone times when we Germans were still a forest folk; and the forest was the most magnificent church, the most splendid cathedral, that the lord of all worlds had built with his own hands.* (1994: 109)

The third movement, the closest in spirit perhaps to Williams's *Superman* titles, is described as presenting "the forest spirit of this symphony in a more down-to-earth, conventional manner" (*ibid.*: 114), though it also comes in for criticism for its large-scale repetitions (a criticism we might also level at Williams). The programmatic implications of Bruckner's symphonies are perhaps particularly ripe for quasi-religious mythologizing. Thus, when talking of the spiritual pilgrimage narratives of Bruckner's Fourth and Fifth symphonies, the semiotician Robert Hatten can talk of the works being endowed with "mythic power" (2001: 179).

Nor, it seems, was Bruckner the naïve Catholic that many accounts of his life have sought to emphasize: Carl Hruby, in his reminiscences of the composer, noted that

> On the subjects of religion and the Christian faith, Bruckner expressed himself
> more candidly and dispassionately than one would have expected from such a
> deeply pious man ... At one point ... someone brought up the subject of David
> Strauss and his Leben Jesu, and to my complete astonishment I discovered that
> Bruckner had read it. My amazement increased when I heard how calmly and
> objectively Bruckner spoke about this work. (Hruby, in Johnson, 1998: 33)

Richard Heller's observations of the composer also suggest a less than dogmatic Christianity, since Bruckner was often criticized for the "strange form" of his devotions (Heller, in *ibid.*: 172). Furthermore, the anthroposophist Erich Schwebsch later interpreted Bruckner as a great mystic, the producer of a cosmic art – a viewpoint that, according to Constantin Floros, prepared the way for the writings of Oskar Lang, Fritz Grüninger and Ernst Bloch, and influenced Kurth (Floros, 2001: 292).

Bruckner is also deeply embedded in a discourse of absolute music, however. The twentieth-century German musicologist Carl Dahlhaus, in particular, argued that Bruckner's symphonies were not an expression of extramusical ideas (as Constantin Floros might suggest) but represented a metaphysics of absolute music, filtered through Wagner and Schopenhauer (J. Williamson, 2004: 118). Following the death of Wagner in 1883, Bruckner was even appropriated by Viennese Wagnerites as the true inheritor of Beethoven (Notley, 1997: 425), thus tying him into a discourse of absolute music that arguably grew out of the same climate that challenged the received truths of Christianity. The concept of absolute music, after all, is often said to have developed around 1800 in the writings of Wackenroder, Tieck and E. T. A. Hoffmann (see Dahlhaus, 1989: 10) simultaneously with the more general challenging of Christian modernity. In addition, symphonic contemplation – influenced by Schopenhauer's conception of music as a copy of the Will itself – increasingly became associated with quasi-religious or substitute religious experience: Johann Nikolaus Forkel, for example, advocated a quasi-religious worship of the works of J. S. Bach as early as 1802 (*ibid.*: 78); and by 1918, subsequent to Nietzsche assigning music a prominent role in the rebirth of Germanic myth in the 1870s (Nietzsche, 1967), Paul Bekker would note that the symphony was "in accord with the goals of religion", such was its oratorical power to mould a community in the ways that masses, oratorios and Passions had previously done (Notley, 1997: 435). August Halm's interpretation of Bruckner's symphonic output in the 1910s likewise took the dedication of the Ninth Symphony to 'Almighty God' as its starting point: "A new religion of art is being created, and Bruckner's entire symphonic oeuvre served this creation, so that that dedication ought to be inscribed above all of Bruckner's symphonies" (Dahlhaus, 1989: 40).

Through the use of melodic, gestural and rhythmic features that evoke Bruckner's music, Williams's *Superman* music emphasizes further the narrative and symbolic resonances with the nineteenth century's search for a new mythology that are present in the film. Moreover, it is significant that these allusions are preserved in the music of the film's sequels, which retain many of Williams's themes despite the absence of the composer himself.[14] This retelling of the music's story is an integral part of Superman's status as mythic narrative, as we shall now discover.

Eternal recurrence and the oneiric climate

> *"You act like you've been here before."*
> Kitty Kowalski to Lex Luthor, *Superman Returns*

In a 1972 article entitled 'The Myth of Superman', Umberto Eco argued that something fundamental separated the comic-book character from other universal and unchanging heroic figures of mythology – namely, his presence in a market that demands development, in common with the novelistic character. For Superman to act, Eco argued, meant taking a step towards his own death, in a way that the heroes of classical myths could avoid, separated as they were from contemporary society. The narrative paradox that resulted – that Superman "possesses the characteristics of timeless myth, but is accepted only because his activities take place in our human and everyday world of time" (Eco, 1972: 16) – could only be solved by a paradoxical solution to time. Thus, causality is broken between *Superman* stories, and Superman begins each week as if the previous week's story had never happened; it is only in this way, Eco argues, that the character can avoid "consuming himself". As he puts it:

> The stories develop in a kind of oneiric climate – of which the reader is not aware at all – where what has happened before and what has happened after appears extremely hazy. The narrator picks up the strand of the event again and again as if he had forgotten to say something and wanted to add details to what had already been said. (ibid.: 17)

The word *oneiric* is derived from the ancient Greek *oneiros*, meaning 'dream'. Personifications of dreams, the *oneiroi* are alternatively described as the brothers or the sons of Hypnos, the embodiment of sleep. More than that, though, in contrast to the lower irrational class of dream active only in sleep (the *enhupnion*), the *oneiros* was a serious dream that continued to operate after waking and, as the ancient Greek author Artemidorus (2nd century AD) claimed, "comes true either for good or for bad" (quoted in Kenaan, 2004: 256). It thus had a prophetic quality that is the product of the mind, while the *enhupnion*, in being concerned with things pertaining to the body, indicated the present. Artemidorus also states of *oneiroi* that:

> some of them come true at the very moment of perception, so to speak, while we are still under the sway of the dream-vision. Hence it bears its name not without reason, since it is simultaneously seen and comes true. (quoted in Irby-Massie and Keyser, 2002: 350)

It is perhaps unsurprising, then, that the word 'oneiric' has also been used in connection with cinema and its dreamlike qualities.[15] Eco's use of the term, however, suggests something more of the idea of prophecy; in other words, a narrative climate in which the major events of Superman's existence have a fixed inevitability, despite the fluidity of the more novelistic events surrounding them. The oneiric climate thus negates the cause and effect of everyday experienced time and prevents the character developing: in short, it allows Superman to attain mythic status. The frame provided by the moving picture arguably represents another manifestation of this oneiric climate and provides an experience of time in which, as Eco puts it above, "what has happened before and what has happened after appears extremely hazy". Bordered by the music of the opening and closing credits of *Superman*, the character's adventures seem contained by the cinematic frame.

Eco's 'oneiric climate' and its repetitive strands of narrative might also point us in the direction of Nietzsche's idea of Eternal Recurrence – a cycle of opposites whose symbols include the *ouroborus* or the serpent biting its own tail and whose explication may be read as an attempt to unite myth and philosophy (see Yelle, 2000). And it is in this way, perhaps, that the character's name, in referencing the mature work in which Nietzsche deals most extensively with Eternal Recurrence, *Also Sprach Zarathustra*, is strangely appropriate (although *übermensch* is now more commonly translated as 'overman' than 'superman'). Yet the idea of the cycle of time is also dramatized in the film version of *Superman* as the world is literally turned back, ringed by the figure of Superman attempting to bite his own tail in order to 'resurrect' Lois (the 'death and transfiguration' love theme here is wonderful misdirection – like Superman, Lois can never die; or at least she must be resurrected in order for the mythology of Superman to be preserved).

Superman II is a particularly clear dramatization of Eco's point. Beginning with a retelling of the opening scene of *Superman* (the capture and sentencing of the criminal General Zod and his friends), it adds new details and edits dialogue. The title sequence that follows includes, as we have discovered, a visual recap of the first film. Moreover, that visual reminder is supported by Ken Thorne's bombastic rescoring of John Williams's music (all thumping timpani and rattling snare drum), itself a retelling of an already told story. At least the opening part of the film, then, suggests a kind of temporal paradox, a break of narrative continuity from the first film. The idea of temporal paradox is even more overt, however, in *Superman Returns* (Bryan Singer, 2006). As the restarting of a franchise, following the rather lacklustre sequels of the mid-1980s, *Superman III* (Richard Lester, 1983) and *Superman IV: The Quest for Peace* (Sidney J. Furie, 1987), *Superman Returns* faced a number of problems. Supposedly taking place just five years after *Superman II*, it is set, nevertheless, in the present day. Certain features of the film, though, refer back subtly to the first *Superman* movies: the Kryptonite-containing meteorite stolen by Lex Luthor (Kevin Spacey) is labelled 'Addis Ababa 1978', the same meteorite referred to in the original film; Kitty Kowalski (Parker Posey) notes Lex's familiarity with Superman's Fortress of Solitude, clearly referencing the plot of *Superman II*; and, as pointed out earlier, the title sequence references the flying text of the original (even if it has a more dynamic background). Furthermore, given Brandon Routh's remarkable physical resemblance to the deceased Christopher Reeve, his performance as Superman properly deserves the Freudian label 'uncanny'.

Beyond these ghostly resemblances and subtle references, however, *Superman Returns* actively draws attention to its temporally paradoxical nature when seen as part of a continuing narrative: not only is Marlon Brando's performance as Jor-El reused, but John Ottman's score also makes prominent use of John Williams's thematic material and, as discussed above, retains an altered version of the *Superman* March for the film's titles. He also incorporates into his score Williams's Love theme, the theme for Krypton and the variant of Superman's theme used for Clark and his rural life in Smallville. The music, it seems, has become as indispensable to the Superman myth (at least in its film manifestation) as the red cape and kiss-curl of the superhero's image. The mythic qualities of the character, including the music that defines him, are of greater importance than the idea of narrative causality; and the viewer, happily recognizing Brandon Routh as Superman partly because of the music, can overlook the troubling temporal paradox created by the film's modern setting. Whereas other re-launched film franchises – such as *Batman Begins* (Christopher Nolan, 2005) and its sequel, *The Dark Knight* (Christopher Nolan, 2008) – will tend to act musically as if the previous films did not exist (though they might make affectionate nods to their predecessors), in making a deliberate attempt to link itself to the earlier films through its music, *Superman Returns* partakes of the idea of Superman as myth despite its obvious temporal paradox.

Hollywood, then, has built on Superman's mythic character and, at least on the big screen, further cemented it in a particular visual and aural design.[16] That aural design – in tying Superman overtly to the concerns of German romanticism through the symphonic discourse of Bruckner and Richard Strauss, coupled with the decision in later films to re-use Williams's original themes – suggests that film-makers continue to regard the man of steel, fundamentally, as a mythic rather than novelistic character. Since Williams's scores of the late 1970s are frequently heard as reviving the classical film-scoring practices of Korngold and Steiner,[17] these 'symphonic' attributes are evidently nothing new in film music. Indeed, the *Superman* score reminds us (lest we forget) of the proximity of this nineteenth-century discourse to that 1930s generation of classic-era film composers, most of whom were of European provenance. Fantasy cinema of the 1930s, in particular, frequently drew upon nineteenth-century musical idioms, even if sometimes it was the modernist attributes of composers like Mahler that appealed (see Winters, 2009). Yet, the subject matter of *Superman* also implies that Williams is engaged in more than a nostalgic nod to early Hollywood. While certainly adept at using other instrumentation and styles – evident in his jazz-influenced score to *Catch Me If You Can* (Steven Spielberg, 2002), for example – his music for *Harry Potter and the Philosopher's Stone* (Chris Columbus, 2001) likewise opted for late-nineteenth-century orchestration and gestures, indicating not so much a personal stylistic choice as a recognition that fantasy cinema often warrants a more traditional approach to scoring.[18] Similarly, as Janet Halfyard notes, the late-romantic musical idiom of Danny Elfman's score to *Batman* (Tim Burton, 1989) "effectively renders the music timeless ... despite the fact that it could logically evoke nineteenth-century Germany" (2004: 61); moreover, it was an idiom that seems to have been requested by the film's director (*ibid.*: 11).

By drawing upon nineteenth-century musical gestures, fantasy films like *Superman* can tap into a discourse of absolute music without actually subscribing to its aesthetics and in so doing buttress their claims to occupy a mythic narrative space. Like their paradoxically timeless narratives, these films' musical languages can revisit the past and retell already told stories, whether they be of classical scoring practices of the 1930s or of nineteenth-century German orchestral music. As such, they will always have new details to add: Williams's *Superman* score, for example, also features modernist glissandi and "quasi-aleatoric" passages (Larson, 1985: 300) and is doubtless not overly restricted by the musical language established in the titles. Williams clearly has not set out with *Superman* to write a nineteenth-century symphony, yet considering his score within such contexts illuminates an aspect of the fantasy narrative's mythic qualities. Moreover, the fact that contemporary fantasy films continue to invoke many of these orchestral idioms, when other genres are more reluctant to do so, suggests the genre's roots in myths and nineteenth-century discourse continue to shape our musical expectations in the cinema.

Notes

1. 'Superman Returns to Krypton' (*Superman* #61). A similar story is found in 'Superman's Return to Krypton' (*Superman* #141; 1960): see Fingeroth (2007: 66). In *Superman Returns* (Bryan Singer, 2006), Clark has attempted to discover the remains of his planet.
2. Despite this, Müller appears to have shunned the nationalist implications of Aryanism after German unification: he denied there were any racial implications in his philology and praised the Jews for their ancient culture, arguing that no religious group had a monopoly on truth. See Strenski (1996: 62–3).
3. Though Wagner's last opera, *Parsifal*, moves back towards the realm of Christianity in its use of Christian symbols and rituals, it is, as Bryan Magee takes pains to point out, not a Christian work. Rather, redemption is achieved only through a Schopenhauerian denial of the will. See Magee (2001: 264–85).
4. From a religious perspective, this need not be a negative comment, since allegory has always played an important role in theological teaching. For religion's place in film, see Lyden (2003).
5. The comic-book writer Frank Miller even claimed Superman was a golem. See Fingeroth (2007: 23).
6. See Halfyard (2004: 39).
7. See Chapter 3 in G. S. Williamson (2004).
8. We might also point to the film's fondness for crystalline ice structures in its depiction of Krypton and the Fortress of Solitude – images that may recall the mountain films of Weimar cinema *Der Berg des Schicksals* (Arnold Franck, 1924) and *Im Kampf mit dem Berge* (Arnold Franck, 1921). Siegfried Kracauer regarded this worship of nature as symptomatic of a prevailing attitude of anti-rationalism (Kracauer, 2004: 112).
9. The image of *The Daily Planet*'s revolving globe seen in this opening section might also remind us of the old studio logo for Universal Pictures in the late 1930s. The connection is strengthened markedly by the similarity of its accompanying fanfare to Williams's March (section C in Table 6.1).
10. In the region 2 DVD (*Superman: The Movie - Expanded Version*), one has the option of watching with a 5.1 music-only track.
11. Many pop music songs of the 1980s onwards, for example, employ a sudden tonal shift for the last iteration of the chorus, followed by a 'repeat and fade'. Admittedly, we may also point to the breakthrough moment in the fourth movement of Mahler's First Symphony (rehearsal figure 34), with its sudden tonal shift to D major. Although tonality may not be considered a major structuring

factor, the cue's ending in G major clearly also acts as a dominant preparation for the Planet Krypton cue that immediately follows.

12. Though I open myself here to Abbate's charge of being in thrall to the "cryptographic sublime" (2004: 524–5), such musical sphinxes were common throughout the nineteenth century. Schumann, for example, used a BACH motif in his Piano Quintet in E flat, Op. 44, shortly after an allusion to Bach's 'Es ist vollbracht' from the St John Passion. See Reynolds (2003: 154).

13. The 'Bruckner rhythm' is a distinctive rhythmic motif used throughout Bruckner's works, but particularly prominent in the opening movement of the Fourth Symphony. It consists of a duplet followed by a triplet. This rhythm also features in John Ottman's score for *Superman Returns* in the scene in which Clark recollects the discovery of his powers as a youth.

14. *Superman II* (1980) and *Superman III* (1983) were scored by Ken Thorne; *Superman IV: The Quest for Peace* (1987) was scored by Alexander Courage; and *Superman Returns* (2006) by John Ottman.

15. See, for example, Bergstrom (1999). The use of the word is not explained but is evidently a reference to the film's "hypnotic, dreamlike quality" (p. 116).

16. Superman on television (*The New Adventures of Superman*; *Smallville*) or the serialized Larry Crabbe versions are beyond my scope here, although Williams's main theme was used in the *Smallville* episode 'Rosetta' (season 2, episode 17), which featured the then wheelchair-bound Christopher Reeve as Dr Virgil Swann, who reveals to the young Clark Kent the truth of his origins on Krypton, again ignoring the paradoxes of the presence of both actor and music to connect the series to the Superman myth. I am indebted to Janet Halfyard for this observation.

17. Williams's *Superman* music also shares motivic links with the classic-era scores of Erich Wolfgang Korngold. See Winters (2007: 41).

18. Though the *Harry Potter* franchise is ultimately locked into a novelistic development process that will preclude any revisiting of the past in the manner of Superman's oneiric climate, the later orchestral scores by Patrick Doyle, Nicholas Hooper and Alexandre Desplat continue to reference Williams's themes.

References

Abbate, C. (2004), 'Music: Drastic or Gnostic?' *Critical Inquiry*, 30(3), 505–36.

Bergstrom, J. (1999), 'Oneiric Cinema: "The Woman on the Beach"', *Film History*, 11(1), 114–25.

Campbell, J. (1993), *The Hero with a Thousand Faces*, London: Fontana Press.

Dahlhaus, C. (1989), *The Idea of Absolute Music*, Chicago: University of Chicago Press.

Eco, U. (1972), 'The Myth of Superman', *Diacritics*, 2(1), 14–22.

Fingeroth, D. (2007), *Disguised as Clark Kent: Jews, Comics, and the Creation of the Superhero*, London: Continuum.

Floros, C. (2001), 'On Unity between Bruckner's Personality and Production', in C. Howie, P. Hawkshaw and T. Jackson (eds), *Perspectives on Anton Bruckner*, Aldershot: Ashgate, pp. 285–98.

Halfyard, J. K. (2004), *Danny Elfman's Batman: A Film Score Guide*, Lanham, MD: Scarecrow Press.

Hatten, R. S. (2001), 'The Expressive Role of Disjunction: A Semiotic Approach to Form and Meaning in the Fourth and Fifth Symphonies', in C. Howie, P. Hawkshaw and T. Jackson (eds), *Perspectives on Anton Bruckner*, Aldershot: Ashgate, pp. 145–84.

Irby-Massie, G. L., and Keyser, P. T. (2002), *Greek Science of the Hellenistic Era: A Sourcebook*, London: Routledge.

Johnson, S. (1998), *Bruckner Remembered*, London: Faber and Faber.

Kenaan, V. L. (2004), 'Delusion and Dream in Apuleius' "Metamorphoses"', *Classical Antiquity*, 23(2), 247–84.

Kracauer, S. (2004), *From Caligari to Hitler: A Psychological History of the German Film*, rev. and expanded edn, edited by L. Quaresima, Princeton: Princeton University Press (first published in German in 1947).

Kretzschmar, H. (1994), 'Anton Bruckner, Symphony No. 4', in I. Bent (ed.), *Music Analysis in the Nineteenth Century*, Vol. II. *Hermeneutic Approaches*, Cambridge: Cambridge University Press, pp. 109–17.

Larson, R. D. (1985), *Musique Fantastique: A Survey of Film Music in the Fantastic Cinema*, Metuchen, NJ: Scarecrow Press.

Lyden, J. C. (2003), *Film as Religion: Myths, Morals, and Rituals*, New York: New York University Press.

Magee, B. (2001), *Wagner and Philosophy*, London: Penguin.

Nietzsche, F. (1967), *The Birth of Tragedy* and *The Case of Wagner*, trans. W. Kaufman, New York: Vintage Books.

Nietzsche, F. (1978), *Thus Spoke Zarathustra: A Book for All and None*, trans. W. Kaufmann, New York: Penguin Books.

Notley, M. (1997), '"Volksconcerte" in Vienna and Late Nineteenth-century Ideology of the Symphony', *Journal of the American Musicological Society*, 50(2/3), 421–53.

Parkany, S. (1988), 'Kurth's "Bruckner" and the Adagio of the Seventh Symphony', *19th-Century Music*, 11(3), 262–81.

Raglan, Lord (1936), *The Hero: A Study in Tradition, Myth and Drama*, London: Methuen.

Rank, O. (2004), *The Myth of the Birth of the Hero: A Psychological Exploration of Myth*, expanded and updated edn, trans. Gregory C. Richter, Baltimore: The Johns Hopkins University Press (first published in German in 1909).

Reynolds, C. A. (2003), *Motives for Allusion: Context and Content in Nineteenth-century Music*, Cambridge, MA: Harvard University Press.

Schelling, F. W. von (1800), *System des transcendentalen Idealismus*, Tübingen.

Schlegel, F. von (1968), *Gespräch über die Poesie*, Stuttgart: Metzlersche Verlagsbuchhandlung (first published in German in 1800).

Segal, R. A. (2004), *Myth: A Very Short Introduction*, Oxford: Oxford University Press.

Strenksi, I. (1996), 'The Rise of Ritual, and the Hegemony of Myth: Sylvain Lévi, the Durkheimans, and Max Müller', in L. L. Patton and W. Doniger (eds), *Myth and Method*, Charlottesville: University of Virginia Press, pp. 52–81.

Sturma, D. (2000), 'Politics and the New Mythology: The Turn to Late Romanticism', in K. Ameriks (ed.), *The Cambridge Companion to German Idealism*, Cambridge: Cambridge University Press, pp. 219–38.

Wertham, F. (1955), *Seduction of the Innocent*, London: Museum Press.

Williamson, G. S. (2004), *The Longing for Myth in Germany: Religion and Aesthetic Culture from Romanticism to Nietzsche*, Chicago: University of Chicago Press.

Williamson, J. (2004), 'Programme Symphony and Absolute Music,' in J. Williamson (ed.), *The Cambridge Companion to Bruckner*, Cambridge: Cambridge University Press, pp. 108–20.

Winters, B. (2007), *Erich Wolfgang Korngold's* The Adventures of Robin Hood: *A Film Score Guide*, Lanham, MD: Scarecrow Press.

Winters, B. (2009), '"There Have Been Developments": Frankenstein's Monster Finds a (Mahlerian) Voice', *Interdisciplinary Humanities*, 26(2), 116–27.

Yelle, R. A. (2000), 'The Rebirth of Myth? Nietzsche's Eternal Recurrence and Its Romantic Antecedents', *Numen*, 47 (2), 175–202.

7 Music and Fantasy Types in Tim Burton's *Edward Scissorhands*

Alexander G. Binns

The aim of this chapter is to show how music plays a central role in the presentation of fantasy in Tim Burton's 1990 film *Edward Scissorhands*, how the idea of fantasy is constituted as a genre and to explain how its parody of this genre through music might be understood in terms of broader narrative strategies, particularly those drawn from literature and proposed by, among others, Jacques Derrida.

The identities of spaces and locations are important to the way in which *Edward Scissorhands* unfolds and they help us to understand how reading this film straightforwardly as a fantasy film is problematic. The use of music to delineate spaces and locations is, of course, an approach central to the structures of many films and of itself does not represent a new approach to understanding music's function in cinema. However, in *Edward Scissorhands*, it is the responsibility of music, as well as other components of the filmic narrative, to effect a distinction not only in the types of spaces but also in these spaces' generic identities. As will be argued, however, this distinction is part of a critique of these genres.

Similarly, music has functioned elsewhere as a way of differentiating narratives – or narrative spaces – and in itself, therefore, this does not represent a radical departure from common practice. What is interesting about its use here is the way in which the music tells us, as spectators (but also as critics) something of the quality of the location in question. Popular music and, in particular, the deployment of well-known pre-existing music (most often here by Tom Jones) enables that space within the filmic narrative to 'feel' different from the world we come to understand as that configured by Edward Scissorhands himself, whose identity is thus framed as Other and whose domain offers some of the classical presentations of a fantasy environment. By contrast, the use of popular music helps to secure a sense of familiar place and of 'self' within the suburban space. This is the place against which the space of the castle is defined and against which the realm of fantasy is to be read.

Although discussions of film music (and indeed, music more generally) as constructing a sense of self and Other are not new, the binary of the fantasy/fairy-tale world set against the real/suburban world in *Edward Scissorhands* does not map straightforwardly onto this notion. Rather than operating to provide further support to the construction of the film's fantasy world – the aim of most film music in immersive fantasy – here, the music helps to ensure a more uneasy separation of sumptuous fairy-tale fantasy and suburbia. It is, in part, the switch between the commissioned orchestral score and the use of pre-existing popular music that achieves this. Previously, theories of pre-existing music have sought to explain how its use widens the possible types of identification with it. Anahid Kassabian (2001) has described such music as creating an 'affiliating identification' among spectators because it seeks to broaden the range of meanings drawn from the varying previous experiences spectators may have had with the music. However, in this film, such a reading is not so straightforward and the role of music in foregrounding the idea and identity of the fantasy (the extent to which the two areas of the plot 'know of' each other; how the levels of the film's engagement with fantasy and storytelling emerge) is important.

Edward Scissorhands takes place, in broad terms, within one narrative. That is to say, the characters from each space are aware of the others and can interact and infiltrate both spaces. This makes the film stand out from common practice, in which fantasy worlds adjunct to the constructed 'real' world are much more carefully and prohibitively circumscribed. Access to them is not easy and their existence is often mediated by magic. This is not the case in *Edward Scissorhands* but, because it also draws on the visual trope of fantasy so heavily, uses music to suggest a different world and makes every effort to effect a difference between the two spaces, it makes sense to see the film in terms of fantasy, albeit one whose generic status is unstable and inviting critique.

The use of music, in particular, helps to negotiate the type and extent of fantasy in this film. Given that *Edward Scissorhands* is not an 'immersive' fantasy, such as that found in the works of J. R. R. Tolkien, music helps to marshal the audience into and out of moments of connection with the fantastic. In terms of music, this film, however, presents an interesting case study of fantasy because it also forces us to consider the ways in which musical categories remain a powerful means of differentiation; and it is differentiation that is key to the status of fantasy in *Edward Scissorhands*. Popular music and the specially commissioned orchestral underscore still wield strong referential clichés and cultural categories and it is, in part, because of these that *Edward Scissorhands* produces the type of fantasy that it does. This chapter, therefore, does not attempt to offer an as-yet-undiscovered understanding of how music works in this film or to force a singular way of comprehending music's role. Instead, it aims to put forward a starting point for interpretation that may subsequently allow for further theoretical elaboration.

Film outline

Edward Scissorhands is Tim Burton's fourth film and like its predecessors it uses a specially composed score by Danny Elfman, Burton's long-time musical collaborator, as well as public-domain music. The original score for the film is richly orchestral and also makes use of a large choir (which sings without words). The film is set in two very distinct locations, though both are geographically close to each other: the 'real' suburban environment – vivid green lawns, leading down to the street, and with one-storey houses painted in differing but equally bright colours set out in open plan – and its counter, the castle and the hill or mountain at the top of which it sits, representing everything that the bright and colourful suburb is not. It is dark, almost black and white by contrast; it is shadowy; it is old, even antique and thus mysterious and, crucially, seems to put itself beyond historical time. It is here that the 'unfinished' Edward lives, his inventor having left him incomplete and with scissors for hands. This space is also constructed historically within the film, because we witness not only the contemporary location but also its past involving the inventor. We do not have the same purchase on the suburb's history and this serves to reinforce the status of the suburb as normative.

After this introduction, the connection between the two locations is made clear when one of the main characters, Peg Boggs (Dianne Wiest), an Avon Lady, decides to venture up to the castle after a day of weak sales in the suburb. The entrance to the mountain path that leads up to the castle is to be found at the end of the suburb's cul-de-sac and thus it provides a physical link between the two spaces. Until this point, no non-diegetic music has been presented (apart from that found in the narratorial opening). However, as Peg sits in her car and turns the wing mirror, which reveals the gate and path leading to the castle, we encounter the first use of the original score, indicating at once the distance – in terms of narrative – that this location suggests. After entering it, she encounters Edward (Johnny Depp) for the first time and, taking pity on his apparently tragic situation, brings him back to her house in the suburb. From then on the film deals with the ways in which Edward is assimilated into the world of the suburb – in school, life and, of course, love. It is interesting to note the heightened presentation of these suburban tropes (the rather ersatz presentation of which constitutes a kind of fantasy through exaggerated realism).

The neighbours at first accept him and suggest that his skills with his scissor hands can be used for cutting hedges (topiary becomes an option) and this eventually leads him to work in a hair salon, run by one of the neighbours, Joyce (Kathy Baker). However, misunderstanding and discrimination lead most to fear Edward and from this point forward the film deals with the ways in which suburban America can be seen as a hostile and closed space. Peg's daughter, Kim (Winona Ryder), falls for Edward and her current boyfriend, Jim – the neighbourhood bully – attacks him, causing Kim to announce that their relationship is over. However, because of an incident in which Edward accidently cuts Kim's face, the neighbours begin to distrust Edward and Jim turns against him more vociferously. He is chased back to his castle on the hill, where a mob gathers outside. Kim comes to find Edward but is pursued into the castle by her rage-filled boyfriend, who is eventually stabbed (again by accident) by one of Edward's scissor hands in a fight started by Jim. Jim finally falls to his death from a castle window, but Edward is protected by Kim, who claims he also died in the fight. We learn that the narrator – the elderly lady who begins and closes the film – is in fact Kim herself and thus, she quite literally becomes the film's narrative voice. The connection between Kim and Edward and between the narrated opening and closing parts is musical but they are also linked through the use of snow and ice (even in a Florida-esque suburb) and by Edward's seemingly magical performances in which he creates figures out of ice. *Edward Scissorhands* is thus a film about isolation and the ways in which difference is managed, a common topic within the fairy-tale or German Expressionist cinema. This film, however, also draws on seemingly solid American tropes of discovery and alienation and demonstrates how difference is also manifested and constructed musically.

The identity of fantasy

It is important at this stage to set out the type of fantasy under discussion here. As outlined above, describing *Edward Scissorhands* as a fantasy film is not straightforward, and yet a certain amount of play is made with generic types – especially the lines between fantasy and what might be termed proto-horror. It seems reasonable, therefore, to explain in what ways its generic status as fantasy is insecure. Tolkien, as mentioned above, articulated and practised a type of fantasy that is significantly dissimilar to the way the story is presented in *Edward Scissorhands*. He stipulated that:

> If you are present at a Faërian drama you yourself are, or think that you are, bodily inside its Secondary World. The experience may be very similar to Dreaming and has (it would seem) sometimes (by men) been confounded with it. But in Faërian drama you are in a dream that some other mind is

weaving, and the knowledge of that alarming fact may slip from your grasp. To experience directly a Secondary World: the potion is too strong, and you give to it Primary Belief, however marvellous the events. You are deluded—whether that is the intention of the elves (always or at any time) is another question. They at any rate are not themselves deluded. This is for them a form of Art, and distinct from Wizardry or Magic, properly so called. They do not live in it, though they can, perhaps, afford to spend more time at it than human artists can. The Primary World, Reality, of elves and men is the same, if differently valued and perceived. (1966: 72–3)

For Tolkien, therefore, a central tenet was the totality of the fantastic realm; not merely that it made coherent sense – that it was internally logical – but that it also took for granted its identity, space and world and that (in his case) the readers found themselves inside this world, though it was clearly not the real world. The difficulty with using this as a working definition of fantasy with respect to *Edward Scissorhands* is its dependence on the distance and totality of the fantastic from the spectator's world and the avoidance of drawing attention to the tropes of fantasy's generic identity that are brought to the fore in Burton's film.

A defining attribute of fantasy is, of course, this very distinction from reality (howsoever this may be conceived). It is not enough for this distinction merely to be presented. Instead, its very distance from what is perceived or understood as real constitutes, in film, its identity. In other words, the ways in which this departure from a supposed reality are presented determine the extent to which a text or context is considered fantastic or the extent to which it engages with established models of fantasy. And yet, there are clearly varieties of fantasy: those whose status as fantasy is total and which do not involve a critique of their own identity; those which play with the idea of their own fantasy identity and invite attention to their own unreality as a feature of the narrative. *Edward Scissorhands* takes for granted the fantastic realm (especially that obvious fantasy of the world of the castle). But it also connects this freely to the purportedly real world of the suburb and it is this that problematizes the categorization of fantasy.

Once again, however, because the space of the castle is presented as strongly fantastic, it is easier for this to be understood as fantasy – it uses the visual signs and characteristics associated with fantasy. And yet, it might also be feasible to regard it as a kind of alter ego to the hyper-reality presented in the suburb. It is as though the castle space, in this context, stands as the darker, introverted side of the bright suburb. Thinking of it in this way helps to connect it with a range of issues that preoccupy Burton more widely: an inner reality of isolation and a counter to the brilliance of the suburb, which by contrast is inhabited by many.[1] Nonetheless, the use of fantasy as a narrative trope here at least suggests that the frameworks of the generic expectations of fantasy might also be brought into a discussion of the film, especially given the use of orchestral music (versus the use of pre-existing popular music emanating from the suburb) as a signature for the castle space. Furthermore, the fact that the film takes for granted the slippage between spaces as normal within its own narrative would also suggest that fantasy is an appropriate description of *Edward Scissorhands* since internally this transition is not questioned.

In more general ways, fantasy has largely been linked with fiction in literary terms and has proven difficult to differentiate historically because of the diversity of ways it presents itself. This difficulty lies in the central premise of fantasy as a manifestation of the impossible – walking down the street is possible (even if its presentation in film is manifestly constructed); flying down the street is regarded as beyond the realms of possibility (filmic cutting and real-time issues notwithstanding) and is thus presented as 'fantasy'.[2] As a result, the constitution of fantasy is not so much generic as what William Irwin has described as "an overt violation of what is generally accepted as possibility; it is the narrative result of transforming the condition contrary to fact into 'fact' itself" (Irwin, 1976: x). However, Irwin continues that such an overt violation is only possible with the complicity of the audience in their suspension of disbelief. He identifies the pact of successful fantasy, therefore, as one that functions as a kind of game in which the spectator must be a willing participant.

Music is indispensable in the production of fantasy narratives and, in particular, the production of fantastic subjectivities. A distinction should be made between fantasy and the fantastic as a narrative condition, and the genre of fantasy which presupposes certain generic types and properties. This is especially important when examining *Edward Scissorhands* because the construction and then blurring of small-scale generic boundaries is central to the film. Its overarching status as fantasy, however, is not compromised in this process. Indeed, the use of music helps to thematize this play between fantasy, reality and the seemingly ordinary whilst exaggerating and thus drawing our attention to what makes up that ordinariness.

Edward Scissorhands, therefore, presents a case for understanding fantasy along musical lines and also demonstrates the sense in which fantasy is broadly and complexly conceived. It does this by highlighting the very tropes that have commonly constituted the genre and then sets these against and alongside commonly non-fantastic environments. Fantasy in this context is part of a series of binary oppositions within the narrative, each necessary in marking the 'return' to the real world and thus of drawing one's attention to the caricature of fantasy that is presented. This is interesting for the present discussion because music is partly responsible for the characterizing and caricaturing of each space (a key function of film music more generally).

It is also possible, however, to read the film as a whole as operating within a kind of fantasy setting. Geography (the mountain and castle where Edward lives) circumscribes the central and most visible area of fantasy, but the fact that Edward transgresses this by entering the 'other' world – and is accepted into it – might suggest that the film mobilizes the idea of fantasy more widely. This does not take away from the crucial separation of spaces within the film's narrative, however. The specific choice and placing of public-domain music, which is usually presented diegetically – belonging to the inhabitants of the suburb and defining their identities – and Danny Elfman's original soundtrack help to mark out this distinction and in so doing construct spaces of fantasy in which the depth or extent of the fantastic is mediated by its musical dimension. In this way, the fantastic is determined by music in relation both to its other more intense identities in the film, but also in relation to what constitutes fantasy-cinema music more widely. A concatenation of contemporary fairy-tale visually and an orchestral (and crucially) choral soundtrack proves to be a rich territory for the consideration of music's role in articulating fantasy in cinema. As a result, the distinctions between the dominant focus of each narrative are articulated through musical differences as the characters move between domains.

Like much of Burton's work, *Edward Scissorhands* plays on the boundaries of and tropes presented by traditional non-fantasy cinema and fantasy cinema in that it takes place both within a contemporary, seemingly real world as well as a fantastic other. To achieve this shift, the idea of fantasy, as well as the moment the fantasy commences, is *invoked*. That is to say, the idea of a world adjunct to the real one is a commonly explored theme and is marked by different musical language. For example, Burton's 1988 film *Beetlejuice* achieved this by distinguishing the reality of the New England environment and the house the protagonists had recently purchased from the expression-istic and surrealist world that also unfolds – a space whose music is much less tonally secure. The distinction in *Edward Scissorhands,* by contrast, is much less clear. Music serves as both a way of invoking fantasy (here constituted as a mixture of urban fairy-tale and gothic luxury) and of ensuring a kind of generic security. It achieves this sense of generic security by drawing on the idea of the fairy-tale – of the gothic narrative – both as a trope of enticement (important to fantasy more generally, drawing us into the fantasy space) and also as a way of creating a striking contrast to suburban space. How music contributes to the narrative in *Edward Scissorhands* is very closely connected to the conditions of fantasy that emerge, but as has been noted, the space of the castle (Edward's realm) is part of the suburb in that it can be readily accessed. It is visually very different but otherwise it does not display the same fantastic characteristics that are found in *Beetlejuice*, where the ghosts' movements between the house, its exterior, the model of the town and the 'spirit realm' often trigger moments of extreme visual and musical rupture. This serves to highlight that *Edward Scissorhands* is *about* fantasy as much as it *is* fantasy and therefore presupposes an understanding of fantasy as a genre.

Marina Warner has noted how the historical understanding of fantasy has developed with a distinction between the visual and the rational:

> 'Fantasy', the Latinized version of the Greek, has acquired a stream of distinct associations with the result that shades of difference now operate to distinguish imagination from fantasy in common usage, in ways that effloresce from definitions attempted by Renaissance philosophers. Pietro Pomponazzi (d.1525) restricted fantasy to the sleeping mind alone, and granted imagination a connection with conscious perception. Imagination still carries these more positive, rational, even comic overtones: in common parlance, 'Use your imagination' does not mean the same as 'Go ahead, fantasize', but rather evokes conscious, responsible, and sympathetic behaviour, by contrast with 'You're fantasizing', which calls to inner realms of the unconscious and dream. (2006: 122)

Warner's sketch of fantasy departs from Tolkien's, who preferred to avoid considering sleep and the idea of fantasy as an emerging or transient condition. For Warner, fantasy has often been presented as closely related to a form of irrationality. Extending Warner's use, it is not difficult also to read fantasy and madness as connected, particularly as these are both unified as Other. This joining of fantasy and madness as a discursive form is especially pertinent because it is explored within *Edward Scissorhands*, in which difference – and in particular the difference that Edward presents – is framed as threatening (sexually and/or violently). This trope is also found elsewhere, with Park Chan-Wook's 2006 film *I'm a Cyborg But That's OK* providing a useful example. Madness here uses fantasy as a central tenor of its own identity and of how it is constituted. It does not seem unreasonable, therefore, to read this approach in *Edward Scissorhands* and in the way in which Burton explores ideas of isolation, difference and its sometimes awkward interaction with society.

Edward Scissorhands maintains this by musically dividing the 'real' world, with its obtainable – read 'desirable' – attributes from the fantastic, with its innocent, misunderstood and withdrawn identities. It is not only presented as innocent but is also constructed as both threatening and threatened, and it is here that music participates in refining the audience's ideological identification with these categories and their associations. Indeed, the music helps to forge some of the associations such as the ways in which Edward's identity is always only marginally assimilated into the suburban narrative and to highlight moments of incongruity. In so doing, the music helps to entrench the sense of fantasy that Warner outlines above: one in which dreamlike, unconscious and implausible events and moments take their place alongside purportedly more rationalized behaviour. However, *Edward Scissorhands* also offers a more complex presentation of fantasy because the film both presents the fantastic and also runs an implicit critique of fantasy alongside, part of which is contained within the music. It is not possible, for example, to understand the ways in which this critique is operating, without first attending to the ways in which the music is working with and promoting the interplay of fantasy and reality within the context of this film. As a result, although the generic labelling of *Edward Scissorhands* as a fantasy film still stands, while music participates in creating this idea (mainly through the use of larger referential clichés that have come to be associated with fantasy – wordless choir, generally tonal but full orchestral writing and a close tracking of action or sentiment presented visually but supplemented musically), it also seems to rationalize the absurdity of the fantastic at other moments, usually ones which present the diegetic music of the suburb. Of course, the conceit that this highlights is, ultimately, to cast the film's narrative as fantasy. Simply by highlighting when it is not so, the film can at other moments reinforce the fantasy narrative's voice more strongly. A paradox emerges, therefore (about which more below), in which the fantasy is strengthened through its connection with the non- or less fantastic.

Music, geography and fantasy

The geographical identity of fantasy in *Edward Scissorhands* is central and is one of the dimensions that music is responsible for embodying. The castle of fairy-tale proportions at the top of the mountain is the first fantastic territory to which the spectator is exposed. This is made more apparent by the way in which it is differentiated from the hyper-realized suburban territory in which the film proper begins. Essentially a film founded on extremes and the extent to which those extremes are reconcilable, *Edward Scissorhands* sets up a binary between two worlds, each of whose identifying characteristics are exaggerated for fairy-tale effect.

In the concept of alterity, the difference between two terms constitutes not only their shared identity but also functions to create a value judgement, weighting one of the terms against the other morally. This is a useful way of understanding how the narrative operates here and seems to connect more widely with the themes of isolation and distance that occupy Burton more generally. Narrative, of course, is a notoriously problematic notion to frame and in the context of film music, its identity is problematized yet further by the sense in which the music is understood as diegetic or non-diegetic. For example, Ben Winters (2010) has suggested that previous scholarship on the purely narrative status of film music is not always a useful way of under-standing its effect. Earlier theorists – usually with academic backgrounds in literature departments – framed their arguments as though the music itself had a narrative impulse.[3] An understanding of film music's role in the production of narrative and its position as a means of forging difference between components or spaces within the story is the one most germane to *Edward Scissorhands*. It is central because music's role mediates what might be termed 'narrative voice' and the 'narratorial voice'. These terms, drawn from Jacques Derrida and thus borrowed from a literary context, help to identify some of the ways in which music provides a localized supplement and a broader narrative signposting. Derrida states:

> The narrative voice ... is "a neutral voice that utters [dit] the work from the placeless place where the work is silent." The placeless place where the work is silent: a silent voice, then, withdrawn into its 'voicelessness' ['aphonie']. This 'voicelessness' distinguishes it from the 'narratorial voice', the voice that literary criticism or poetics or narratology strives to locate in the system of the narrative, of the novel, or of the narration. The narratorial voice is the voice of a subject recounting something, remembering an event or a historical sequence, knowing who he is, where he is, and what he is talking about. (Derrida, 1979: 104)

The distinctions that Derrida outlines can be read in *Edward Scissorhands* because of the way the film begins with an overt narratorial voice – the effect of which is to start the story which follows. This unfolding of the story – in broad terms – can be considered that narrative voice, though within this there are further knots of narrative significance: music whose narratographic identity is bound up both in the narrative voice and the narratorial voice. I say 'bound up' so as not to suggest that the music itself constitutes either of these, for it does not. However, it is a crucial pillar in the construction of each of them. A particular feature is the complicity of music in the (con)formation of ideological distinc-tions with respect to character, morality and larger ideological codes. Indeed, Derrida follows his passage, quoted above, in aphoristic vein by suggesting that the narratorial voice and, more specifically, "all organized narration is 'a matter for the police', even before its genre (mystery novel, cop story) has been determined)" (*ibid.*: 105). Here Derrida seems to be suggesting that the demand for narrative presented by the narratorial voice requires a response. Interestingly, in the case of *Edward Scissorhands*, part of that answer may emerge from the way the music helps to condition the narrative subsequently. Music is present in the initiating of the story (the narratorial voice) and then in the distinction of the spaces within the subsequent narrative.

This position problematizes the more straightforward distinction between music's role as supplement to the narrative voice and its role as supplementing the narratorial structures within the film world proper. But perhaps this distinction need not worry us too much. Similar agonizing over the differences between diegetic and non-diegetic music may also prove less useful and it might be more prudent to consider the function and identity of film music here as much more fluid, less fixed and more open to change and reinterpretation with other components of the cinematic narrative. Nonetheless, the role of music in *Edward Scissorhands* does suggest that, at times, it functions along expected ideological parameters; but these are not the only ways in which it contributes to narrative.

One of the more conventionally framed uses of music (but central here nonetheless) is the use of the underscore to foreground subject positions with characters or ideas. For example, non-diegetic music is initially associated with Edward's world in the castle but it is not present when he moves to the suburb, whose identity, as previously noted, is constructed musically through the use of diegetic, popular music. Not only does this heighten the sense in which both of those areas are narratively separate, but it also helps to lessen the sense of Edward as a purely fairy-tale figure and helps to make more plausible his presence in the 'real' world.

The connection, therefore, between music and place in film is clearly central. In Michael Curtiz's 1942 film *Casablanca*, the use of the 'Marseillaise' at the opening as the visuals sweep over a map of 'French Morocco' does a similar kind of ideological gelling, creating a link between the place and the sense of ownership or identity with it. Similarly, Edward's owned space, at the start of the film at least, is that of the castle. It is not until later that the associations with this place are brought musically into play within the suburb. When we witness these scenes (the virtuosic performance with his scissor hands in the high school to create a long and intricate set of interconnected paper figures and, more especially, a scene in the latter half of the film and also at the close in which the character Kim dances around the suburban house garden at night, which is covered by the snow-like ice from a sculpture created by Edward with his scissors), we are forced to understand, as in Derrida's suggestion of narrative and the demand for a police confession, that these are moments alien to the geography of the suburb. The music helps to link these feelings – for they are felt more than articulated – both to the subjectivity of Edward and also to the world of the castle in which this kind of music and these kinds of events, we are told, belong. It also describes how music functions in an important but more oblique fashion, operating in what Claudia Gorbman famously called "that gray area of secondary perception least susceptible to rigorous judgement and most susceptible to affective manipulation" (Gorbman, 1980: 183). Until the Otherness of the castle location is defined, there is no sense in which the accentuated suburbia should be considered normative. However, the fact that the music of Edward's domain and the narratorial opening of the film are the same suggests a generic dominance, but the normativity established by the suburb subsequently destabilizes this straightforward reading. Furthermore, the use of music in *Edward Scissorhands* does present some interesting divergent and even paradoxical uses.

If one accepts the idea that *Edward Scissorhands* constitutes a fantasy film, then a paradox seems to emerge in which the extent of the use of music is complicit. The film is narratively framed by moments of telling, in which the 'enclosed' story is meant to be understood as a modern-day fairy-tale. This legitimizes, to a certain extent, what takes place within the film and allows all of it to constitute fantasy. This claim is also supported by the fact that both the opening and closing 'once upon a time' and 'happily ever after' sections respectively are richly scored, using both full orchestra and the supplement of a wordless choir. The closing scene also presents the viewer with a further paradox: the story that unfolded as a fairy-tale turns out to be the real story of the now-older lady who is recounting it. However, this does not undermine the idea of understanding the interior narrative as fantasy, because the film in general plays with the notions of what constitutes fantasy and how this is presented. Returning to the claim made at the outset – that *Edward Scissorhands* does not present a total 'immersive' fantasy but rather uses music, among other elements of the film, to critique and interrogate the genre – it follows that the overt use of the typical storyteller's end to the tale (only for the viewer then to learn that it was the storyteller's actual history) is, likewise, part of the film's broader parody.

The music of the suburb

Although the suburb contains distinctive music, the fact that it does not have its own scored music – that instead public-domain music emanates from here – suggests that the spaces are defined in different ways and that the narrative or ideological centre of the film is pushed towards the musically most intensive space. Though this is a far from uncommon use of film music, in *Edward Scissorhands* it is important because the distinction is not merely one of place but also one of genre or, at least, of playing with generic models. Edward's castle is clearly supposed to be understood as the more fantastic location but the fact that it is an area known by and accessible to those from the suburb complicates both its own identity and that of the 'ordinariness' of the suburb. This does not necessarily mean to suggest that the space of the castle, albeit scored in ways that suggest a richly fantastic environment, constitutes fantasy whereas the suburb does not. Instead, it is the foregrounding of fantasy, the access to fantasy and its potential here to be negative, lonely and isolating that is explored through the polarization of the suburb and the castle.

Although 'diegetic music' has increasingly become a theoretically imprecise and unstable term (see, for example, Binns, 2008; Stilwell, 2007; Winters, 2010), most of the music contained within the world of the suburb is what is commonly known as diegetic music and, within the context of fantasy narratives, this helps to specify this location as normative and thus enables the more fantastic identity of Edward's castle to emerge as Other. By virtue of being specially composed, the music associated with the castle (Edward's space) also creates a musical subjectivity, in which the psychology of the character associated with it, or even the location itself, is 'projected' through the music. This is different from the function of the pre-existing diegetic music used in the suburb, where music operates as an aspect of the scene – it justifies and enriches the characters by telling us what their musical interests might be – rather than supplementing them in a psychological manner. This serves to heighten further the distinctions between suburbia and the 'fantasy' of the castle.

The fact that the concentration of non-diegetic music is located within Edward's castle space seems to license this proposition, following, as it broadly does, the logic of Hollywood scoring practice. Similarly, the fact that no diegetic music is heard in the domain of the castle highlights the difference (and even threat) that Edward seems to pose in the suburb. Here, his superhuman abilities are marked by music which strongly activates within spectators the feeling that he is Other to the suburb's identity; that he is to be constructed in narrative terms as representative of instability – a threat to the status quo precisely because (his) music at these moments is from elsewhere. The rather rough binary serves to highlight the ways in which a central feature of *Edward Scissorhands* is both a moral narrative and an ideological separation of ideas. The two locations of the narrative operate as signifiers for larger ideological tropes (isolation and innocence within the castle; threat, mob rule and ostracization within the suburb) and their clear separation is central for this to be effective. Music's role in this process is also central because it is largely the responsibility of the music to reinforce the separation of locations and yet the paradox here (particularly within the context of *Edward Scissorhands*) is that the suspension of disbelief that is central both to fantasy and to the fairy-tale more generally is invoked at the start, when the storytelling scene starts the film (all of which is thus to be seen as a story). Following this narrative 'framing of the story' moment, the film moves into the 'real' world of the film, as presented by the geographical narrative of the suburb, only to be again internally critiqued through a staging of the castle/suburb dynamic. This dynamic is not merely one that separates two parts of the story. Its importance lies in the ways in which these differences form the story itself. For the moral within the moral (or the story within the framed storytelling mode) to be successfully conveyed, music enables a distinction to be *felt* by embodying the different locations with separate identities – one more closely associated with the Derridean narratorial voice than the other.

Part of the way in which classical Hollywood underscores operate is to mask the inherent artificiality of the fractured film narrative by using music not only to create a type of sonic continuum but also to foreshorten the distance between the film itself – that is to say, the flat screen – and the spectator. In so doing, this quite obviously heightened artificiality enables the spectator to identify with the narrative being played out and thus more easily to suspend disbelief. At the same time, however, it can also weaken the spectator's critical reading of what is on screen and thus has the potential for strong ideological manipulation, not least because music operates in the perceptive background and is, by definition, unseen. This is the most frequently used scoring model in classical Hollywood cinema, and yet in *Edward Scissorhands* there is a sense in which this practice is both in evidence and in reverse. It is almost as though the music here is used to activate those familiar conditions for which it is dutifully deployed in other mass-entertainment films, only to undercut those conditions through the critique provided by the two starkly different locations. When Edward's music sounds in the suburban scenes, it is both underscoring – constructing – the magic that attends them, but it is also making plain the sense in which he is magical and thus alien to that location. To be sure, in the context of the story, Edward's magical existence and actions are believed, but they are presented as unreal, as something that does not or should not happen in the suburb; the music, in these instances, provides the primary force behind this reading. In this way, music helps to bind and weave together not only the entire narratives of the two locations, but also moments of intersection, of memory and of reference.

It should be stressed that these moments are not to be seen as narrative, not even in the sense that Carolyn Abbate (1991) proposes, in which very special moments of musical recall might constitute moments of musical narration. These moments do, however, highlight how music is conscripted to put forward an interpretation for the audience that requires both the separation of spaces (suburb/castle) and the connection or conflict between them at other times. Returning briefly to Derrida but to a different text, 'Plato's Pharmacy' in *Dissemination* (1981), we are reminded of what he terms the 'Pharmakon', something that is both itself and the opposite within the same context. Here, this approach could be read into the use of music, allowing an interpretation of the music to shift away from how it moves the plot forward and turn instead to an arena of interpretation in which the music's relationship to narrative itself is brought under review. The binary that has been outlined above need not cause an interpretative dilemma, nor should it be seen as inconsistent with an understanding of the function of music here. Instead, it is hoped that music is read as broadening narrative possibilities interpretatively. Indeed, following on from Anahid Kassabian's idea that popular music soundtracks widen the identificatory possibilities between the spectators and the film scene, here we might offer a parallel claim: that the orchestral underscore can also be understood as diverse and even subversive with respect to traditionally constituted narrative formats and allow for their self-critique. It does not offer the wider identificatory possibilities that Kassabian suggests popular music so often does, but it need not occupy such narrow ideological confines either.

Edward Scissorhands, therefore, can be read as both fantasy/fairy-tale and a critique of a modern-day fairy-tale or fantasy narrative at the same time. The extent of critique never quite results in satire, nor does it set out to destabilize the suburb, which, although clearly an accentuated collection of suburban archetypes, nonetheless is sufficiently distinct from the castle domain for the real/make-believe polarity to retain its legitimacy. Usually, the use of music makes film scenes appear more real (in spite of its obvious artificiality) and yet here it is the less-musical suburb, set against the musical-associative castle, that is rendered 'real'. The trope of enticement through music, therefore, lies not in the framing of 'reality' but in the framing of the conspicuously unreal and connecting this to something which has an aura of reality, but whose structures (the suburb) are exaggerated.

Notes

1. I am very grateful to Janet Halfyard for suggesting this line of interpretation. See Halfyard (2004) for further discussion of the idea of duality in the construction of Burton's narratives; and Burton (2006: 84–100) for the director's own discussion of themes in this film.

2. In this context, however, fantasy is to be differentiated from science fiction. The latter is based upon supposedly scientifically provable or, at least, logically reasonable scenarios. Fantasy, by contrast, is not, often invoking magical or supernatural practices instead.

3. Claudia Gorbman's now famous *Unheard Melodies: Narrative Film Music* (1987) and Caryl Flinn's *Strains of Utopia: Gender, Nostalgia and Hollywood Film Music* (1992) both tend to present non-diegetic music in particular as offering a distinct voice within film, rather than emphasizing its role as a influential constituent in the emergence of narrative.

References

Abbate, C. (1991), *Unsung Voices: Opera and Musical Narrative in the Nineteenth Century*, Princeton: Princeton University Press.

Binns, A. (2008), 'Desiring the Diegesis: Music and Self-seduction in the Films of Wong Kar-Wai', in D. Cooper, C. Fox and I. Sapiro (eds), *CineMusic? Constructing the Film Score*, Newcastle: Cambridge Scholars Publishing, pp. 127–40.

Burton, T. (2006), *Burton on Burton*, rev. edn, edited by M. Salisbury, London: Faber and Faber.

Derrida, J. (1979), 'Living on: Border Lines', in H. Bloom (ed.), *Deconstruction and Criticism*, New York: Continuum, pp. 75–176.

Derrida, J. (1981), 'Plato's Pharmacy', in J. Derrida, *Dissemination*, trans. B. Johnson, Chicago: University of Chicago Press, pp. 67–186.

Flinn, C. (1992), *Strains of Utopia: Gender, Nostalgia and Hollywood Film Music*, Princeton: Princeton University Press.

Gorbman, C. (1980), 'Narrative Film Music', *Yale French Studies*, 60, 183–203.

Gorbman, C. (1987), *Unheard Melodies: Narrative Film Music*, Bloomington: Indiana University Press.

Halfyard, J. K. (2004), *Danny Elfman's* Batman: *A Film Score Guide*, Lanham, MD: Scarecrow Press.

Irwin, W. R. (1976), *The Game of the Impossible: A Rhetoric of Fantasy*, Champaign: University of Illinois Press.

Kassabian, A. (2001), *Hearing Film: Tracking Identifications in Contemporary Hollywood Film Music*, London: Routledge.

Stilwell, R. J. (2007), 'The Fantastic Gap between Diegetic and Nondiegetic', in D. Goldmark, L. Kramer and R. Leppert (eds), *Beyond the Soundtrack: Representing Music in Cinema*, Berkeley: University of California Press, pp. 184–204.

Tolkien, J. R. R. (1966), 'On Fairy Stories', in *The Tolkien Reader*, New York: Ballantine Books, pp. 3–84.

Warner, M. (2006), *Phantasmagoria*, Oxford: Oxford University Press.

Winters, B. (2010), 'The Non-diegetic Fallacy: Film, Music, and Narrative Space', *Music and Letters*, 91(2), 224–44.

8 The Tritone Within

Interpreting Harmony in Elliot Goldenthal's Score for **Final Fantasy: The Spirits Within**

Scott Murphy

It may seem, at the least, off-track to investigate the musical score of a film whose most glowing accolades and central claim to cinematic fame stem from the artistry and technical achievements of its visuals. *Final Fantasy: The Spirits Within* (Hironobu Sakaguchi and Moto Sakakibara, 2001), henceforth *Spirits Within*, is generally considered to be the first full-length computer animation film to feature photorealistic human characters, clearly setting a new standard for the industry. Moreover, the film treats the viewer to splendorous and breathtaking images of landscapes, cityscapes and dreamscapes, eye candy that even the film's harshest critics cannot help but savour. Popular film critic Roger Ebert, one of the film's most public advocates, well summarizes this view: "The reason to see this movie is simply, gloriously, to look at it".[1] However, when the film was released on 2 July 2001, during the lucrative summer season, far too few moviegoers 'looked at' the film for it to recuperate the four years and US$137 million that the film's director Hironobu Sakaguchi, the creator and director of the extremely successful *Final Fantasy* role-playing videogame series (henceforth *FF*), had invested in the film.

In critical reviews, several possible explanations were floated for the film's failure, and at least three of them share a common structure of ambivalence.[2] Firstly, the widely disparaged script attempts to amalgamate Hollywood action-film clichés with convoluted New Age mythology; those anticipating a popcorn blockbuster may have found the film tainted by the elements of a spiritualist narrative or vice versa. The following synopsis of the film's plot foregrounds this opposition. On the one hand, the narrative co-opts a familiar alien-invasion model: aggressive phantoms from another planet infest twenty-first-century Earth, killing most of the human population by either wresting the spirits from their bodies or infecting them with alien particles. Those remaining alive have retreated into 'barrier cities' that keep the phantoms at bay for the moment. The Deep Eyes Squadron, led by Captain Gray Edwards, combats the phantoms with bravado and firearm/artillery warfare reminiscent of both military/sci-fi cinematic hybrids such as *Aliens* (James Cameron, 1986) and the stylized violence of many popular role-playing games. The biggest gun, the orbiting Zeus space cannon, is under the control of General Hein, a ruthless antagonist suffering from the loss of his family to the phantoms, who plans to destroy the phantoms with one blow. On the other hand, Dr Aki Ross and her mentor Dr Sid espouse the Gaia hypothesis, which claims that every planet contains a spirit or Gaia, and they warn that Hein's cannon may harm or even destroy Earth's Gaia. Rather, they propose a means of disabling the phantoms by assembling eight spirits from seemingly innocuous life forms into a wave pattern that may neutralize the wave pattern of the phantoms.

A second area of critique emerging from the film's reviews is that while Sakaguchi's film makes a few oblique references to his videogame series of the same name, this was not enough to appease the substantial game-playing segment of the market that had anxiously awaited the film and that Sony, the parent company of both the film's distribution studio (Columbia Pictures) and the videogame's platform (Playstation), had hoped to tap. Additionally, the verisimilitude of the film's human characters, as achieved particularly in remarkable close-ups, suffers from certain unreal bodily appearances, positions and motions. However, this negative assessment stems not from such lapses per se, but rather from the very accuracy of the anthropomorphous representation. As Taylor and Hsu put it: "*Final Fantasy*'s humans, in some ways, were so realistic that they were unsettling to watch" (Taylor and Hsu, 2003: 105).[3]

The third critique, which engages a special case of ambivalence, alludes to roboticist Masahiro Mori's theory of the 'uncanny valley', which speculates that, for example, prosthetic hands designed with minute details of human anatomy can become 'too real', such that:

> *when we notice it is prosthetic, we have a sense of strangeness. So if we shake the hand, we are surprised by the lack of soft tissue and cold temperature. In this case, there is no longer a sense of familiarity. It is uncanny.* (Mori, 1970)

The late music theorist David Lewin once opined that while theory in and of itself cannot validate or authenticate criticism, it "can be used to qualify it, to sharpen and develop one's own discrimination, and to communicate critical experiences to others" (Lewin, 1969: 64). Such is the case here: Mori's theory (or its epistemic ancestors and siblings from Sigmund Freud, Julia Kristeva and so on) resonates with the notion that the film's close-but-not-quite-right simulation of human appearance and motion creates far less empathetic connection between the celluloid characters and the audience than that achieved by either live acting or more conventional Disney or anime-style representation.

Although theories of media music have multiplied in the past two or three decades, few have provided comparable resonances for media-music criticism that wilfully taps into the structure of ambivalence.[4] I propose that at least two psychological theories may serve this purpose. First, theories of the uncanny (*das Unheimliche*) could ally with some of these criticisms, either in general cases where a particular image/music amalgam precariously straddles two opposing interpretations instead of conforming to only one of them (closer to the undecidability of psychologist Ernst Jentsch's *Unheimliche*)[5] or, in special cases, where a particular image/music amalgam pushes both the familiar and the strange into uncomfortably close psychological quarters (closer to Freud's refinement of Jentsch's theory[6] and the *Unheimliche* to which Mori refers). For one example of the former, Jack Sullivan pans John Addison's "skilful boilerplate" music accompanying the main title for *Torn Curtain* (Alfred Hitchcock, 1966) for being "too mild for the apocalyptic images on the screen but too dour for counterpoint" (Sullivan, 2006: 285). If one brings to the film the expectation that the music will work either with or against the images – the oft-cited parallel/counterpoint opposition – then this critique seems to suggest that the occupation of an unallied region in between these two accepted modes of presentation demotes the art *a priori*. For an example of the latter, Robynn Stilwell has noted moments in the soundtrack for the television programme *The X Files* (Fox, 1993–2002) where the diegetic sound-universe – the sonically real – encroaches upon the non-diegetic musical score – the sonically imaginary – and vice versa (Stilwell, 2003). Although Stilwell does not associate this blurring with the uncanny, its parallels with the programme's macabre and paranormal themes unquestionably invite it.

Yet theories of the uncanny in media music relate best to those ambivalences that are relatively immediate in both time and perception, in that, like shaking the prosthetic hand, the two contrasting interpretations that subconsciously trigger the uncanniness are either simultaneous or chronologically contiguous. However, my interest in the score to *Spirits Within* revolves around a related but nonetheless distinct kind of ambivalence, in which an appreciable span of time separates the two contrasting interpretations and which may require conscious deliberation.[7] In media music, such ambivalence may arise when two chronologically independent but related mappings between a segment of music and an image, character or other narrative object appear to contradict one another in some fashion.

Consider the case of leitmotivic association gone awry. Put coarsely, in a Hollywood score that associates distinct musical themes (leitmotifs) with concrete narrative objects (characters, places, items and so on), the association is typically construed as a function: f (theme) = narrative object. Often the function is bijective, in that there is exactly one narrative object for each theme and vice versa. Sometimes the function is injective (one-to-one) but not bijective, in that there may be multiple themes associated with a single narrative object, such as Goldsmith's three themes for *Patton* (Franklin Schaffner, 1970).[8] But an association of multiple narrative objects with a single theme challenges the traditional 'functional' behaviour of a film's leitmotivic structure. This situation arises for one of Erich Wolfgang Korngold's themes in his score for *The Sea Hawk* (Michael Curtiz, 1940). A soaring string melody, first heard as the secondary subject in the main title, receives its associational 'baptism' as it accompanies the moment when English slaves trapped below in a Spanish galley realize they are rowing in the English Channel. One might infer from this initial association and others from the beginning of the film that involve variations on the theme, that this melody signifies 'England'. A subsequent appearance of the theme later in the film highlights the moment Captain Thorpe (Errol Flynn) and his men, left to die in the sweltering jungles of Panama, find the beach, complete with means of rescue in the form of a nearby longboat. Although the specific 'England' association might still apply tangentially (Thorpe and company have a chance to make it home), Royal S. Brown entertains broadening the signification of the theme (which he names the 'romantic' theme) to "feelings ... of heroic optimism heavily tinged with a sense of freedom" (Brown, 1994: 101).

Nonetheless, Brown ultimately finds the 'romantic' theme "problematic in its dramatic implications" (*ibid.*) and also dubs it the 'floating' theme, since it "attaches itself to various characters and situations" (*ibid.*: 98) and thereby frustrates any clear, concrete signified at what I will call the *basic level*. For Brown, the 'floating' nature of this theme becomes at once most logically apparent and most dramatically pertinent during a scene towards the end of the film, when Thorpe and his love interest Doña Maria (Brenda Marshall) confess their true feelings toward one another. The theme accompanies the beginning of the scene, when Thorpe learns that Doña Maria, the half-Spanish, half-English niece of the film's Spanish antagonist, is planning to stay in England instead of accompanying her uncle back to Spain. When she professes her love for Thorpe, the score immediately changes to another theme. Brown's reading of the appropriateness of this theme capitalizes on its 'floating' nature, which avoids "allowing too much of the viewer/listener's pleasure to get caught up in the narrative events"; therefore, "most of [its] effect/affect remains in the domain of music" (*ibid.*: 113). But it may also be read as appropriate given its associations from earlier in the film: just as the English prisoners long for the shores of Dover, and Thorpe and his men long for the cool refreshment and familiar sight of the ocean, so does Doña Maria long to be in her rightful romantic place with Thorpe (and in her rightful ideological place with England). In short, the 'romantic' theme is a 'homecoming after oppression' theme. Yet it permits the more general association – on what I will call the *superordinate* level – precisely because of the abnormal one-to-many mappings of musical idea to narrative object on the basic level.

One may argue that such one-to-many mappings, as they frustrate basic-level linguistic function, not only fail but also transcend linguistic function altogether, thereby achieving the mythic. James Buhler takes this approach when discussing a particular scene in *Star Wars* (George Lucas, 1977):

> *When Luke steps outside with the two suns hanging in the sky as background, a full statement of the Force theme accompanies him despite the fact that at this point in the film nothing about the Force has been revealed. The 'primal baptism' that will link signifier to signified does not occur until Ben explains the Force to Luke later in the film. Moments like this one when the music seems not entirely bound up with its semiotic function are what gives the music its mythical character. The music seems to intuit connections that are beyond immediate rational comprehension. This semiotic failure is the mark of the mythic, pointing to a realm beyond reason, beyond language – a realm [which] cannot be represented other than through this failed link between signifier and signified in music.* (2000: 44)

However, for certain films such as *The Sea Hawk*, the *Star Wars* films, *Spirits Within* and others, I propose a happy medium between requiring only the 'calling-card' basic-level associations of musical themes and distinctive pitch collections with narrative objects and dismissing linguistic function altogether in favour of the mythic. Like the uncanny response, the immediate response to these atypical associations may short-circuit rationality. But unlike the uncanny response, reflection and study may lead one to intuit superordinate connections that, while not immediate, are nevertheless within the realm of rational comprehension. Moreover, it seems that one-to-many mappings of music/narrative associations enable such superordinate associations: they propel music's ability to signify higher-level concepts without necessarily escaping linguistic gravity altogether. From this perspective, I see these particular employments of associational musical ideas as invitations to the listener, akin to how cognitive psychologists Sandra Waxman and Dana Markow view the roles of words in early language acquisition (from whose field I borrow the terms 'basic level' and 'superordinate'):

> *Words serve as invitations to form categories .... We claim that words focus attention on commonalities among objects, highlighting them especially in cases where the perceptual similarity among objects may not be as apparent as at the basic level. Thus, novel words invite infants to assemble together objects that might otherwise be perceived as disparate and distinct entities. This modest invitation has dramatic consequences, for by engendering such groupings, words provide infants an opportunity to consider these objects*

> *together, to compare them, and, in so doing, to discover deeper and perhaps*
> *more subtle commonalities among them.* (1995: 298)

This interpretative trajectory – a conflict among basic-level associations that leads to discovering superordinate associations – characterizes some of my critical experiences with the musical and dramatic aspects of *Spirits Within*; but to qualify, sharpen and communicate these experiences, theories of the uncanny are inappropriate. Rather, I have found Leon Festinger's psychological theory of cognitive dissonance to offer firmer footing, as it accommodates the aforementioned 'reflection and study' of initial basic-level contradictions. Although fifty years old, this theory still plays a supporting role in some modern studies in social psychology, as well as a recent musical analysis (Sauer, 2007). Roughly summarized, it holds that two of a person's cognitions – those things that a person knows about the world or personal beliefs and opinions – may be consonant or dissonant with each other. For two cognitions that are relevant to one another, they are consonant if they do not contradict one another, and they are dissonant if the obverse of the one does not contradict the other. Contradictions arise through logical inconsistencies or violations of cultural or experiential norms. Festinger hypothesizes that cognitive dissonance impels the one who experiences it to reduce it somehow, either by eliminating or reducing one of the contributing cognitions or by adding a new cognitive element that reconciles the two dissonant elements. The first example of such reconciling that Festinger presents in his 1957 book *A Theory of Cognitive Dissonance* involves two cognitions of the Micronesian Ifaluk society: all people are good, and young children go through a period of "strong overt aggression, hostility, and destructiveness" (Festinger, 1957: 23). To reduce the dissonance between these cognitions, the Ifaluk introduced a new cognition, a belief in "the existence of malevolent ghosts which enter into persons and cause them to do bad things" (*ibid.*). This reconciles the two dissonant cognitions, in that it does not require a dismissal of one or both of them, but rather finds a way for both of them to coexist.

This manner of reconciliation characterizes a turning point in my criticism of the score to *Spirits Within*; this turning point divides this chapter into two parts. The dissonances reviewed in the first part involve technical incongruities among multiple basic-level associations between distinctive musical tokens and narrative objects. The second section then introduces a new cognition that seeks to reconcile these seeming dissonances. Like any criticism, the following narrative is ultimately a personal one, and the reader may find my reconciliatory element as plausible as the Ifaluk's belief in ghosts. But I still find it compelling, if only because the reconciliatory element that shifts my critical narrative closely parallels that which shifts a primary component of the film's narrative: a reassessment of the spirits without and within.

Preparing the dissonance

Sakaguchi's choice not to employ Nobuo Uematsu – the beloved composer used for the entire *FF* series – as the composer for *Spirits Within* alienated many videogame enthusiasts.[9] Despite Uematsu's strong following, as evinced in numerous recordings of his *FF* music in both its original form and in numerous arrangements for various ensembles, Sakaguchi hired Brooklyn-born composer Elliot Goldenthal. Like his teachers John Corigliano and Aaron Copland, Goldenthal has succeeded in composing outstanding music for both the concert hall and the movie theatre, although the latter has brought him more name recognition. His twenty-seven feature film scores (as of 2010) include critically acclaimed and eclectic scores for directors such as his longtime companion Julie Taymor and Neil Jordan, as well as effective scores for films in the science-fiction, action and horror genres by other directors.

Despite the film's poor showing at the box office, *Spirits Within*'s film score has garnered ample praise from aficionados of soundtrack recordings.[10] Lay critical reception of the film's score primarily, and in many cases exclusively, relies on the commercially released compact disc recording of Goldenthal's original music. The *Spirits Within* soundtrack recording is well representative of its film score, as it generally captures the experience of many of the composer's idiosyncratic musical soundscapes, including thematic and orchestrational signatures. Yet the soundtrack recording fails as a dependable primary source for the music as it operates within the film and an explanation of why this is so enables a discussion of the music's dramatic associations in the film. This failure extends beyond the customary differences, such as the practical limitations and/or marketing difficulties of including a film's entire score on a single compact disc – in the case of *Spirits Within*, the compact disc contains 56 minutes and 28 seconds of music whereas the film's music (including the two songs) totals 78 minutes and 13 seconds – or the industry's rampant practice of including music on the soundtrack recording that is not heard in the film.[11] Rather, the soundtrack recording, both among and within each of its tracks, is a veritable scramble of the original score. In addition to a convolution of the overall chronology of the film's music, ten out of the sixteen orchestral tracks are assemblages of non-adjacent passages from the score. Moreover, the labelling of the compact disc tracks breaks some of the bonds between Goldenthal's music and the narrative elements of the film, which is a primary concern of this study. While a few of the track titles are faithful to their narrative association, such as 'Code Red', 'Entrada', 'A Child Recalled', 'The Eighth Spirit' and 'Adagio And Transformation', others mislead. For example, none of the three different segments stitched together to form 'Blue Light' has anything to do with any part of the film that features that colour as a narrative symbol. 'Flight To The Wasteland' and 'Winged Serpent' may each begin with music associated with their titular counterparts but they each end without this association.

The track named 'The Kiss' is perhaps the most deceitful of all. Praised by several online reviewers as one of the finest cues on the soundtrack and as revealing Goldenthal's gentler, more lyrical side,[12] the track begins with music that indeed accompanies the kiss between the two lead characters, as well as the preceding dialogue. As the scene changes – with an ingenious visual transformation of a spaceship into a bullet – the music darkens while General Hein prepares to commit suicide. The compact disc track follows suit, up to the moment where Hein changes his mind and sets a course for the Zeus cannon. While the film's music turns sinister, the corresponding moment on the soundtrack recording lurches into a saccharine dominant-seventh chord complete with a rapturous string melody and predictable harp arpeggios, the quintessential cliché for romance. Nothing remotely close to this is heard in Goldenthal's music during the film.

Another example of this track-title/filmic-association mismatch is where I wish to begin my study of the score. The music transcribed in Figure 8.1 is included on the CD's third track, entitled 'The Phantom Plains', yet, when this same music occurs in the film, it accompanies neither phantoms nor plains. Rather, it first accompanies the scene when Aki awakens from the dream that opens the film. She is seen alone and, after untethering herself from her reclined chair, weightless inside a dark room-sized compartment, presumably aboard a spaceship. As she saves the record of her dream, her voice-over explains that such dreams may be the key to removing the phantom threat: "I have vowed to end that fear." She floats toward a window, through which the curvature of a blue planet can be seen just below; she ends her voice-over with the question, "Will I be in time to save the earth?" The film cuts to an external sweeping shot of a spaceship bearing USAF insignia, which breaks orbit and descends into Earth's atmosphere above the east coast of North America.

There are several ways to read how music interacts with the film in this scene. In his commentary, Goldenthal focuses on certain timbral and textural connections. For example, the glass harmonica that opens the cue connotes

Figure 8.1 Author transcription – 'Aki Awakens', from *Final Fantasy: The Spirits Within*, composed by Elliot Goldenthal (2001)

both the "fragility of this woman Aki" and the "sense of floating". The pounding percussion that concludes the cue "underscores that it's almost a paramilitary operation". In between, he implies that the "grandeur of space and Earth" and the "majesty of this beautiful blue planet" are captured, at least in part, by "this giant E♭ chord".[13] While the timbral and textural resplendence of the individual E♭ major and A major triads, along with their expansive timespans, certainly convey majesty and grandeur, their relationship to one another also signifies space in particular within the intertextual realm of Hollywood film music. This can be understood by focusing on the intervallic structure and progression of the chromatic harmonies. E♭ and A, as the roots of the two major triads in this cue, are a tritone apart. Elsewhere I have recounted how numerous Hollywood science-fiction films from the 1950s to the present have associated the tritone harmonic progression between two major triads – what I call the major tritone progression – with outer space in general and, from *Star Wars* to films from the early twenty-first century, with external, establishing shots of outer space and celestial objects in particular (Murphy, 2006). Therefore, filmgoers consciously or subconsciously attuned to the musical accompaniment for similar scenes in previous science-fiction films may channel such intertextual experience into Goldenthal's majestic music, thus reifying *Spirits Within*'s computer-generated universe as, at the least, embraced by a larger cinematic cosmos.

Yet subsequent scenes in the film refine, or perhaps redefine, the significance of the major tritone progression, turning the immediate generator of its associational meaning from intertextual to intratextual. Major tritone progressions between two major triads appear sprinkled throughout the score, but many of them are nestled within longer progressions and merely contribute to an overall triadic chromaticism that Hollywood composers often use to conjure the fantastical without abandoning the familiar. I focus here only on those two-chord harmonic progressions that are singled out in one or more of the following ways: (1) oscillation between the two chords; (2) sheer volume and relative dominance on the soundtrack; (3) synchrony with a significant visual or dramatic moment. A few scenes spotlight the major tritone progression in such ways and collectively suggest a consistent intratextual meaning for the musical gesture. Aki's descent to Earth at the beginning of the film takes her to 'Old New York City', a phantom-infested part of Manhattan where she finds the sixth spirit and encounters both hostility from the phantoms and assistance from Captain Gray Edwards's Deep Eyes Squadron. Predictably, the phantom's threat grows as Aki and the soldiers near evacuation: at the height of the tension, when Gray is the last to scramble up to the evacuation site, he misses a step. As one of the soldiers catches his hand, the mounting score suddenly bursts into a repetition of Aki's 're-entry' cue at its first major tritone progression and proceeds to the end of the same cue as the party is saved.

A strikingly similar usage takes place in a battle scene later in the film, when, after the phantoms have killed the Deep Eyes Squadron, Gray is seemingly alone and outmatched in his firefight. Aki and Dr Sid appear in her ship, and Gray perilously but bravely leaps towards the ship's open side door in a slow-motion shot, accompanied by a powerful four-second A♭ major triad. As Gray hangs onto the edge of the ship, the full orchestra invokes the major tritone progression by shifting to a D major triad, which concludes as Dr Sid grabs Gray's outstretched hand; the musical cue concludes with the same 'paramilitary' percussion. These two scenes rework the associativity of the major tritone progression 'from within', adding to its intertextual affiliation with extraterrestrial settings an intratextual affiliation with superhuman protagonist heroics, particularly those of a salvatory nature that recall Aki's hope "to save the earth". Any dissonance here between the intertextual code insinuated during the film's opening and the intratextual code that develops as the film progresses is mild at most; there is sufficient intertextual support among other Hollywood film scores for the major tritone progression's broader association with the heroic and the extraordinary (Murphy, 2006: note 4).

Goldenthal associates the *minor* tritone progression – the tritone progression between two minor triads – most consistently with General Hein and his ambition to vanquish the phantoms, although this association is only hinted at early in the film. When Hein first appears, arguing with Sid and Aki in front of the council about the next course of action against the phantoms, music enters when the Gaia theory is broached. The first triadic progression in halting trochees that accompanies Hein's belittling of the theory includes but does not stress the minor tritone progression: C minor–B minor–C minor–A minor, C minor–F♯ minor–C minor. Another single minor tritone progression in quiet but ponderous chords (F minor–B minor) begins the music that accompanies the scene change before Hein's next appearance. During Hein's third appearance, the same F minor–B minor incipit underscores his menacing close-up and utterance: "By tomorrow morning, the council will be at our feet." Later in the film, as Hein considers suicide, the score provides a clear minor tritone progression (F♯ minor–C minor) exactly when he changes his mind. Undulating F♯ minor and C minor triads accompany Hein's communication with a beleaguered council member and receipt of the Zeus cannon access codes, and the same undulation occurs threefold during a subsequent scene as Hein continues to fire the cannon into the phantom crater even though it is overheating and ineffectual. Pivotal moments in each of Hein's final three scenes concretize the link between the F♯ minor–C minor undulation and his single-minded belligerence: as he seeks to override the cannon's safety shutdown; as the cannon is brought back online for Hein to fire manually; and as Hein desperately attempts to fire it despite the system overload.

This intratextual association between the minor tritone progression and the film's villain is scarcely contested by intertextual associations in Hollywood film music, which are considerably more diffuse than that of the major tritone progression.[14] Hence, there is little to no cognitive dissonance from outside the film that complicates this associative bond. Moreover, this association and the film's association with the major tritone progression are mutually consonant. The major/minor duality comports with the protagonist/antagonist duality, owing to well-worn correlations in western music. Major and minor triads in particular are mirrored images or 'inversions' of one another, in that the stack of a major third plus a minor third forms a major triad, whereas the stack of a minor third plus a major third forms a minor triad. Furthermore, the major tritone progression is an inversion of the minor tritone progression: play one progression 'upside down' and you hear the other. This inversional relationship is depicted in Figure 8.2. The particular triads in this diagram are those that, based on the previous summaries, constitute the most common progression for each association: E♭ major–A major for the protagonist's progression and F♯ minor–C minor for the antagonist's progression. Each note is labelled by both its diatonic letter name (C, E♭, etc.) and its chromatic pitch-class number

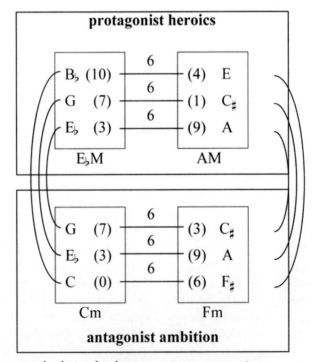

Figure 8.2 Inversional relationship between tritone progressions

(0 for C, 1 for D♭, etc.) and the latter allows the representation of chromatic relations and transformations. The horizontal lines show the pervasiveness of tritone (six-semitone) pairings between notes in each chord; note how two numbers connected by a horizontal line differ by six. The vertical arcs pair up individual notes that are inversions of one another; note how two numbers connected by a vertical arc sum to ten. This musical inversional relationship corresponds to a moral inversional relationship between good and evil.

However, another association in the film perturbs this consonance. During the film's climactic scene at the phantom crater, Aki and Gray search for the eighth and final spirit while under siege from both Hein's cannon blasts and the phantoms. Although Aki finds the eighth spirit and completes the wave pattern, a blow from the cannon disables their ability to transmit the pattern to the alien phantoms and mortally injures Gray. He professes belief that his spirit will indeed live on and then wilfully accepts death as the alien Gaia comes into contact with his extended arm and hand. As he does so, the pattern passes from Aki into his departing spirit, accomplishes the transmission and extinguishes the phantom threat. Tritone progressions boldly punctuate both Gray's profession of belief and the passing of his spirit. In fact, the latter of these two climactic moments strongly resonates with the visual motif of the outstretched hand and its consistent association with the major tritone progression. Yet, the tritone progressions during this climactic scene are neither major nor minor, but a blend of the two: an F major triad progresses to a B *minor* triad after Gray's profession of belief, and an E minor triad alternates with a B♭ *major* triad during his spirit's passing. Why would such a heroic, honourable sacrifice be accompanied by a 'hybrid' tritone progression equally similar to antagonist and protagonist progressions?

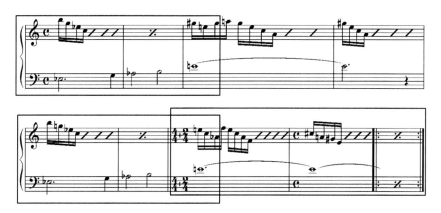

Figure 8.3 Author transcription of 'Barrier City' cue in *Final Fantasy: The Spirits Within*, composed by Elliot Goldenthal (2001)

Another potential dissonance is evident if one listens closely to Goldenthal's use of non-diatonic collections, instead of chromatic triadic progressions. After the Deep Eyes Squadron rescues Aki at the beginning of the film, their ship heads to 'New York City' and the viewer is afforded the first long look at a barrier city, during which the music transcribed in Figure 8.3 provides accompaniment. The intertextual resonances of the treble arpeggios within the realm of film music are particularly strong: the tempo and repeating sixteenth-note cascades harken back to Bernard Herrmann's main title for *The Day the Earth Stood Still* (Robert Wise, 1951) and the harmony of a minor triad (C–Eb–G) with a major seventh (B) invokes Herrmann's 'Hitchcock chord', particularly the *Vertigo* (Alfred Hitchcock, 1958) vintage one given Goldenthal's realization. Yet the intratextual connections this music forms with other parts of the score engage other aspects of its pitch content. Each of the three boxes in Figure 8.3 encloses a span in the music that projects, in its entirety, a 'hexatonic' collection: a six-note collection whose pitches, when placed in scalar order, form the intervallic pattern of alternating minor seconds (one semitone) and minor thirds (three semitones). For example, the notes in the first or second enclosures are exactly the six pitches C, Eb, E, G, Ab (G♯) and B. The notes in the third enclosure, while different, nonetheless also constitute a hexatonic collection. The 'hexatonic sound', at once magical and unsettling, becomes particularly modernist when its tonal and triadic potential is suppressed or obfuscated, as in the few other twentieth-century compositions from Gustav Holst, Arnold Schoenberg and Béla Bartók among others that employ it as baldly as in Goldenthal's cue.[15] Three other scenes later in the film conspicuously and exclusively present a single complete hexatonic collection. First, Goldenthal uses only the notes C, Db, E, F, G♯ and A throughout a vigorous and dissonant musical cue that accompanies the sweeping first view of the Zeus cannon and Hein's ship that approaches it. Second, when the waveform is completed inside Aki's last dream, the harmony resolves to a broad C major triad (C, E, G) against which an expansive melody pits the succession Ab, G, Eb, then B, resulting in the hexatonic collection C, Eb, E, G, Ab and B. Third, after Gray's spirit passes into the alien Gaia, the 'healing' of the phantom spirits first begins during an ecstatic, mighty swell of the notes Eb, G, Bb and Cb through the entire range of the orchestra. The music suddenly thins to these four notes in soft high strings and a celesta as a shaft of blue light rises from the crater above the earth; poignant melodies in solo trumpet and cor anglais subsequently add the notes D then F♯ to this four-note harmony to complete the hexatonic collection: D, Eb, F♯, G, Bb, B.

All four of these hexatonic cues (of which only the last appears on the soundtrack recording) differ markedly from one another with respect to orchestration, texture and rhythm, as well as the manner in which the six notes are distributed into harmonic and melodic dimensions. These musical differences well match the visual and narrative differences among the specific scenes they accompany. Yet the fact that all four cues utilize a special arrangement of a set of six pitches for an appreciable span of time – at least twelve seconds – suggests a special relationship among them. Since there are 924 possible ways of choosing six notes out of the twelve in the chromatic scale, and there are only four different hexatonic collections, there is less than one-half of a one percent chance that any randomly chosen six notes will form a hexatonic scale. This distinctiveness of the hexatonic collection, which would be even higher without the six-note restriction, approaches that of a musical *leitmotiv*. Yet much like the 'floating' theme in *The Sea Hawk*, the hexatonic collection, as an intratextual signifier in *Spirits Within*, frustrates a basic-level signified: it does not seem designed to accompany a particular character, place or object, and its party affiliation with either the protagonists or antagonists is split or neutral. Instead, any association consonant with all four moments will need to entail a superordinate signified.

The last cognitive dissonance to be reviewed here, and the one that prompted my reconciliatory solution, originated with Goldenthal's commentary on the Special Edition DVD. In his introduction, the composer states his intent to take the auditor "through some scenes and ideas that will make maybe the listening a little clearer". His articulate and enlightening commentary throughout the film certainly accomplishes this in several ways, such as identifying names and intertextual significances of particular timbres and effects and revealing subtle large-scale thematic processes. A comment on the music for one of Aki's dreams caught my attention in spite of its banality. The dream begins, as previous ones have, with Aki encountering warring aliens on a strange planet, followed by their sudden destruction in a massive nuclear conflagration. But this dream goes on to reveal that the firestorm destroys the alien world, and a small chunk of the planet on which phantom forms of the aliens presumably travel is hurtled into space in front of the explosion. Goldenthal describes his accompanying music – one of the few moments in the musical score that is not available either on the soundtrack recording or free of commentary on the DVD – as a "large, sort of brass, almost fanfare to signal the death of a planet". The dream ends as the planetary fragment rockets past the film's point of view, and the music ends with synchronous D and G$\sharp$ pitches that echo for three seconds into the next scene. Goldenthal remarks on this conclusion, "And [it is] the interval of a tritone that we're left with, which we all know is the 'devil in music', that something right is not exactly happening." This characterization of the tritone as the *diabolus in musica* perfectly falls in line with both customary intertextual interpretations relating the interval to "evil, danger, and mystery" (Cooper, 2001: 63) and the narrative moment this bare tritone accompanies in the film: it is but a short step from 'devil' and 'something's amiss' to 'murderous alien phantoms headed for Earth on a hunk of rock'. But how can one accept the intertextual interpretation of the tritone as *diabolus* when the same interval presides over a harmonic progression – the major tritone progression – that has been consistently associated with noble heroics in the film?

Resolving the dissonance

It is after Aki's dream of the alien planet's demise – which, incidental to the bipartite organization of my chapter, comes exactly halfway into the film – that she understands, in her words, "what the phantoms really are". During an expositional scene a bit later in the film, Aki, Dr Sid and the members of the Deep Eyes Squadron address a cognitive dissonance between the belief that the phantoms en masse have attacked Earth in the manner of an invading army and the observation that many of the larger phantoms that roam the wastelands seem unconnected to any martial assault. Aki reconciles these dissonant cognitions by introducing a new element not unlike that which, in Festinger's analysis, the Ifaluk introduced to reconcile observations involving aggression: "They're not an invading army. They're ghosts." Her dream just prior to this suggests that the horrific death of the alien planet's inhabitants, along with the death of the alien planet-as-organism, confuses their disembodied and suffering spirits, which consequently become hostile phantoms and unwitting passengers on the meteor that slams into Earth.

This reconsideration of the phantoms not as evil and hostile invaders but as exposed and disturbed souls strongly parallels a germane re-evaluation of the tritone as the *diabolus in musica*. With which musical-dramatic situations involving the tritone is this extra-musical association relevant and with which situations is it not? The answer reveals a slippery but still negotiable slope. The tritone interval, when presented as a bare simultaneity, unquestionably exhibits a palpable sensory dissonance; in one celebrated example, it serves well as the first sound from the 'devil's fiddle', at the beginning of Camille Saint-Saëns's 'Danse macabre' (1875). But add two other notes and the severity of the tritone dyad can be ameliorated by a much more pleasing, although not entirely stable, dominant-seventh chord, which can then easily resonate with gentler extra-musical associations: consider the *Spirits Within* soundtrack's version of 'The Kiss' discussed earlier. Melodic tritones, while avoiding the harmonic harshness of the interval, nonetheless can still convey the *diabolus* association, especially when divorced from a tonal framework, as in the opening of Franz Liszt's 'Dante' Sonata (1849), which corresponds to 'The Inferno' of Dante's *Divine Comedy*. Yet melodic tritones nestled within a diatonic setting hardly agitate sweeter extra-musical references: for example, parents of small children do not shy away from singing the tritone leap in the middle of Johannes Brahms's famous 'Wiegenlied' ('Lullaby'). Furthermore, although the tritone is the least frequent interval in the diatonic collection (for example, the white notes of the piano), it is therefore also the most representative of any such diatonic collection and thus is the most efficient in the perceptual process of 'key finding', a vital component of tonal listening. Nonetheless, this superlative efficiency requires at least one other pitch to be present for the identification of the diatonic collection to be unequivocal.[16] Lastly, once a major or minor key has been established, notes within the key separated by a tritone are perceived to have the strongest incentive to 'move' to nearby stable pitches.[17]

This brief musicological survey suggests that, like the phantom presence in *Spirits Within*, the tritone interval is more appropriately compared to *anima* (life, soul) or *animus* (vivacity, spirit) rather than *diabolus*. In many diatonic harmonies and tonal settings, the tritone is 'the spirit within', its harshness and mystery tempered by its comfortable surroundings. In such environments, the tritone both encapsulates the diatonic collection of which it is a part and also spurs notes to proceed to other notes in the collection, thus lining it up with the Aristotelian notions that the soul is "the essence of the whole living body" and "the source or origin of movement" (Aristotle, 1992: 191). But expose the tritone by removing its common-practice harmonic and diatonic insulation and its latent qualities of abrasiveness and ambiguity will rear their ugly heads; only in such specific situations is the *diabolus* label suitable – reconfigured to mean not the Devil in particular, but a malicious incorporeality in general. I do not mean to suggest that a generalization of the tritone's association from *diabolus* to *anima* is appropriate in all cases, but it is relevant to *Spirits Within* for two reasons: the moment in Goldenthal's score when the tritone is the most bare is when the spirits of the alien planet and its inhabitants are rent from their material dwellings (and the true nature of the phantoms is thus laid bare); and the association of the tritone with *anima* or *animus* helps to reduce the cognitive dissonances presented earlier.

I will begin with the film's associations of the major tritone progression with protagonist heroics and the minor tritone progression with antagonist ambition. While the association of the tritone with *diabolus* accords with the latter but certainly not with the former, the *anima/animus* reading accommodates both proposed associations. Although neither progression occurs within a diatonic context, the tritones for which they are named are still curiously hidden from immediate aural perception. First, the exclusive employment of major or minor triads produces euphony in the vertical dimension. The familiarity of these consonant harmonies puts all the progressions that involve them at home with humans; note their ubiquitous presence during the film's character-driven scenes. Second, Figure 8.2 was used to show, via horizontal lines labelled with sixes, how tritone (six-semitone) pairings saturate the major and minor tritone progressions in the horizontal dimension. However, the actual voice leading for Hein's minor tritone progression only engages intervals of 1 (G–F♯), 2 (E♭–C♯) and 3 (C–A) semitones, and the only line in the realization of the heroic major tritone progression that moves by tritone is the bass. So, while the tritone is present, its presence is not directly manifest in either progression. And yet these two progressions boast the highest possible number of tritone pairs within the confines of a triadic progression (zero is the fewest, three is the most). In light of the tritone as *anima/animus*, these musical features match the moments that they accompany: within the confines of human form, the accompanied characters are extraordinarily, hyper-humanly 'anima-ted' as they fight against the phantoms and for the lives of themselves and others.[18] How the characters channel this intense drive through moral decisions then distinguishes them on the surface; likewise, the quality of the triads (major versus minor) provides an analogous outward distinction for these two progressions.

Recalling another cognitive dissonance proposed earlier, the variety of the four scenes during which a complete hexatonic collection is presented – the introduction of the barrier city, the introduction of the Zeus cannon, the completion of the waveform and the healing of the phantom spirits –precludes associating a basic-level signified with the distinctive collection. However, as with an interpretation of *The Sea Hawk*'s 'floating' theme as a 'homecoming after oppression' theme, a single superordinate association may also be drawn from these four scenes: each depicts an effort to remove the phantom threat. The realization of the hexatonic collection that accompanies each of these scenes supports this association. Since Goldenthal permits the dissonances of the collection to occur as harmonic simultaneities, the resulting sound has less in common with the consonant triadic progressions that often underscore the characters in the film; therefore, it makes sense that the collection be associated with something other than a character. Moreover, the very structure of the hexatonic collection, when combined with the association of the tritone with *anima/animus*, also supports the 'removing the phantom threat' appellation, in that the hexatonic collection does not contain a single tritone. This is a relatively exclusive property among six-note collections, in that only 5.2 percent of them do not have the six-semitone interval.[19] Furthermore, since Goldenthal evenly distributes the six pitches of the hexatonic in such a way that most, if not all, of its fifteen pairs of pitches are sounded harmonically, any tritone that would otherwise be in the collection would be exposed as a harsh dissonance without any chordal or diatonic amelioration. The hexatonic collection, in Goldenthal's uniform texture, clearly associates with a 'removal of the phantom threat' association because the tritone, as a harmonically exposed *anima* (and thus *diabolus*), is also notably absent.

Within this association, however, there is a strong difference in the way the objects and events in these four scenes address the phantom threat. The first two scenes represent militaristic solutions and the last two involve scientific endeavours. On the one hand, the barrier city and Zeus cannon both become weapons – the former for political gain, the second in combat – that Hein brazenly wields despite the lives lost by doing so. On the other hand, the completing of the waveform and the subsequent healing of the alien spirits brings to fruition the theories and efforts of the protagonists. The film's symbolic primary colour scheme also follows this organization: the yellow of the barrier city's shield and the Zeus cannon's beam contrasts with the blue of the alien (and, for that matter, human) spirits at peace; together, these colours complement the red of the phantoms. The music also articulates this contrast in a manner already discovered earlier in this chapter. Figure 8.4 provides the pitch content for the opening of each of the 'Barrier City' and 'Healing of the Phantoms' scenes. The first five pitches in each melody are written out horizontally, while the four-note harmony that provides accompaniment is spelled out vertically on the left side. The bold melodic notes are those pitches not in the accompanying harmony; thus, the union of a four-note harmony plus the two novel melodic pitches it accompanies results in a hexatonic collection. These two cues have more in common than the hexatonic sound: in both, the

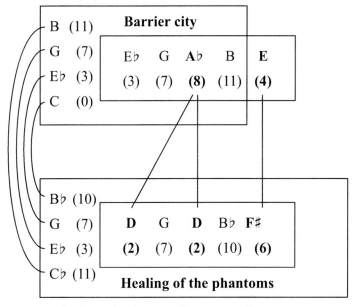

Figure 8.4 Inversional relationship between hexatonic collections

Figure 8.5 Author transcription of the 'Adagio' and climactic scene in *Final Fantasy: The Spirits Within*, composed by Elliot Goldenthal (2001)

melodies rise on brass instruments (horns for the 'Barrier City', trumpet for the 'Healing of the Phantoms') and the harmony scintillates above the melody in shimmering strings and keyboard instruments. The vertical arcs and lines of Figure 8.4 reveal that the harmonies and novel melodic pitches, in order of presentation, are inversions of one another; moreover, the mirrored pitches sum to ten, the exact inversion used in Figure 8.2. This musical consistency accords with the consistency between the protagonist/antagonist opposition and the contrast of methods each side employs to combat the phantoms.

Lastly, the tritone as *anima* or *animus* can help to reconcile my cognitive dissonance involving the striking 'hybrid' tritone progressions that invigorate the film's climactic scene, but this will require a more detailed analysis. Figure 8.5 is the 'Adagio', as Goldenthal calls it in his commentary and on the soundtrack; to save space, the harmony has been abbreviated to chord symbols. The caesura marks (') divide the music into phrases, and the lines of dialogue from Aki and Gray have been placed above the music in regular and italic font, respectively, along with major visual events in brackets.

In the context of major and minor tritone progressions, I suggested the name 'hybrid' for a tritone progression such as F major–B minor in bars 22–23 because, although the roots (F and B) span a tritone, it involves one major and one minor triad each. However, a reconsideration of the major and minor tritone progressions as three horizontal tritone pairs (depicting an abundance of *animus*) encased with a progression of major and/or minor triads (depicting human *corpus*) puts the root's tritone motion on a level playing field with the other two tritone pairs. Figure 8.6a shows the results when the F major–B minor hybrid is conceived in the same fashion: the progression drops from three tritone pairs to two. Thus, from this perspective, the F major–B minor progression, which accompanies Gray's profession of faith, is not a hybrid of the major and minor tritone progressions, but a reduction in *animus* from either of them. Figure 8.6b reveals the same reduction for the E minor–B♭ major triads, which first unfold when Aki (by request) leaves Gray's side in bars

a. Gray's profession of faith

b. Aki leaves Gray's side

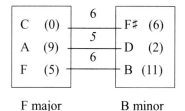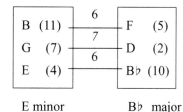

Figure 8.6 Two 'abnegating' harmonic progressions

18–19 and undulate during the release of Gray's spirit in bars 26–28. Note that the G–D pair in Figure 8.6b (the altered tritone) is articulated as the melody in bars 18–19: had this been a *major* tritone progression, the melody would have required a noticeable tritone leap.

This decrease in *animus* corresponds with Gray's abnegation, a "willful resignation as spiritual acceptance of a (tragic) situation that leads to a positive inner state, implying transcendence" (Hatten, 1994: 287). His decisions are still internally heroic and ultimately salvatory; hence, the two tritone pairs still supersede mundane single-tritone diatonicism and partially resonate with the associations the film has made with the major tritone progression. But if Goldenthal had used the major tritone progression at these points, the inevitable evocation of hyper-*anima*-tion associations would have been out of place, for Gray's final decisions externally manifest themselves not through action but through acceptance and submission. Thus, while the use of a hybrid tritone progression could simply be read as representing the bittersweet quality of the scene, the notion of tritone as *animus* speaks particularly to the kind of (in)action that ultimately triumphs. It also strengthens Christological readings of this moment: Gray saves human civilization not through outward struggle, but by 'yielding up his spirit'.[20]

How does this music account for the fact that Gray sacrifices not only *amimus* through his surrender, but also *anima* through his death? Based on the musical analogues I have suggested, a human life would correspond to a progression of major and/or minor triads (depicting human *corpus*) with at least one tritone in the abstract voice leading, particularly if the progression can be situated within a single diatonic collection, thereby anticipating a resolution to the tonic chord of one of those keys. The 'Adagio' opens up with such progressions. The B minor–C major progression in bars 1–2 contains one tritone (F♯–C) that is within E minor, to whose tonic chord the music soon arrives (bar 5). The E minor–F♯ major progression unequivocally points back toward B minor, whose tonic chord immediately follows in bar 8. But in bars 11–14, key finding of this sort begins to falter. In both melody and harmonic progression, there is no tritone during this span; it is only the lingering rhetorical assertion of B minor from earlier in the music and the modal change to a dominant F♯ major triad that nudges B over F♯ as the tonic note. The third and fourth phrases (bars 15–18 and 19–22) each lack a single tritone and a sense of an unequivocal tonal identity has vanished. The A minor–E minor progression sounds like a plagal IV–I motion, but then the E minor–A minor sounds like a modal V–I motion. Thus, a sense of tonic aimlessly vacillates without a tritone – for example, involving a passing F or F♯ in between the melody's E and G, making A or E sound more like tonic, respectively – to bias the listener one way or the other. And since both E minor and A minor function as tonic while they sound, there is no impetus pressing the harmony forward and fuelling the undulation. The fourth phrase (bars 19–22) creates the same phenomenon even more strongly. Therefore, in keeping with the proposed associations, these two phrases signify human death: the major and minor triads are present and even situated within a diatonic collection, but there is no 'tritone within' to give them tonal life.

However, this Adagio music has been heard earlier in the film, which could potentially dilute the exclusivity of this interpretation. Goldenthal explains in his commentary that the Adagio music that accompanies this scene is the "actual culmination of all the little bits and pieces that started almost in reel one ... and now the theme is in its entirety". A soft F major–B minor progression follows Aki's surgical rescue of Gray early in the film and each chord supports two statements of the four-note motif from bars 11–12 of the Adagio.[21] Then the A minor–E minor–A minor progression of bars 15–17 plays under the dialogue of the scene's conclusion, although it does not accompany death. The Adagio music then accompanies the scene with the kiss between Aki and Gray. Yet it breaks off at bar 14: the F♯ major triad resolves to B minor (with a lingering A♯), stopping just before the Adagio's 'death' diatonic progressions and the 'abnegating' chromatic progressions. Therefore, while the tritone-supported tonality-finding opening of the Adagio (bars 1–14) accompanies the human activity of romance and its return in the climactic Adagio reminds the listener of those associations, bars 15–28 feature the harmonic progressions that I have associated with 'death' and 'abnegation', which have not been so heavily foregrounded in Goldenthal's score at any earlier time. Such a novel foregrounding also takes place in the visual realm during the final scene, after the phantoms have been healed and after the musical cue, which concludes with a variant of the 'death' harmonies in bars 11–12, 16–17 and 19–21, has stopped. Aki cradles Gray's body in her arms as the two of them are lifted on a platform out of the crater. It is at its end that this film, which has painstakingly tried to bring its characters to life, spends the most time – 44 seconds distributed over six scenes, the fifth being a close-up – showing a corpse. While the musical score stands in silence during these shots, they are still bookended by the 'death' and 'abnegation' harmonic progressions, as the music of the Adagio returns one last time in the song 'The Dream Within', sung by Lara Fabian over the end titles. The 'abnegation' progression from bars 26 to 28, extended to a four-chord undulation between E minor and B♭ major in the song, is clearly one of the song's climaxes, in that it supports the highest vocal pitches. Yet, just as the film ends with life (a lone hawk flying above the elegiac scene), so the song ends by returning to the tritone-affirmed tonality of bars 1–7, which ultimately rest on a final B major triad.

Conclusion

Relative to the extraordinary technical and artistic mastery required to achieve photorealistic humans with computer animation or to simulate anthropic appearance and motion flawlessly with an android, the deviations from perfection that push the replica into the uncanny valley can be quite minute: a bit of stiffness in the gait, the absence of normal intermittent blinking and so on. And yet the intensity of some of the possible responses – derision, antipathy, repulsion, horror – is strikingly out of proportion with the apparent triviality of the nonconformities that produce such responses in the first place. I contend that an analogous disproportionality, albeit leading to an ultimately positive outcome, underlies this musicological analysis. Compared to the technical and artistic mastery evident in Goldenthal's score, the cognitive dissonances presented in the first part of this chapter – the hybrid tritone progression accompanying a noble sacrifice, the one-to-many basic-level mappings of the hexatonic collection and the oddity of the *diabolus in musica* undergirding the hyper-heroic tritone progression between two major triads – are quite minute. And yet, as argued in the second part, they invited me to discover deeper and perhaps more subtle meanings, which involved a re-imagining of the tritone as *anima/animus in musica* – a re-imagining that parallels, within the narrative itself, the protagonists' re-imagining of the evil marauders as exposed and confused spirits. So whereas sheer closeness in terms of the uncanny effect inevitably creates an immediate and profound negative affect, sheer closeness in terms of cognitive dissonance has the potential to enrich the artwork significantly by encouraging a closer, contemplative survey of the intricacies of its semantic and dramatic landscapes. In the case of *Spirits Within*, the music may not have saved the film from box-office failure, but its potential to broaden and enhance the film's narrative asks us to look at the film – as well as to listen to it – once more. By doing so, we can move beyond the box-office recoil – the instinctive and sudden withdrawal of the salutatory hand which the film's potential audience initially extended in 2001 – and instead ponder the film before us, however different from our original preconceptions, on its own terms.

Notes

1. R. Ebert, 'Final Fantasy: The Spirits Within', *Chicago Sun-Times*, 11 July 2001 (http://rogerebert.suntimes.com/apps/pbcs.dll/article?AID=/20010711/REVIEWS/107110301/1023; accessed 15 July 2007).
2. The critical reviews of the film surveyed for the chapter were sampled from the 169 online reviews linked by the *Internet Movie Database* (http://www.imdb.com/title/tt0173840/externalreviews).

3. This kind of concern may also apply to intimately familiar animated objects besides humans. Sharon Calahan, the director of photography and lighting for the Pixar animated film *Ratatouille* (Brad Bird, 2007), recognized this when depicting food: "We didn't want something to look really photo-real ... If it starts looking too real, it starts getting pretty disturbing." See K. Severson, 'A Rat with a Whisk and a Dream', *New York Times*, 13 June 2007 (http://www.nytimes. com/2007/06/13/dining/13rata.html?em&ex=1182052800&en=74af2c169733fb 0a&ei=5070; accessed 15 June 2007). Another negative criticism related to this particular kind of ambivalence is articulated in Sobchack:

> The film attempts to achieve indexical, photorealistic 'human characters' in a world that is emblematic, symbolic, irreal – and thus it visibly *equivocates* within what, narratively and semiotically, is supposed to be an integrating 'perceptual realism'. That is, without textual purpose ... *Final Fantasy* solicits from the viewer two different and incompatible modes of epistemological apprehension and aesthetic judgment. (2006: 176).

4. This is not to say that binary pairs (for example, diegetic/non-diegetic, parallel/ counterpoint) have not been unpacked in the musicological literature. For example, David Neumeyer's classification scheme (1997; 2000) expands the diegetic/ non-diegetic pair into ten binary pairs. However, by translating a one-dimensional uncertainty into a multi-dimensional certainty, ambivalence is taken out of the equation as a variable in its own right.

5. "In telling a story one of the most successful devices for easily creating uncanny effects is to leave the reader in uncertainty whether a particular figure in the story is a human being or an automaton and to do it in such a way that his attention is not focused directly upon his uncertainty, so that he may not be led to go into the matter and clear it up immediately" (Jentsch, cited in Freud, 1953: 227).

6. "The uncanny is that class of the frightening which leads back to what is known of old and long familiar" (Freud, 1953: 220).

7. Such 'intellectual uncertainty', as opposed to subconscious uncanny effects, is one way Freud distinguishes his approach to *Unheimlichkeit* from that of Jentsch.

8. An injective but not bijective leitmotivic function is not typically construed as ambivalent since, as in the case of *Patton*, the two or more musical themes are considered to bring out different aspects of the narrative object with which they are all associated. Yet it is less intuitive to invert this relationship and to consider how two or more different narrative objects can bring out different aspects of a musical theme with which they are all associated.

9. It is helpful to compare this decision with that for the film version (Christopher Gans, 2006) of the videogame *Silent Hill* (Keiichiro Toyama, 1999; Masashi Tsuboyama, 2001; etc.), in which the cinematic score attributed to Jeff Danna conspicuously includes parts of Akira Yamaoka's music for the game.

10. The great majority of online reviews from film music websites give Goldenthal's music extremely high marks, while a much smaller number (such as that at

http://www.scorereviews.com/reviews/review.aspx?id=304, which self-acknowledges being in the minority) are less dazzled.

11. In light of these constraints, it is curious that some audio from the original score occurs in several places on the soundtrack recording. For example, the music that accompanies 1:17:09 to 1:17:50 on the DVD (NTSC version) is in both Tracks 1 and 15 of the soundtrack CD. It should also be mentioned that, although 78 minutes of the film are underscored with music, it does not follow that one hears 78 minutes of original music: some of the cues are literally repeated, down to the last detail, in the film's soundtrack. For example, 40 seconds of the 'Code Red' cue is repeated during the later car-ride scene.

12. See the previously mentioned reviews on the *Internet Movie Database* and 59 reviews of the soundtrack on *Amazon.com*, online at http://www.amazon.com (as of January 2011) several of which make this comment. One Amazon reviewer ascribes the music on the track entitled 'The Kiss' to how the music operates in the film: "'The Dream Within' is a beautiful song and 'The Kiss' is very romantic and successfully conveys the very touching moment between Gray and Aki." Koalathebear (2001), 'Very evocative', Amazon.com, 27 July (http://www.amazon.com/Final-Fantasy-Original-Picture-Soundtrack/product-reviews/; accessed 7 January 2011).

13. This and subsequent quoted comments by Goldenthal are taken from Elliot Goldenthal (2001), audio commentary on *Final Fantasy: The Spirits Within (Special Edition)*, directed by Hironobu Sakaguchi, Sony Pictures.

14. The most consistent intertextual association I have recognized between the minor tritone progression and narrative elements in Hollywood film music is with danger or threat of harm, more often from circumstances or objects rather than human antagonists. But the supporting themes and scenes for this intertextual association are relatively few, such as the trash compactor scene in *Star Wars* (George Lucas, 1977), the 'Ark' theme from *Raiders of the Lost Ark* (Steven Spielberg, 1981), a terrible snowstorm in *Balto* (Simon Wells, 1995), the approach of an F-5 tornado to a drive-in theatre in *Twister* (Jan de Bont, 1996), and the scene when Neo steps out onto a high, windy ledge of his tall office building in *The Matrix* (Andy and Larry Wachowski, 1999).

15. Hexatonic collections figure prominently in 'Neptune' from Holst's *The Planets* (1916), Schoenberg's *Ode to Napoleon* (1942), the 'Elegia' from Bartók's *Concerto for Orchestra* (1943), and Lowell Liebermann's Sonata for Flute and Piano (1987), as well as Goldenthal's score for *Sphere* (Barry Levinson, 1998).

16. For example, the notes C and F♯ could be in either the one-sharp diatonic collection (the keys of G major or E minor) or the five-flat diatonic collection (the keys of D♭ major or B♭ minor). Adding one of any of the remaining ten pitches would determine the diatonic collection exactly. 'Position-finding' and the special role of the tritone are discussed in Browne (1981) and Brown and Butler (1981).

17. For example, the notes C and F♯ in the key of G major are expected to resolve by step to the notes B and G, respectively.

18. The phrase 'hyper-human' comes from Goldenthal in his liner notes for the soundtrack recording: "*Final Fantasy* presented a strange hybrid between the fantastical and the hyper-human." See E. Goldenthal (2001), *Final Fantasy: The Spirits Within (Original Motion Picture Soundtrack)*, performed by the London Symphony Orchestra, conducted by Dirk Brossé, Sony Classical SK 89707 [CD].

19. The distinctiveness of the tritone's absence is most apparent in a six-note collection. 'Tritone-less collections' are more common among smaller-sized chord groups: 24 percent of five-note collections, 49 percent of four-note collections, and 73 percent of three-note collections do not have tritones, and collections of seven or more notes must have at least one tritone.

20. While it may seem unusual to call forth a Christian interpretation from a film closely allied with *anime*, whose religious and philosophical roots extend into Shinto and Buddhism, other recent Japanese animated films seem to be striking a balance between eastern and western religious symbologies. For one case, consult Kraemer (2004).

21. In his commentary, Goldenthal explains that this is "the first statement of a melody that will be weaved throughout the film representing the romance between the characters". Challenging the association of the four-note motif D–C♯–B–F♯ (or a transposition of this) with romance is its conspicuous and recurrent use during a battle scene where all of the members of Gray's Deep Eyes Squadron are killed by phantoms. It first occurs when Neil is killed in front of Jane, and she furiously blasts the assassin. The second statement of the motif, however, corrupts the final descending perfect fourth into an augmented fourth – a tritone – just as a phantom's tentacles appear from the bottom of the screen, surrounding Jane. She soon falls prey to it, and her lifeless body collapses next to Ryan's. The music's basic-level 'romance' association thus tunes the listener into a suggestive subtext for these supporting characters. However, the same four-note motif persists as Aki risks danger to help the others, and as the injured Ryan comes to the rescue of the ship. As with Jane, the phantom that slays Ryan emerges during a melodic tritone. This infuses the motif with a superordinate 'love of fellow man' association that operates in conjunction with the basic-level romance association; both associations pour into the final 'Adagio' and Gray's sacrifice.

References

Aristotle (1992), 'De anima', translated by J. A. Smith in R. P. McKeon (ed.), *Introduction to Aristotle*, New York and Toronto: Random House, pp. 153–251.

Brown, H., and Butler, D. (1981), 'Diatonic Trichords as Minimal Tonal Cue-Cells', *In Theory Only*, 5(6–7), 39–55.

Brown, R. S. (1994), *Overtones and Undertones: Reading Film Music*, Berkeley and Los Angeles: University of California Press.

Browne, R. (1981), 'Tonal Implications of the Diatonic Set', *In Theory Only*, 5(6–7), 3–21.

Buhler, J. (2000), '*Star Wars*, Music, and Myth', in J. Buhler, C. Flinn and D. Neumeyer (eds), *Music and Cinema*, Hanover, NH: University Press of New England, pp. 33–57.

Cooper, D. (2001), *Bernard Herrmann's* Vertigo: *A Film Score Handbook*, Westport, CT: Greenwood Press.

Festinger, L. (1957), *A Theory of Cognitive Dissonance*, Stanford: Stanford University Press.

Freud, S. (1953), 'The Uncanny', in *The Standard Edition of the Complete Psychological Works of Sigmund Freud*, vol. 17, ed. and trans. by J. Strachey, London: Hogarth Press, pp. 221–52.

Hatten, R. (1994), *Musical Meaning in Beethoven: Markedness, Correlation, and Interpretation*, Bloomington and Indianapolis: Indiana University Press.

Kraemer, C. H. (2004), 'Between the Worlds: Liminality and Self-Sacrifice in *Princess Mononoke*', *Journal of Religion and Film*, 8(1); online at http://avalon.unomaha.edu/jrf/Vol8No1/BetweenWorlds.htm (accessed 3 February 2008).

Lewin, D. (1969), 'Behind the Beyond: A Response to Edward T. Cone', *Perspectives of New Music*, 7(2), 59–69.

Mori, M. (1970), 'Bukimi No Tani [The Uncanny Valley]', *Energy* 7, 33–5 (trans. K. F. MacDorman and T. Minato (online at http://www.androidscience.com/theuncannyvalley/proceedings2005/uncannyvalley.html; accessed 16 July 2007).

Murphy, S. (2006), 'The Major Tritone Progression in Recent Hollywood Science Fiction Films', *Music Theory Online*, 12(2) (online at http://mto.societymusictheory.org/issues/mto.06.12.2/mto.06.12.2.murphy.html; accessed 15 January 2010).

Neumeyer, D. (1997), 'Source Music, Background Music, Fantasy and Reality in Early Sound Film', *College Music Symposium*, 37, 13–20.

Neumeyer, D. (2000), 'Performances in Early Hollywood Sound Films: Source Music, Background Music, and the Integrated Sound Track', *Contemporary Music Review*, 19(1), 37–62.

Sauer, A. S. (2007), 'Cognitive Dissonance and the Performer's Inner Conflict: A New Perspective on the First Movement of Beethoven's Op. 101', *Music Theory Online*, 13(2) (online at http://mto.societymusictheory.org/issues/mto.07.13.2/mto.07.13.2.sauer.html; accessed 15 January 2010).

Sobchack, V. (2006), 'Final Fantasies: Computer Graphic Animation and the [Dis]illusion of Life', in S. Buchan (ed.), *Animated 'Worlds'*, Eastleigh, Hampshire: John Libbey Publishing, pp. 171–82.

Stilwell, R. (2003), 'The Sound Is Out There: Score, Sound Design, and Exoticism in *The X Files*', in A. Moore (ed.), *Analyzing Popular Music*, New York: Cambridge University Press, pp. 60–79.

Sullivan, J. (2006), *Hitchcock's Music*, New Haven and London: Yale University Press.

Taylor, T., and Hsu, M. (2003), *Digital Cinema: The Hollywood Insider's Guide to the Evolution of Storytelling*, Studio City, CA: Michael Weise Productions.

Waxman, S., and Markow, D. (1995), 'Words as Invitations to Form Categories: Evidence from 12- to 13-month-old Infants', *Cognitive Psychology*, 29: 257–302.

9   Scoring Fantasy Girls
Music and Female Agency in Indiana Jones *and* The Mummy *films*

Janet K. Halfyard and Victoria Hancock

In the 1970s, Laura Mulvey asserted that the reading of Hollywood film was "inherently (that is, both theoretically and filmically) gendered" (Kassabian, 2001: 62–3) and it was this observation that triggered the development of a now substantial body of material examining issues of gender in film. This chapter draws on some of the resulting ideas to examine the particular position of women in fantasy action adventures, how the construction of female characters in these narratives has changed over the course of a generation, and the extent to which these changes are both reflected in and enhanced by the music written for such films. The principal examples are taken from the *Indiana Jones* series from the 1980s, in particular *Indiana Jones and the Temple of Doom* (Steven Spielberg, 1984); and the *Mummy* series from the late 1990s and early 2000s, primarily *The Mummy* (Stephen Sommers, 1999) and *The Mummy Returns* (Stephen Sommers, 2002).

Mulvey explores the issue of gender in film in two essays.[1] In 'Visual Pleasure and Narrative Cinema' (first published in 1975), she argues that women in Hollywood film reflect the obsessions of the films' creators in the largely patriarchal Hollywood studio system. Drawing on Freudian theory, Mulvey suggests that in a patriarchal society women stand purely as the male opposite, representing all that is non-male. Woman's lack of a phallus reduces her to the male Other, not even 'woman' (Mulvey, 1989a: 15). As the reflection of male desire, the woman becomes an image or icon, with men controlling the look or gaze, which in turn results in a masculine spectatorship position: the film is automatically read from a male perspective. Women in film, therefore, have two functions, acting as "erotic object for the characters within the screen story and as an erotic object for the spectator" (*ibid.*: 19). This leads to both the protagonist and spectator experiencing scopophilia, the pleasure derived from looking at someone as an erotic object. The woman becomes an object to be looked at, potentially stripped of any subjective voice or position in the narrative.

Mulvey also looks at the traditional division of labour in society, and relates it to the plot space and movement of characters in film. She suggests that in the traditional heterosexual division of labour, men are not sexual objects: they hold the power, they act and control (*ibid.*: 20). Similarly in film they become the narrative agents who control and advance the story, the audience identifying with their viewpoint (which Mulvey sees as a narcissistic pleasure working alongside scopophilic pleasure). Women are conventionally positioned as sexual objects and in film become spectacle, a source of visual pleasure. As a result the male protagonist controls the structure of the film and requires realistic three-dimensional narrative space in which he is free to move. Women, however, are static; the spaces they occupy within the film are more contained, the two-dimensional space of spectacle that is also therefore often less realistic. This creates a greater sense of reality for the male protagonist, aiding the spectator's identification with his narrative agency.

If the male characters control the narrative, then the female characters tend to be occupied in actions against or outside the flow of the general storyline (e.g., instigating a romantic subplot, being placed in danger and/or causing a distraction from the primary events). The woman is therefore important not in herself but in what she causes others to do. As Budd Boetticher describes it:

> What counts is what the heroine provokes, or rather what she represents. She is the one, or rather the love or fear she inspires in the hero, or else the concern he feels for her, who makes him act the way he does. In herself the woman has not the slightest importance. (Boetticher, in Mulvey, 1989a: 19)

In 'Afterthoughts on "Visual Pleasure and Narrative Cinema"' (1989b; first published in 1981) Mulvey addresses the effect a female protagonist has on a film, with the battle between active masculinity and passive femininity as the central issue. For Mulvey, problems are caused in such films by the fact that women are both the controllers of the narrative and the element of desire. This can be seen in genres such as Westerns or film noir, where the female protagonist must choose between her 'true' path of femininity or the 'wrong' primal path of masculinity. Choosing the wrong path is likely to lead to her death, while the 'correct' choice effectively relegates her to a more conventional, passive role in which she hands her agency back to a man and is rewarded with marriage. Mulvey's examples are taken from Westerns and, since her essay was published, films with female protagonists have become more common, finding new ways of expressing the tension between agency and desire, as in *Erin Brockovich* (Stephen Soderberg, 2000) or even *Bridget Jones's Diary* (Sharon Maguire, 2001). However, the old model is certainly not extinct and fantasy displays similar characteristics to those observed by Mulvey. In Peter Jackson's *The Lord of the Rings* trilogy (2001–3), Éowyn disguises herself as a man, goes into battle and slays the Lord of the Nazgûl; although in the original books her desire for battlefield glory is her primary motivation, in the film her love for Aragorn and desire to follow him seems a stronger factor. She slays the enemy who could not be killed by any man, and then gives up her masculine role as warrior and is rewarded with the love of Faramir. Likewise, Elizabeth in *Pirates of the Caribbean* (Gore Verbinski, 2003–7) dons trousers and becomes a pirate, battling foes and clearly rejecting the restrictions of her feminine life with her most famous line "You like pain? Try wearing a corset" as she knocks her opponent unconscious. Yet, at the end of the first film, she is back in her corset and appears to be firmly back in her feminine role, rewarded with the love of Will Turner; at the end of the third film, by which time she has been the King of the Pirates and commanded the pirate fleet, she is stripped of all agency. We leave her on a lonely shore, having finally consummated her marriage to Will, committed to do nothing more than wait for the brief moment in every decade when he will be able to leave *The Flying Dutchman* and visit her. A more passive role for a woman is hard to imagine.[2]

Complementing these ideas on the functional and visual aspects of women in film, theories have also been offered on the gendered nature of film music. Looking at classical Hollywood scoring, Kathryn Kalinak (1982) identified two types of women, clearly categorized by their music: the virtuous wife and the fallen woman. In Hollywood scoring, the fallen woman is represented by "a predominance of orchestral colors associated with popular jazz such as saxophones ... unusual harmonies, chromaticism and dissonance ... dotted rhythms and syncopation; and ... by the use of portamento and blues notes" (*ibid.*: 77). The virtuous wife, meanwhile, tends to be represented by violins and flutes, "lush [harmonies] based on late nineteenth century modules" (*ibid.*) and "lyricism, long phrases, basically even rhythms and upwards leaps in the melodic line" (*ibid.*: 81).[3]

Philip Tagg, in collaboration with Bob Clarida, carried out a detailed study of musical semiotics that was finally published in full in 2003. The study was based on the results of a reception test where participants were asked to write down any verbal-visual associations (VVAs) that came to them on hearing ten short pieces of music. Tagg's 1989 paper, "An Anthropology of Stereotypes in TV Music?",[4] presents an analysis of gender-associative responses by establishing which tunes produced VVAs of a man or men, which of a woman or women, and which of mixed-sex groups. Four of the ten tunes appeared to be characterized as feminine, in that they produced significantly more female VVAs than male; four of the other tunes were predominantly masculine; and two could not clearly be categorized. Tagg then analysed the music's characteristics to see if there were common qualities within the two groups. A summary of his findings is shown in Table 9.1.

Table 9.1 A summary of Tagg's observations of male- and female-coded characteristics

Musical characteristic	Music of women	Music of men
Tempo, note values and division of time	Slower, with longer note values adding to the sense of a slower tempo. Regular division of note values	Faster, containing short notes with syncopation, dotted rhythms, including double dotting and repeated notes
Phrasing	*Legato*, slurring	Articulated, often *staccato*
Dynamics	Dynamic phrasing, frequent use of the *crescendo* and *diminuendo*	Remains at one dynamic level
Instrumentation	Melody lines in the strings, woodwind and piano, accompanied by strings or piano	Melody in electric guitars, brass, synthesizers and percussion, accompanied by brass and synthesizers
Melodic shape	Overall descending tendencies with rising and falling contours. Frequent use of a falling sixth	Overall ascending tendencies

Tagg also found that the music producing female VVAs was associated with pastoral ideas such as nature, reproduction, 'earthiness' and instinct. The masculine tunes, by contrast, generated VVAs of weapons, and law and order. Female figures were never associated with weapons and male figures were not associated with pastoral scenes, thus aligning neatly with traditional feminist theories about gender difference and the balance of power. Tagg also notes Anahid Kassabian's observation on the gender-related test data that:

> by a huge margin, the study's participants found it easier to imagine a single individual as specifically male, and in general found it difficult indeed to picture specifically female people in the scenes they imagined. This is, of course, related to the 'men act and women sit' distinction. (Kassabian, cited in Tagg, 1989: 11)

"The biggest trouble with her is the noise": romance, comedy and screaming in *Indiana Jones and the Temple of Doom*

The three original films of the *Indiana Jones* series all have very different female characters. Marion, in *Raiders of the Lost Ark* (Steven Spielberg, 1981), is feisty and independent and can drink any man under the table, but she is also fairly disaster-prone, as seen most clearly in the sequence where she locks herself into the cockpit of an airplane that she has already set in motion by removing the chocks, and has to be saved (yet again) by Indiana before the plane explodes. Elsa, in *Indiana Jones and the Last Crusade* (Steven Spielberg, 1989) is a deeply problematic character who has a relationship with both Indiana and his father and who turns out to be working for the Nazis. Predictably, her fallen-woman status and desire for power (as represented by the Holy Grail) are punished with her death. The central film of the 1980s trilogy, *Indiana Jones and the Temple of Doom*, has a leading lady, Willie, who appears to be a composite of all the worst attributes available to a female character in a fantasy action narrative, in particular her hatred of the outdoors, her squeamishness about unfamiliar food and indigenous insects (particularly when they turn out to be the same thing), her obsession with her appearance and, above all, her incessant screaming. Fay Wray was perhaps the first leading lady required to scream to excess, in *King Kong* (Merian C. Cooper [uncredited], 1933), but that function of the role became quickly established and is played for comedy in *Temple of Doom*: as Indiana says in the camp one night, as Willie runs around in the background screaming at everything, "the biggest trouble with her is the noise".

Willie's voice is arguably as important a part of her sonic identity as any scored music. We first meet her as a singer in a nightclub (singing Cole Porter's 'Anything Goes' in Cantonese), and from this the move to screaming is a relatively short step. Both types of vocalizing serve to undermine her in some way: she is an ethnic European singing a language that is clearly not her own, and the overall effect is of an artificial construct in which her position is anomalous, even though she clearly feels much more comfortable in the enclosed space of the nightclub than in the three-dimensional outdoor environment to which Indiana takes her. The nightclub is very much the type of space that Mulvey identifies women occupying: its lack of realism and Willie's two-dimensionality are highlighted when the film's title inserts itself between her and the stage set of her performance; and the overall effect of the sequence is to establish Willie and the female dancers as spectacle and a source of visual pleasure.[5] In the later outdoor environment, her screaming replaces the singing and more overtly positions her as out of place, undermining her actions even when they are otherwise effective. She saves Indiana and his young sidekick, Short Round, from being crushed in a secret chamber in Pankot Palace, but her screaming and her squeamish terror of bugs distracts from the fact that she has acted effectively to help the team.

For the first half of the film, there are two main types of scoring: thematic scoring of action associated primarily with Indiana and secondarily with Short Round; and 'ethnic' scoring (that Claudia Gorbman [1987] would describe as both referential and connotative narrative cueing), which formally marks the movement between environments and enhances and, indeed, creates the sense of place as the group moves through different locations: Shanghai, the village from which the mystical Shankara stone has been stolen, the jungle, Pankot Palace and the temple that lies beneath it.

Indiana and Short Round both have their own themes, used almost every time they appear on screen and clearly announcing their actions. Indiana's theme is the march theme from *Raiders*; and, although it is written with a clear Chinese inflection to reflect his ethnic background, Short Round's shares several features of Indiana's, a musical reiteration of their partnership (Figure 9.1). Short Round's theme prominently implements the same leap of a perfect fourth preceded by an ascending stepwise sequence as Indiana's theme; both themes are generally stated loudly, using similar instrumentation that communicates ideas of masculinity (and therefore agency and action), according to Tagg's model. Their themes are sufficiently similar to be played simultaneously, as shown in Figure 9.1c. Willie is musically and socially isolated and excluded from their relationship, which evidently predates her arrival; and Short Round's presence removes the possibility of Willie forming an effective partnership with Indiana in terms of her active participation in events, since that role has already been taken by the precociously capable boy.

The only role left available to Willie is that of romantic interest and the vulnerable woman to be saved from a horrible death in a fiery pit. This thrusts her firmly into the type of passive role described by Mulvey, the opposite of

Figure 9.1 Author transcription of themes from *Indiana Jones and the Temple of Doom* (John Williams, 1984)

the all-male partnership of Indiana and Short Round, representing all that is non-male. Willie becomes an object to be looked at; but perhaps more disturbingly, her inability to cope with the challenging physical environments in which Indiana is entirely at home means she also becomes a character to be laughed at, a second level of objectifying her and stripping her of an effective subjective voice within the narrative.[6] Musically, however, it becomes apparent that both she and Short Round are subordinate to Indiana. Whilst Indiana's theme stands out, instantly recognizable from the previous film, Willie and Short Round often find their themes elided, Willie's theme acting as a B section to Short Round's in several cues and, indeed, in 'Short Round's Theme' in Williams's concert arrangement of music from the film. In effect, Willie's status in the action of the film, as indicated by her music, is very much that of a secondary – and less effective – sidekick.

As romantic interest, musically she does not precisely fit Kalinak's model of either virtuous wife or fallen woman but negotiates a path between them, using both kinds of music that Kalinak describes. The fact that she is a singer, a showgirl, brings certain connotations to her character: flirtatious, playing on her femininity, performing the role of desirable woman in order to achieve a particular end, which in this case appears to be seducing Indiana. 'Anything Goes' is a jazz standard, accompanied here by a big band, and so it alludes to Kalinak's fallen-woman category through the use of saxophones, syncopation, a jazz idiom and chromaticism.

Willie does not, however, continue down this path. After being shot at and chased from Shanghai, jumping from a crashing airplane and then landing in India she stops her confident, flirtatious behaviour and becomes increasingly frustrated and unhappy with the overall situation. Her music after this point moves towards the virtuous-wife category with the introduction of a new theme. We first hear this as Indiana, Short Round and Willie escape from China and we watch an animation plotting their airplane's route across the continent. The theme is not specifically identified as Willie's at this point – there are no characters in shot – but conforms strongly to Tagg's taxonomy of a female-coded theme (see Figure 9.2). The theme is gently flowing, with a regular triplet figure, each beat slurred, and small rises and falls in pitch. The use of the rising and falling intervals creates a 'lilt' and a sense of natural phrasing with an overall descending tendency. There is a strong sense of dynamic shaping created by the contours of the melodic line, and it is orchestrated using violin, flute, oboe and French horn, accompanied by the string section and harp, features that Kalinak identified as part of her description of the virtuous wife's music, although there is a chromatic element in the theme itself (the A natural) and the constant reiterations of the theme in new keys that suggests a lingering element of fallen woman.

Figure 9.2 Author transcription of Willie's theme from *Indiana Jones and the Temple of Doom* (John Williams, 1984)

All of this contrasts sharply with Indiana's march theme, which is faster (allegro to this new theme's andante), uses uneven dotted rhythms and syncopations to give the theme a sense of drive and comes across as strong, punchy and accented, with the orchestration dominated by the brass section. The march has an overall ascending tendency and is almost always played loudly, contrasting with the descending tendencies and more subtle dynamic shaping observed in the other theme. Effectively, these two themes encapsulate almost everything that Tagg observes about female-coded and male-coded music, and it is hardly surprising that the new theme becomes associated with Willie. It is used in several different forms for different types of situation which tend to objectify her as a source of comic or visual pleasure; a staccato, semiquaver version for comic moments when she is being made to look ridiculous, such as when she tries to climb onto an elephant in high heels and ends up facing backwards; a slowed-down form for the rare occasions when she is being calm and rational; and its original, lilting form in scenes where she becomes the potential romantic partner for Indiana, including all three occasions where they kiss. Given how annoying he normally finds her and the way that the same music is used for her comic, annoying episodes as well as for romantic moments, the theme can credibly be read as the way in which Indiana 'hears' her, representing his point of view, whether he is regarding her as an irritating distraction or a romantic one. The theme stands in direct contrast to his own theme, which enhances his position at the centre of the narrative by underscoring his actions and emphasizing his heroism.

Willie's and Indiana's themes parallel the on-screen tension between male protagonist and female distraction, the two themes – like the two characters – a polarization of culturally coded, gendered characteristics that reiterate Willie's isolation within the plot space. Unlike Short Round, her music has no obvious common features with Indiana's and highlights the fact that she is the only female character in the film: her music positions her as Other to them. Her participation in the action is peripheral and distracting, and her sole function as vulnerable woman in need of saving and potential prize for the successful hero is underlined by the overt femininity of her theme. The only time it takes on a remotely masculine tenor is again a moment of making fun of her attempts at action: trying to free a mine cart for the team to escape in, she has to put all her strength into moving the brake and falls head first into the cart, at which point the opening of her theme is stated on the trumpet. The use of Indiana's instrument mocks Willie's attempt to be heroic, brave and helpful; her lack of power causes her literally to land flat on her face.

Despite her subordinate position in the narrative, Willie presents some interesting musical characteristics. She is neither a fallen woman nor a virtuous wife but combines elements from both, thanks mainly to the diegetic music of the opening. As Kassabian suggests (2001: 69–70), the model of two types of scoring for women identified by Kalinak in films of the 1930s and 1940s is too limited and cannot fully account for the scoring of women in more recent narratives, albeit that this is one set in 1935. The strategy underlying Willie's scoring aims at a theme that makes the most overt contrast to the protagonist's music. By being given the song at the beginning, Willie is positioned as altogether too liberated and racy for a conventional virtuous wife; but scoring her by using the musical vocabulary of the virtuous wife brings out the anomaly of her position within the narrative, the fish out of water, the woman in a man's world. For all that it is a film of the 1980s and not the 1930s, it nonetheless quite strongly reinforces classical Hollywood constructions of a woman's role within a fantasy action-adventure as a figure entirely unimportant in herself – important only for what she causes others to do.

"What's a nice place like me doing in a girl like this?" Agency, love and place in *The Mummy* and *The Mummy Returns*

The scoring strategy of the first two films of *The Mummy* trilogy is distinctive and relatively unusual in the way that it both exploits and subverts some of the conventional approaches to scoring ideas of masculine power and women as objects of desire.[7] The opening of the first film appears to strike a completely conventional position: it begins with a male voice-over telling the history of Egypt, thus putting a male voice into an automatic position of authority at the outset of the narrative. This is heard in conjunction with a shot of Pharaoh Seti I in his chariot, clearly powerful and enhanced by the first major theme of Jerry Goldsmith's score, a dramatic one that evokes the power of ancient Egypt through strong brass scoring, the use of a non-western scale and the equally exotic use of a 7/8 metre (Figure 9.3).

This is quickly followed by our introduction to Seti's mistress, Anck-su-namun, and her illicit love for the priest, Imhotep. A second theme is used here, and just as the first theme pointed to the pharaoh's power, this theme points to Anck-su-namun as an object of desire. Whereas the 'Power' theme is

Figure 9.3 Author transcription of 'Power' theme from *The Mummy* (Jerry Goldsmith, 1999)

Figure 9.4 Author transcription of 'Desire' theme from *The Mummy* (Jerry Goldsmith, 1999)

characterized by dramatic brass and a 'down and back up' contour, this theme contrasts in its use of woodwind and 'up and back down' figuration (Figure 9.4).[8] However, the use of these two themes, which dominate the rest of the film, is nothing so straightforward as a simple scoring of masculine power and feminine desirability. This more complex approach to gendered scoring is suggested by Anck-su-namun's declaration to Pharaoh just before she kills herself: "My body is no longer your temple." She rejects her own embodiment as his object of desire and this rejection is then developed through the subsequent rejection of a traditional musical strategy towards gender in the film. Yet she conforms entirely to the conventions of on-screen female desirability – slender, scantily clad in the extreme and ethnically exotic – and the film negotiates a fine balance between the female power and desirability within the narrative.

The strategy the score adopts uses the two themes in a flexible manner: neither of them signifies one person or idea in the more usual way of thematic scoring, as seen in *Temple of Doom*. Instead, each theme relates to a group of people and ideas. The 'Power' theme encompasses Egypt itself, both the landscape and the architecture and fabric of the ancient empire. It is used for Seti at the start of the film, but also – in a recognizable but consistent variation – for Imhotep. We hear this version first as the opening images move from the exterior shots of Egyptian architecture to the inside of Pharaoh's palace; and again after Imhotep has been resurrected and begins his quest for his own full regeneration and the resurrection of Anck-su-namun (Figure 9.5); but in its original form, it is also used for the Magi, who were once Pharaoh's personal guard and now seek to maintain control of Imhotep. Thus, the same thematic idea represents both the villain of the film and those who fight against him, bringing a very specific musical tension to the idea of agency: it does not obviously lie with any one character.

The 'Desire' theme also represents multiple people and concepts. It starts as the love theme for Anck-su-namun and Imhotep, but it too is used to

Figure 9.5 Author transcription of Imhotep's theme from *The Mummy* (Jerry Goldsmith, 1999)

O'Connell's theme

Desire theme

Figure 9.6 Author transcription of O'Connell's theme from *The Mummy* (Jerry Goldsmith, 1999)

represent Egypt, both the landscape and its modern urban areas; it transfers from Anck-su-namun to the central twentieth-century female character, Evelyn ('Evy'), and is used both for her and for her developing relationship with the American mercenary, O'Connell; just as the 'Power' theme has a significant variation used exclusively for Imhotep, so the 'Desire' theme has a significant variation used exclusively for O'Connell and his most decisive moments of action (Figure 9.6). This last use is particularly unexpected. The 'Power' theme arguably represents a masculine principle in the film (power, Imhotep, the Magi) and the 'Desire' theme a female principle (the female characters and their love relationships). Tagg's taxonomy would certainly classify the 'Power' theme as masculine, with its loudness, marked articulation, use of brass and the unusual time signature (which creates a metric feel not unlike that of syncopation for a listener expecting a standard duple or triple metre). Imhotep's variation makes the signification of power even more aggressive with its use of tritones, removing any of the latent lyricism of the original. The 'Desire' theme, on the other hand, displays many of the characteristics Tagg attributes to a reading of femaleness: a gentle tempo with even divisions of note values, a lyrical, legato melody, dynamic shaping of the phrase and the typical up-and-back-down shape of the melodic line. Placing O'Connell thematically into this group rather than that of the 'Power' theme confirms that something quite unusual is occurring in terms of narrative agency within the film.

The key to this conundrum is Evy. On the surface, O'Connell is an Indiana Jones figure: he is operating in a similar era, he is an American man of action who appears to have some archaeological knowledge, and he is certainly in search of ancient treasures. However, where Indiana is motivated by intellect and guided by an unerring moral compass, O'Connell's archaeological interest is focused on material reward, and it is Evy who, like Indiana, is the possessor of knowledge pursuing adventure out of intellectual curiosity and, later on, a desire to prevent power from falling into the wrong hands.[9] Moreover, she is genuinely Egyptian (on her mother's side) and the evocation of Egypt within the music automatically points to her more than it does to O'Connell as the focus of our attention and identification. In a great many ways, Evy is the driving narrative force of much of the film, and her connection to Egypt means that this is reinforced by the constant evocation of Egypt in the music. Her drunken declaration to O'Connell – "What's a nice place like me doing in a girl like this?" – neatly reveals the relationship she has with the narrative space of the film. This is her landscape and she is a mobile figure operating within three-dimensional space, considerably removed from the static women, objectified in two dimensions, identified by Mulvey.[10] O'Connell may have found the key that contains the map to Hamunaptra, but it is Evy who recognizes what it is and who organizes the expedition. She bargains with the warden to save O'Connell's life, absolutely refusing to use feminine wiles to do so; she wins the camel race (her ease on a camel contrasting strongly to Wille's hatred of riding an elephant and again emphasizing her control of the narrative space) and reaches Hamunaptra first, closely followed by O'Connell. Alas, it is also Evy who is responsible for raising Imhotep when she reads from the Book of the Dead, and her authority is regularly undermined by her astonishing clumsiness, but it is a moment of profound narrative control when she resolves a stand-off between the two sides by deciding to hand herself over to Imhotep, instructing O'Connell to rescue her. A far more normal route would see the heroine unwillingly kidnapped and the hero then deciding to rescue her; Evy subverts this process by assuming control of the decision-making. She then saves O'Connell from an unnatural sandstorm by distracting Imhotep with a kiss (the only time she stoops to using her desirability as a weapon and clearly an act of last resort on her part). She finally defeats Imhotep by giving her brother Jonathan the information he needs to take control of Imhotep's mummified soldiers, while she reads from the Book of Amun-Ra to strip him of his immortality. That O'Connell actually kills Imhotep is debatable: Imhotep walks forward and impales himself on O'Connell's sword as Evy reveals that her reading from the Book has made him mortal and therefore vulnerable.

O'Connell is certainly an active player in the narrative but he is rarely the instigator of action, and although he rescues Evy on several occasions, she rescues him just as frequently: she drives the narrative and he reacts. That O'Connell's theme derives from the one associated with her becomes less mysterious: he is the outsider, and so the music associated with Egypt cannot truly belong to him, but he is closely associated with Evy and, by extension, with her 'feminine principle' theme. Giving him his own version of the theme allows him to operate in clear musical opposition to Imhotep without disrupting the overall structure of a narrative that places Evy at its centre. His variation dilutes the exoticism of the scale, making it more appropriate for an American figure, and rewrites the structure and character of the theme to conform strongly to Tagg's ideas of masculine music: fast-moving, brass-dominated, with complex rhythms and dominated by an ascending figure created by separating the original theme into two distinct halves (see Figure 9.6). At the same time, it connects him strongly to Evy; and it is also heard very rarely, being easily the least used of any of the four themes shown here from this film. In effect, although gendered musical codings are still at work in the scoring of this film, their impact on the narrative positions of the male and female characters operates very differently from the more traditional positions of the *Indiana Jones* films.

The Mummy Returns, set nine years later in 1933, is scored by Alan Silvestri but continues Goldsmith's strategy of using thematic material to signify groups rather than individuals and moves even further away from an obviously gendered scoring. Two of the main themes, labelled for convenience as 'Action' and 'Love', again correspond musically to a masculine and a feminine principle (see Figure 9.7). A superficial reading might place 'Action' as O'Connell's masculine theme of narrative agency and 'Love' as Evy's feminine 'object of desire' evocation from O'Connell's point of view, but this would be to misread their use quite substantially. The 'Action' theme is, in fact, first used for Evy as she battles an intruder in her home who is threatening her son, Alex; although it does later become closely associated with O'Connell (who is granted far greater agency in this film than in the first), it is not used in his final battle with the Scorpion King but is reserved for the moment that the otherwise comic character, Izzy, arrives in his dirigible to whisk everyone to safety. Likewise it is used fairly indiscriminately for all members of the team (O'Connell, Evy,

a) Action

b) Love

Figure 9.7 Author transcription of themes from *The Mummy Returns* (Alan Silvestri, 2002)

Jonathan and the Magi, Ardeth) during the battle with the miniature zombie skeletons in the forest by Am Sher, a battle which is genuinely a team effort.

The 'Action' theme again displays some typically masculine characteristics: loud, fast, brass-dominated, punchily articulated and beginning with the rising perfect fifth that is characteristic of the heroic themes written by John Williams for fantasy-action film franchises such as *Superman* and *Star Wars*. While the gender coding of the music is heroic (and therefore, in Hollywood terms, normally written for male, white, heterosexual characters), here it is used for a male, white American but also for an Egyptian man, a half-Egyptian woman and her brother, and the black British Izzy, a group of characters that the music treats very even-handedly in a way atypical of Hollywood conventions.

The 'Love' theme also behaves atypically. Rather than scoring O'Connell's gaze when turned on Evy, it signifies their wider family and is most often used when Evy and O'Connell are talking about their son. Rather than a plot that puts a woman in danger, it is Alex who is kidnapped and who needs to be rescued by both his parents. We hear the 'Love' theme early in the film when O'Connell is talking about how much both Evy and Alex mean to him; again, after Alex is kidnapped, when Evy talks about her love for her son; and again at Am Sher when she and O'Connell discuss gun technique, the importance of which at this point is their determination to save Alex from his kidnappers. We also hear it when Evy kisses Izzy, not because she loves him, but because he has saved her family.

The 'Love' theme also brings into focus a narrative element that has been largely absent from fantasy-action adventures before this: family and, in relation to the women of fantasy films, motherhood. Motherhood is quite antithetical to the traditional position of the fantasy woman. Her role has normally been to be placed in danger so that the hero can rescue her, to scream loudly when faced by danger and to be available as the hero's prize at the end of the story. No part of this role allows for a child: if the woman is a mother, then her own role becomes protective and nurturing rather than conventionally vulnerable and desirable; and a child will limit the extent to which she can be available to the hero as his reward, because her allegiances are already spoken for. In the 1980s *Indiana Jones* films, each film saw Indiana with a new girl to be saved and claimed (a goal unachieved in *Last Crusade*). However, because Evy is the central figure of *The Mummy* rather than O'Connell, the idea that a sequel might not include her would make little narrative sense: if the Indiana/leading-lady roles were entirely reversed, we would find Evy teamed up with a new leading man in the sequel. The writers do not go this far in liberating their heroine from conventional constraints; but instead, in keeping O'Connell in the narrative, they allow for a mature romantic relationship that has developed in the intervening nine years, including the raising of a child.

Fathers are not uncommon in fantasy narratives: *Last Crusade* introduces Indiana's father but is typical in its representation of the father/son relationship: fathers tend to be either absent (often dead) or problematic in that they represent for the son a form of competition as narrative agent. Allowing motherhood into the narrative is a reflection of the more modern idea of women 'having it all', a career and a family. In earlier film narratives, women were required to choose, to be either the (passive) virtuous wife or the (active) fallen woman, but it is worth noting that Kalinak does not require a woman to have fallen (i.e., to be sexually active outside marriage) in order to be a fallen woman. One of the characters she identifies as this musical type is Scarlett O'Hara, who is sexually virtuous – no matter the rumours – but fallen due to her desire for agency and punished accordingly: among other disasters, her child dies and her husband leaves her. She is equally the type of woman Mulvey identifies as making the 'wrong' choice between conventional feminine passivity and masculine agency. However, so is Evy – the difference being that her narrative makes no negative judgements about her choice and rewards her for her agency in *The Mummy* with a husband; and again rewards her in *The Mummy Returns* by not only restoring her son to her but allowing her to be returned to life (quite literally to fight another day) when she is suddenly and almost arbitrarily killed by the resurrected Anck-su-namun at Am Sher. Evy is not punished by the narrative for wanting to be an agent rather than an onlooker in her drama. The notion of 'having it all' is embedded in the musical strategy where both the 'Action' and 'Love' themes are used in relation to her and her trajectory through the narrative of *The Mummy Returns*.[11]

Conclusion

In that our film narratives reflect the ideas, beliefs and values of our culture back at us, we should not be surprised to find that more recent film narratives and their scores reflect the gradual empowerment of women in western society, and not only in fantasy narratives: yet fantasy is a particularly interesting genre to examine in that its storylines are so often set elsewhere and 'elsewhen', not in contemporary culture. The films examined here are all set between 1924 and 1935, a period that predates the main period of twentieth-century feminist activism by several decades; and they all aim to recreate an earlier era, filtered to some extent through the lens of the later one in which they were created. What is perhaps most revealing is the extent to which the 1980s film – made well after feminism had established itself as a cultural force – appears to embrace wholeheartedly an approach to constructing and scoring its main female character that would not have been out of place in the 1930s, an apparently tongue-in-cheek gesture towards an 'authentic' recreation of the period, no matter that the result is arguably the least sympathetic heroine to be found in a fantasy adventure of any era. *The Mummy* films, meanwhile, effectively reinvent their historical setting, giving Evy a physical, intellectual and professional autonomy that is unlikely to have been available to her in the 1930s, much less the 1920s. In giving her this autonomy, the films create a heroine who displays a decidedly modern approach to both her command of her narrative and her desirability: the films do not downplay this at all, and include unquestionable moments when our gaze, with O'Connell's, is fixed on her as an object of desire, as when, in *The Mummy*, she appears in her newly acquired Egyptian apparel, having lost all her other clothes. However, in a construction that has not been widely emulated in other fantasy films as yet, her desirability is always balanced against her control of the narrative, a position supported and enhanced by music which, because of the way in which themes are not fixed in their meaning or implied point of view, allows a variety of different subjective positions to be established among the principal characters. The scores of *The Mummy* and *The Mummy Returns* offer a significantly different model for scoring strong female characters, by placing them at the subjective centre of their narratives, thus allowing them to move beyond the relatively simplistic divisions of good wives and fallen women.

Notes

1. Both essays were reprinted in 1989 in *Visual and Other Pleasures*, a collection of her work.
2. Elizabeth does not feature in the fourth film (*On Stranger Tides*, Rob Marshall, 2011) so this dismal fate appears to be the end of her story and her narrative agency.
3. This musical characterization of women as either bad or good can be seen outside film music, as discussed by Susan McClary in *Feminine Endings* (1999). Her analysis of the musical differences between 'the angel and the whore' (Micaëla and Carmen) in the opera *Carmen* corresponds closely to Kalinak's two archetypes.
4. Philip Tagg (1989), 'An Anthropology of Stereotypes in TV Music?' *Swedish Musicological Journal*, 19–42 (online at http://tagg.org/articles/xpdfs/tvanthro.pdf; accessed 12 August 2008).
5. The lack of realism is highlighted in the song-and-dance number, where the dimensions of the performance space are treated in a surreally flexible way (a fantasy within the film fantasy) that disregards the physical properties of the space and alludes to the cinematic dance sequences of Busby Berkeley.
6. An element of Indiana's agency and authority within these films is the ease with which he moves between environments, whether it is the safe tweediness of his life as a college professor or his self-confidence in the alien environments of jungles, deserts and ancient architecture. Willie's inability to do this is a symptom of her inequality within the narrative spaces he controls.

7. The third film of the series, *The Mummy: Return of the Dragon King* (Rob Cohen, 2008) is clearly a vehicle for Brendan Fraser and is the only film of the series not set in Egypt or directed by Stephen Sommers. It is not discussed here.

8. Tagg identifies both of these contours as belonging primarily to female-coded music. Here, the mirror-image shape of the melodic contours acts instead as a point of contrast between the various concepts and characters associated with these themes.

9. One particular scene effectively recreates a scene from *Raiders* with gender roles reversed. In the ruins of Hamunaptra, Evy gets drunk and tells O'Connell that she is going to kiss him: they lean towards each other, and O'Connell puckers his lips expectantly, only for Evy to fall asleep before the kiss is realized. This mimics the scene in *Raiders* when an injured Indiana falls asleep on Marion just as she expects him to kiss her, and her disappointment matches O'Connell's closely.

10. One could argue that the exoticism of the music associated with Evy is an Orientalist gesture that conflates the exotic with the erotic, particularly in relation to the female. Although Edward Said largely avoids the issue of gender in *Orientalism* (1978), the female is part of the Orient's binary opposites (alongside the irrational, the exotic and the heathen) set against the male, rational, Christian and ultimately superior positioning of the west. However, *The Mummy* subverts many (although not all) of the conventions of representing east/west and ideas of Otherness by treating eastern and western, male and female, very even-handedly: the themes of both the masculine and feminine principle are equally inflected by exotic, oriental modes and it is the group of American explorers and their Hungarian guide, Beni, who are positioned most obviously as morally weak and materially grasping in the manner normally reserved for 'Orientals'.

11. It is perhaps not coincidental that *Indiana Jones and the Kingdom of the Crystal Skull* (2008), made almost twenty years after *Last Crusade*, also brings the ideas of family and motherhood into the plot, while at the same time re-engaging with the trope of absent and problematic fathers when Indiana discovers he has a grown-up son by Marion.

References

Gorbman, C. (1987), *Unheard Melodies: Narrative Film Music*, Bloomington: University of Indiana Press; London: BFI.

Kalinak, K. (1982), 'The Fallen Woman and the Virtuous Wife: Musical Stereotypes in *The Informer, Gone with the Wind*, and *Laura*', *Film Reader*, 5, 76–82.

Kassabian, A. (2001), *Hearing Film: Tracking Identifications in Contemporary Hollywood Film Music*, London: Routledge.

McClary, S. (1999), *Feminine Endings: Music, Gender and Sexuality*, Minneapolis: University of Minnesota Press.

Mulvey, L. (1989a), 'Visual Pleasure and Narrative Cinema', in L. Mulvey (ed.), *Visual and Other Pleasures*, London: Macmillan, pp.14–26 (first published in 1975 in *Screen*, 16.3: 6–18).

Mulvey, L. (1989b), 'Afterthoughts on "Visual Pleasure and Narrative Cinema" Inspired by *Duel in the Sun* (King Vidor, 1946)', in L. Mulvey (ed.), *Visual and Other Pleasures*, London: Macmillan, pp. 29–38 (first published in 1981 in *Framework*, 15–17: 12–15).

Said, E. (1978), *Orientalism*, New York: Pantheon.

Tagg, P. (1989), 'An anthropology of stereotypes in TV music?' *Swedish Musicological Journal*, 19–42 (online at http://tagg.org/articles/xpdfs/tvanthro.pdf ; accessed 12 August 2008).

10 Creating Magic with Music
The Changing Dramatic Relationship between Music and Magic in Harry Potter *Films*

Jamie L. Webster

The *Harry Potter* phenomenon is wide-reaching and culturally significant. Following the magical journey of an unassuming boy who discovers his wizarding heritage, enters the Hogwarts School for Witchcraft and Wizardry in a magical parallel world and matures throughout his seven years as a student there into a hero in the fight against dark magic, the story of Harry Potter has captured the hearts, minds and imaginations of adult and youthful readers alike. The seven-novel series has influenced an entire generation of readers worldwide and the *Harry Potter* films have been seen by millions of viewers.

J. K. Rowling's first novel in the series, *Harry Potter and the Philosopher's Stone* (released as *Harry Potter and the Sorcerer's Stone* in the USA, and hereafter referred to by that title), was published in 1997, followed by *Harry Potter and the Chamber of Secrets* (1998), *Harry Potter and the Prisoner of Azkaban* (1999), *Harry Potter and the Goblet of Fire* (2000), *Harry Potter and the Order of the Phoenix* (2003), *Harry Potter and the Half-Blood Prince* (2005) and *Harry Potter and the Deathly Hallows* (2007), which completed the series. The magic at the core of the story captured worldwide attention – while some fans cite the fantastical landscape as a reason for their devotion to the books, some critics cite the inclusion of sorcery as a reason to ban or restrict children's access to the books.[1] In contrast, very few have taken notice of Rowling's many descriptions of music-making in the novels, although there is a significant relationship between her descriptions of magic and music-making in Harry's world.

The subsequent *Harry Potter* films became high-profile productions, then box-office and critical successes. The producers took many steps to ensure that the films would capture the magic of Rowling's original story: they hired well-known film-makers, successful composers and a legion of British and Irish stage and screen veterans; they used British and Scottish historic and outdoor locations and they budgeted for high-end special effects. This chapter examines the role music plays in capturing and conveying the magical elements of Rowling's story.

Any perusal of *Harry Potter* internet fan site discussions – such as those on *HPana*, *MuggleNet*, *The Leaky Cauldron* or review sites such as *The Internet Movie Database* – reveals that fans perceive strong aesthetic differences between the different films. Although viewers have different personal preferences, the web-based discussions and reviews reveal two areas of consensus. On the one hand, fans and critics tend to agree that all the films in the series follow the main events of Rowling's original narrative, that they all belong to the fantasy genre and that they become increasingly darker in tone and subject matter as Harry matures over the course of the series. On the other hand, viewers tend to acknowledge subgenres within the series – the first two films are the faithful 'classics', the third is the 'art film', the fourth is the action-packed 'thriller', and the fifth is the 'psychological drama'.[2] Similarly, all of the orchestral soundtracks have been described as 'colourful', yet listeners use different words to describe the music of each film – characterizing the first two soundtracks as theatrically 'magical', the third as hauntingly 'enchanting', the fourth as 'brooding' and 'regal' (but not magical) and the fifth as 'dramatic' and 'elegant'.[3] It appears from this that the relationship between music and the *Harry Potter* narrative leads the films to be perceived as simultaneously unified yet distinct from each other: some are perceived as more 'magical' than others.[4]

The films feel different from one another in large part because of different director/composer partnerships (see Table 10.1).[5] The *Harry Potter* film franchise experienced four completely different director/composer collaborations over the course of the first five films, each taking its own approach to the dramatic role of magic and fantasy in the narrative. While a few other film series have included some aesthetic changes, this is the first time that such distinctly different approaches have been employed in a serial film saga of this magnitude.[6]

When directors and composers make production choices about visual and audio aesthetics, it affects the way viewers experience the film. One marker of these aesthetic differences in the *Harry Potter* films is witnessed in the changing musical representation of magic in the wizarding world. That is to

Table 10.1 Director/composer collaborations for the first five *Harry Potter* films

Film title	Director	Composer	Year
The Sorcerer's Stone	Chris Columbus	John Williams	2001
The Chamber of Secrets	Chris Columbus	John Williams	2002
The Prisoner of Azkaban	Alfonso Cuarón	John Williams	2004
The Goblet of Fire	Mike Newell	Patrick Doyle	2005
The Order of the Phoenix	David Yates	Nicholas Hooper	2007

say, even though magic is at the core of the original narrative, the film music reveals that magic is presented very differently in each of the films – with more or less emphasis, given more or less importance. Following the theories and models of Claudia Gorbman (1987), Kathryn Kalinak (1997) and Anahid Kassabian (2001), this chapter provides an example of how film music can be organized (as music itself, and with film images) in order to guide cinematic interpretations. My analysis is also informed by the work of other music scholars such as musicologist Mary Ann Smart (2004), who has explored how music can mimic drama with musical metaphors; musicologists Roland John Wiley (1985) and Thérèse Hurley (2007), who have discussed historical musical codes for the fantastic; musicologist Susan McClary (1991), who has interrogated historic significations in musical structure that affect the interpretation of musical meaning in contemporary times; and the late music theorist Steve Larson, who, in conjunction with philosopher Mark L. Johnson (Johnson and Larson, 2003) and music theorist Leigh VanHandel (Larson and VanHandel, 2005), has explored how the metaphorical process of mapping physical motion onto musical motion in melody, harmony and time affects listeners' understanding of and emotional response to music.

In this chapter, I examine the use of traditional musical codes for the dramatic signification of magic in the first five *Harry Potter* films, including the application of music to magical events in the narrative, the use of instruments as signifiers of the fantastic, and the use of musical elements – melodic, rhythmic, harmonic – to evoke the supernatural. Additionally, I explore the use of the *Harry Potter* main theme, 'Hedwig's Theme', as a specific example of the changes occurring in the films as a whole; and demonstrate how the direct relationship between music and magical events in the first two films is complicated and disrupted in the subsequent three. The different approaches to the film scoring are an essential aspect of how the idea and importance of magic within the narrative shifts over the course of the series.

A literary perspective: the relationship between music-making and magic in J. K. Rowling's *Harry Potter* novels

There are many examples of music in Rowling's narrative and most of these are directly linked to magical activities, events and power. One enchanting aspect of Rowling's storytelling style is her way of weaving information from real-life disciplines – including language studies, botany, alchemy, astronomy and astrology, folklore and mythology – into her narrative about an unfamiliar realm, namely, the magical world. Although Rowling does not include the discipline of music as an official course of study at Hogwarts, she frequently describes musical performances, events and participation in these as a way to propel narrative progress and establish a colourful socio-cultural landscape in the magical world, where, for example, music is performed formally and informally for school ceremonies and athletic events. Sometimes there is a magical component to even mundane music performances, as when a suit of armour and a poltergeist sing Christmas carols (Rowling, 2000: 395), when music sounding like "a thousand fingernails scraping an enormous blackboard" plays at Nearly-Headless Nick's deathday party (Rowling, 1998: 131), and when winged cherubs deliver singing love-grams on Valentine's Day (*ibid.*: 238). Music is also used ritually for magical events and as part of magical transactions, such as incantations with rhyme and rhythmic lilt. However, in the film version, most diegetic musical events are normalized in order to minimize the relationship between music and magic.

The relationship between music and magic as portrayed in the books is established early on in Harry's experience at Hogwarts. Upon his arrival as a first-year student, a magical singing wizard's hat sorts new students into four school houses with which the students will be affiliated for the duration of their education. Thus a singing performance helps to establish the hat's powerful authority as a magical judge of each student's character.[7] On the same evening, students and staff sing the school song together – all singing the same words but each individual choosing a favourite tune. When the song finishes, the headmaster, Albus Dumbledore, wipes his eyes and exclaims, "Ah, music. A magic beyond all we do here!" (Rowling, 1997: 128). The performance of the song demonstrates an unusual level of tolerance for individuality in the social organization of Rowling's magical world, and Dumbledore's statement establishes that the performance of music has magical properties. Later in the same novel, Harry and his friend Hermione exhibit the mythical power of Orpheus by soothing a three-headed dog to sleep with flute music (*ibid.*: 275–6). This instance establishes a specific and time-honoured way that music is used to serve magical ends.

None of these latter musical events appears in the first film or in any of the other films. The hat sorts the students but does not sing. Likewise, students and staff do not sing the school song, nor does Dumbledore make any statement regarding the power of music.[8] Harry and his friends do not use flute music to magically soothe the three-headed dog to sleep because the dog is already asleep when they encounter it.[9] Similarly, examples of music-making from the second novel are either eliminated in the film version, or negotiated differently so that magic is taken out of the music equation and vice versa.

The most abundant number of musical events occur in Rowling's fourth novel, *The Goblet of Fire*, and many of these events have a magical component. For instance, male spectators at the Quidditch World Cup tournament are mesmerized to the point of bewitchment by the seductively dancing Veela, woodland sprites from European folklore (Rowling, 2000: 103); spectators of all genders are bedazzled by the choreographed formations of a horde of tiny leprechauns (*ibid.*: 104); and an extremely hairy wizarding rock-band sensation named the Weird Sisters plays music on an eclectic assortment of instruments (such as bagpipes, lute and guitar) at the Hogwarts Yule Ball (*ibid.*: 419). Additionally, a magical clue to Harry's task in the Tri-Wizard Tournament is delivered to him in song by a chorus of mer-people (*ibid.*: 365, 460).

Some of these events are represented in the film version of *The Goblet of Fire*, though the majority of them are normalized in order to represent the familiar rather than the fantastic. For instance, the dance of the leprechauns looks more like a glittery fireworks display than an act of musical magic. Likewise, the Veela do not dance at all – though two gender-specific choreographies are performed by visiting foreign students to Hogwarts. These performances include magical manoeuvres – as when the boys make sparks with their staves, and when the girls conjure butterflies from their arms – but have no magical consequences. A band implied to be the Weird Sisters performs at the school dance but they are neither extremely hairy nor are their instruments eclectic – aside from a bagpipe solo, the band plays standard rock on standard rock instruments and the characters themselves are played by familiar real-life rock performers.[10] As such, the representation of the band relates more closely to the real world than to Rowling's descriptions of a magical world. Harry does receive the magical clue disguised in the mer-song but the performance of the song is normalized by using one lyric soprano singer, following the familiar folklore of a single siren's song rather than Rowling's more mysterious description of a "chorus of eerie voices" (*ibid.*: 460). Another musical ensemble that emphasizes the familiar is also added into the film version of *The Goblet of Fire*. Like the third film, which adds a school choir, the fourth film adds a school band, whose instruments look as Dr Seuss might have drawn them but sound like a standard English brass band playing a normal tune, with no special magical effect.

Although I have pointed out some ways that the *Harry Potter* films differ from the *Harry Potter* books, it is not my intention to elevate one set of choices over another. Literary fidelity need not be a measure of cinematic success.[11] However, different choices create different effects that affect audiences in different ways. Rowling creates a direct connection between music and magic by showing how music-making is part of magical social organization and establishing that music-making in the wizarding world is a potential vehicle for magical power. In contrast, the *Harry Potter* film directors generally ignore – or at least dilute – the connection between music and magic by omitting many of the examples of music-making in the narrative and by adapting those remaining in such a way that their magical effect is minimized.

One reason for these choices is that source music functions differently in literature and in film. The inclusion of music-making in a written text can breathe life into the story. In film, however, source, or diegetic, music is often less emotionally powerful and tends to ground the narrative in the naturalness of realism. This is exactly the experience of music-making in the *Harry Potter* films – the use of source music tends to emphasize connections with the familiar – by using a contemporary rock ensemble to represent a wizard rock group, for example – and dilute connections with the fantastic, by eliminating or giving less attention to examples of music-making with magical effects. As an alternative, the *Harry Potter* films generally rely on non-diegetic underscore to breathe magical life into film.

Figures from cinema: the relationship between non-diegetic music and magic in the *Harry Potter* films

> *Composing for* [fantasy films] *is a gift. The composer no longer has to deal with restrictions which he would probably have with a more realistic picture. The music is always present in the picture. The orchestra keeps playing and the ear of the listener can accept the bombardment of music even if what his eyes see doesn't agree with what his ears are listening to. Music in these types of films plays a very important part because only music can make the audience believe what they see. Only music can make fantasy, reality.* John Williams[12]

Much as Rowling establishes a relationship between music-making and magic early in the *Harry Potter* novels, film-makers establish a relationship between non-diegetic music and magic early in the *Harry Potter* films. At the beginning of *Harry Potter and the Sorcerer's Stone*, the presence of music aligns with the presence of magic while the absence of music aligns with the absence of magic.[13] Music is heard from the Warner Bros fanfare (itself a signifier of the magic of movies) through the first scenes of Hogwarts staff delivering the orphaned infant wizard, Harry Potter, to his (non-magical) aunt and uncle's doorway under the cloak of night. These opening images are musically supported by John Williams's now famous 'Hedwig's Theme' waltz as well as many other shorter musical gestures and phrases played on harp, celeste and other orchestral instruments. In other words, non-diegetic orchestral music supports magical characters who attend to magic-related business and is also performed on instruments that historically have magical associations in music and drama.[14]

To make a transition for the viewer from the infant Harry to the same character ten years later, the camera closes in to focus on a lava-like flash which emerges through baby Harry's lightning-shaped scar (another visual signifier of his inherent magical qualities), then explodes to the far reaches of the screen before fading away from both the screen and the scar on the (now) ten-year-old Harry's forehead. Harry opens his eyes as an almost-eleven-year-old in his cramped, dusty bedroom – a small cupboard under the stairs in the home of his emotionally stingy Aunt Petunia and Uncle Vernon Dursley and their atrociously ill-behaved son, Dudley. From this moment of Harry's awakening in the Muggle – that is to say, the non-magical – world, all orchestral underscore is silenced. There is no magic in the Dursley home and, in fact, the Dursleys are categorically anti-magic, with Uncle Vernon railing against the mere mention of the word 'magic'. Because there is no magic, there is also no music.

Music does not return to the soundtrack until Harry awakens to his magical ability. While at the zoo for his cousin Dudley's birthday, Harry apologizes to a boa constrictor in a glass case who has been rudely disturbed by Dudley's behaviour. The snake looks up at Harry, acknowledges him with a wink, and music re-enters the soundtrack. Although Harry does not realize it at first, he has the magical power to communicate with snakes. The audience learns of this magic before Harry learns of it himself, because his supernatural ability is accompanied by music that alerts the viewing audience to the magic of this event.

From this point, the film alternates between musical silence and the musical accompaniment of 'Hedwig's Theme' until Harry's eleventh birthday arrives. When he receives a mysterious letter in the post, music enters the liminal space during which Harry holds the envelope in his hands but has not yet opened it. Although Uncle Vernon ultimately confiscates the letter (still unopened), we know that its contents are magical because orchestral music enters to tell us so. Magical owls aggressively bring more letters for Harry, though Uncle Vernon tries to fend them off, and 'Hedwig's Theme' accompanies each delivery. As the inevitability of Harry receiving his magical letter becomes clearer, the music of 'Hedwig's Theme' returns louder and with fewer interruptions until it completely fills the aural space. Clearly stated, the musical soundtrack persists in gaining the attention of the listener, thus subverting the silence of realism just as the magical letters persist in subverting the Dursleys's denial of magic. At last, Hagrid, acting as a representative of Hogwarts, breaks down a door to deliver the letter on Harry's eleventh birthday and the promise of magic that was guaranteed by the organized alternation of music and silence comes to fruition. Harry, reading the letter with Hagrid, learns that he is a wizard and that he has been invited to attend the greatest wizarding school that ever was: Hogwarts School of Witchcraft and Wizardry.

Because a precedent is set early on in this film that music accompanies magical events and characters while non-magical characters are not supported by it, music in general becomes a signifier for the fantastic. Furthermore,

Table 10.2 The alternation of background music and silence as a representation of magical and non-magical narrative events

	Opening scenes with music	*Opening scenes without music*
1.	Arrival of Hogwarts professors	
2.		Harry's awakening inside the Dursley house
3.	Harry's conversation with snake	
4.		At the Dursley house
5.	The arrival of owls with Hogwarts letters	
6.		At the Dursley house
7.	The arrival of more owls	
8.		At the Dursley house
9.	[and so on]	

the pattern of applying background music – sometimes as long as a theme, sometimes as brief as a few notes – to magical events in the narrative continues throughout the first two *Harry Potter* films.[15] This approach aligns with statements made by the director Chris Columbus, who sought to make a clear difference between the Muggle and magical worlds by using drab, subdued colours in the Dursley home and bright, rich colours at the Hogwarts School.[16] The director's goal was reflected by Williams's score, in which music is absent from the Muggle world except when magical events take place there but is fully used to support scenes of the magical world, infusing Columbus's version of Rowling's wizarding world with orchestral colours and vitality. Thus, the wizarding world is portrayed as both highly magical and highly appealing.

Music saturates the soundtracks of the first two films, and the most often deployed themes – including 'Hedwig's Theme' – are in dancelike triple metres, include plenty of chromaticism and employ unexpected harmonic progressions, strategies that tend to provide an atmosphere of the fantastic by mimicking irrationality, an important property of the magical realm.[17] Furthermore, these themes align with film images to support various fantastical aspects of the magical world. Because orchestral music also conveys human emotion in the first two films, specific instruments sometimes serve as indicators of magic within the drama. The celeste often signals that general magic is afoot, while harp and unseen choral voices often signal other-worldly, supernatural or mysterious events.

The pattern of relating non-diegetic music to magical events continues in varied form in the third film, *The Prisoner of Azkaban*. Williams's music reflects Alfonso Cuarón's intent to stay true to the spirit of the story rather than to the letter, as Columbus had intended.[18] As in the previous two films, music saturates the soundtrack and many of the prominent themes are in triple metre and/or use chromaticism. However, some instruments are employed differently for the signification of magic, and the relationship between non-diegetic music and magic is complicated by the frequent inclusion and incorporation of source music, an ambiguity or slippage between source and non-diegetic music that Kassabian refers to as "source scoring" (2001: 45).

Unseen choral voices and celeste (used less often in this film) align with images of other-worldly occurrences, as they do in the previous films, and *col legno* strings and tolling bells are added as signifiers of malevolent magic. However, other instruments are emphasized as well – though not always in the service of magic. Early instruments, such as a Renaissance ensemble of woodwinds and tambourine, align with images to signify the exotically medieval – though not necessarily magical – qualities of the wizarding world. Similarly, a harpsichord leitmotif cues the audience to mysterious clues (often, though not always, seen by way of a magical map), but does not directly signify magic. Likewise, a harp is used in the service of folklike melodies as well as in the service of magical signification. The way that Williams incorporates instruments that may have been part of the history and setting of Hogwarts creates an aura of authenticity and bridges the gap in a small way between the non-diegetic music narrating the fantasy for the viewer and the sound-space inhabited by the characters themselves.

Regarding Kassabian's notion of source scoring, sometimes what appears to be source music is seamlessly blended into the non-diegetic music and vice versa, thus seeming to slip across the diegetic boundaries. For instance, the school choir song 'Double Trouble' begins as underscore while students arrive at Hogwarts, develops as source music when we see the choir members sing, then continues in the background once the scene involving the choir has ended. In another, more subtle example, a double-reed melody is initially presented as non-diegetic music over photographic images of the Weasley family's Egyptian vacation, yet is later revealed to be source music from a child musician charming a snakelike rope in the background of the next, wider-angle shot of the room in which the photograph is being admired. This kind of source scoring is used regularly in subtle and complex ways throughout the film, especially for segues between scenes and to link seemingly separate narrative ideas.[19] Because this approach effectively confuses viewers' perceptions about what is real and what is fantasy, it adds to the implicit dialogue about the role of magic in the narrative. Equally, the regular slippage between source and non-diegetic music sutures the relationship between reality and the magical world. This marks a significant shift from the magic versus non-magic dichotomy presented in the first two films.

This new approach is highlighted in one scene from *The Prisoner of Azkaban*, when source and non-diegetic music alternate to signify reality in the magical world versus fantasy in the magical world. During Professor Lupin's lesson, students hear swing music on Lupin's gramophone when they are in control of their perceptions, and film viewers hear dissonant non-diegetic music played by orchestral instruments when a shape-shifting Boggart challenges the students' control over their emotions. The Boggart transforms into the physical form that is frightening to each individual student, causing them to dwell on the fantasy of their fears. Lupin teaches the students a spell that transforms the frightening images into something funny so that they can regain their grasp on reality (see Table 10.3).

This alternation between musical signifiers for fantasy and reality is similar to the alternation between background music and silence as a representation of magic and the absence of magic observed in the first two films (see Table 10.2). However, Williams's and Cuarón's new approach suggests that the real world and magical world co-exist: fantasy can exist within the characters' diegetic reality and vice versa. As such, this example demonstrates that both real-world issues (fear and control) and magical world events (shape-shifting Boggarts) can be accommodated by the narrative. On the one hand, this approach both enriches the narrative and makes the relationship between non-diegetic music and magic less direct. Unlike the music from the first movies which 'tells' the viewer that the story is magical, this new approach allows the viewer to experience fantasy as the characters themselves might experience it. On the other hand, the approach clearly continues to reflect

Table 10.3 The alternation of dissonant, non-diegetic orchestral music and source music as a representation of fantasy and reality within the magical world

Images with non-diegetic orchestral music	*Images with source swing music*
1. Boggart appears as Professor Snape[a]	
2.	Professor Lupin starts the swing record[a]
3. Boggart appears as a spider	
4.	Spider stumbles wearing roller skates
5. Boggart appears as a cobra	
6.	Cobra becomes a jack-in-the-box clown
7a. Boggart appears as a Dementor/	
7b. (then) appears as a full moon	
8.	Full moon becomes a deflating balloon

[a] These two events occur before the main alternating sequence but are included in the table to show how each genre of music is established as a signifier of subjectivity.

the appeal of the magical world, this time by aligning the pleasurable sounds of big-band music with images of benevolent magic, much as the previous films align orchestral music with Harry's introduction to magic. The most cheerful, energetic music – Lupin's swing music – aligns with the most absurdly fantastical images: a giant spider wearing roller skates is more fantastic than a giant spider without them.

The relationship between music and magic is remarkably different in the fourth film, *The Goblet of Fire*. In published statements, Mike Newell expressed his intent to limit extravagant visual effects to those required by the story and to make a stylistic break from the lighter tone of the previous films to reflect the inherent malevolence of teen culture and the critical narrative progress of Voldemort's regeneration.[20] This shift in the approach is also reflected in Doyle's film music. First, the pattern of representing magic with non-diegetic music and the lack of magic with the absence of music is entirely disrupted, in part because the film narrative does not begin at the Dursleys' home in the non-magical world: there is no clear visual contrast between Muggle and magical realms. In addition, the fourth film includes the least amount of non-diegetic music and the most examples of source music, including tournament fanfares, folk music, school songs and hymns, and music for different dances. This grounds the narrative in the familiar rather than in the fantastic. As such, music does not often parallel magical gestures or magical events except when source music is already present. For instance, when Professor Moody takes a swig from his hip flask (later revealed to hold magic polyjuice potion) during the Hogwarts Yule Ball, a flute from the waltz orchestra descends with his physical gesture. However, when Professor Moody takes a swig from the flask in other scenes without source music, his physical gesture is not accompanied by any music at all. Furthermore, Doyle rarely uses instrumental signifiers for magic such as harp, celeste or choral voices in the service of cueing magical events; most non-diegetic musical themes are diatonic, with the exception of leitmotifs for Voldemort; and all non-diegetic themes are in martial or hymnlike duple metre.[21] According to convention, as well as following Johnson and Larson's and Larson and VanHandel's theories of metaphor in music, diatonicism and duple metres tend to provide an atmosphere of order and rationality and align with normal listener expectations, rather than disrupting them with non-diatonic pitches or uneven rhythms. Ultimately, realistic familiarity is emphasized in the music more than magic or fantasy.

That being said, non-diegetic music is used prominently to signify dark magic in the lengthy scene depicting the physical regeneration of the adversary Lord Voldemort and the reorganization of malevolent magical forces around him in a mysterious graveyard.[22] The length of this scene is 9 minutes 53 seconds and non-diegetic music is heard for 9 minutes 38 seconds of it. The duration and prominence of musical underscore in the scene is unlike any other in *The Goblet of Fire*. The effect of this isolated occurrence is that Harry's magical world seems more normal, while only the rise of evil is represented as truly fantastic. Although certainly a standard mode of cinema (and not, for instance, a propaganda statement in favour of evil), the musical emphasis on the rise of evil magic funnels the dramatic tension and spectacle into this scene similarly to the way that the musical emphasis on benevolent magic in the earlier films adds to the excitement and spectacle of the fantasy world in general.

Table 10.4 shows how malevolent magic – as well as emotion – is emphasized with music in the graveyard scene, but benevolent magic is not; and illustrates

Table 10.4 The alternation of silence and non-diegetic music as a representation of benevolent and malevolent magic

	Images without music	*Images with music*
1.	A portkey transports boys from Hogwarts to a graveyard	
2.	Harry and Cedric wonder where they are	
3.		Harry recognizes the mysterious graveyard
4.		Cedric acknowledges the role of the portkey
5.		Wormtail arrives and kills Cedric
6.		A potion is made on behalf of Voldemort
7.		Voldemort regenerates in physical form
8.		Voldemort beckons his minions (Death Eaters)
9.		Voldemort chastises his minions
10.		Voldemort addresses Harry
11.		Voldemort explains Harry's protective magic
12.		Voldemort claims supremacy over Harry
13.		Voldemort tortures Harry
14.		Voldemort challenges Harry to a duel
15.		Harry's wand locks with Voldemort's wand
16.		Voldemort's murder victims emerge as spirits
17.		The spirits give protective advice to Harry
18.		Harry releases his wand lock with Voldemort
19.		Harry escapes by way of the portkey
20.		Voldemort expresses frustration at his failure
21.	Harry (with Cedric's body) returns to Hogwarts	
22.	The school band begins to play a victory march	

the striking difference between the use of non-diegetic music in *The Goblet of Fire* compared with the preceding three *Harry Potter* films. Instead of alternating orchestral music with specific images (as was done in the preceding films), it is applied without break to the many events that occur during the roughly 10-minute-long graveyard scene. While there is no music present before or after malevolent magic is immediately at hand, there is non-stop music throughout the rise of Voldemort and the gathering of his evil forces. While the majority of this musical underscore is built on dissonance, the exception occurs when acts of benevolent magic (sections 16–18) are accompanied by a lyrical, diatonic leitmotif signifying Harry's inner emotions but not signifying magic itself.[23] In other words, the music privileges emotion and heightens the rise of evil but does not generally acknowledge magic or fantasy. Ultimately, the music for the fourth film makes the story dramatic and 'real', but not necessarily magical.

The pattern of equating non-diegetic music with magic is reinstated in the fifth film, *The Order of the Phoenix*, again in varied form. Nicholas Hooper's music reflects David Yates's desire to focus on the emotional and psychological aspects of the story, while still taking the magical component seriously.[24] Non-diegetic music is regularly aligned with magical events, and musical themes for magical and emotional ideas often include established instrumental signifiers of both benevolent magic (celeste, harp, treble choral voices and windchimes) and malevolent magic (*col legno* strings, bass choral voices and prepared piano). The seamless integration of source scoring with digital sound effects (and vice versa) both enriches and complicates the relationship between music and magic, much as the integration of source music and non-diegetic music does in the third film.

For example, the opening scene of the fifth film manages to include source music, source scoring, non-diegetic music, musical silence, heightened source sounds and instrumental signifiers for benevolent and malevolent magic. Although the organization of music and image recalls the original relationship between musical silence in the Muggle world and non-diegetic music when magic is present, it does not follow Williams's model rigorously. When the narrative begins, implied diegetic sounds – a weather forecaster announcing a heatwave and piano music – fade in over the orchestral main title music, then fade out as the camera focuses in on the opening shot of Harry sitting alone in a park. A wind instrument echoing the sound of cicadas, a hot-weather insect, continues before being replaced by other diegetic sounds such as squeaky playground equipment when dialogue begins. A few instruments enter softly on slowly changing pitches to reflect Harry's rising emotions as he and his cousin Dudley exchange insults, establishing low-volume underscoring as a signifier of Harry's personal emotions. Then, fuller-volume instruments along with sound effects enter as foreboding clouds encroach and the hot sky above them turns dark and erupts into a rainstorm. Abruptly, only narrative sounds continue as Harry and his cousin run for cover from the storm, until the magical, malevolent Dementors – who by implication brought the summer storm – descend upon them in an underpass. At this point, dissonant orchestral strings, a low-voiced choir and heightened narrative sounds, such as a spluttering underpass light, enter the viewer's aural sphere to reflect the malevolent magical presence, much as 'Hedwig's Theme' entered the aural sphere to reflect a benevolent magical presence in the earliest films. Harry responds to the Dementor attack by casting the protective Patronus charm, which is accompanied by treble choir voices and sound effects. In contrast to the low-volume underscoring of Harry's emotions, full-volume underscore, including instrumental signifiers for the fantastic such as choral voices, is thus established as a signifier of magical events.

Hooper's approach synthesizes elements from the previous films and adds some new ideas. As in the first three films, the music highlights the fantastic by regularly aligning with images of magical events and by using specific instrumentation to signify magical events. As in the fourth film, the music is also grounded in the familiar by favouring diatonicism and standard harmonic progressions. The music, however, breaks from the previous approaches by employing energetic, compound metres and polyrhythms and by including modern orchestral percussion instruments from different world traditions.

Furthermore, several examples of Hooper's source scoring parallel Harry's visual experience of the wizarding world in such a way that the magical world itself seems to exude music.[25] This approach allows the viewer to experience the fantasy realm as the characters might and increases the energy and the emotional appeal of magic. For instance, when Harry enters the Ministry of Magic, complex musical underscoring represents what he sees as his eyes travel across different pockets of activity, opulence and edifices of power. The music begins when Harry enters the building, becomes louder as he sees grander and more magical aspects of the Ministry, then becomes softer and changes course when Harry leaves the main floor of the building in a lift. An ostinato in the strings suggests the turning sound of the wheels of business – dozens of actual wheels are shown turning like ceiling fans in the windows of the ministry's atrium; the tinkle of the glockenspiel imitates the sparkling twinkle of architectural ornaments, golden statues and glossy glass panes in the atrium; and the melody played by low brass parallels the din of human voices and activity heard within the cathedral-like space. Similar to the approach in the third film, this amplifies the experience of magic in the magical world and also subtly blurs the distinctions between reality and fantasy rather than clarifying the differences as the first two films do, or ignoring the differences as the fourth film does.

Applications of and variations on John Williams's 'Hedwig's Theme' in the first five films

John Williams's 'Hedwig's Theme' has become emblematic of the *Harry Potter* production series as a whole. Although all three composers have used the first melody from Williams's original three-section theme, each has moulded the tune to fit the interpretation of the film at hand. The changes to 'Hedwig's Theme' over the series of films provide specific evidence of the changing dramatic relationship between music and magic.

The Sorcerer's Stone includes over twenty-five separate statements of 'Hedwig's Theme' (at least one phrase in length).[26] The melodies for the three sections of the theme are shown in Figure 10.1, with the most commonly heard harmonies.[27] The first and second sections are heard most often, but all sections are aligned with images to signify the wonders, mysteries and idiosyncrasies of the magical world, and to identify key points in the narrative. Many of the statements of the theme feature celeste and sometimes include harp and

a) Section I

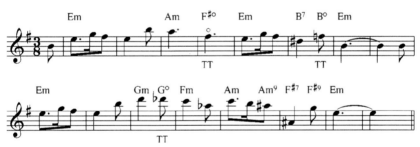

b) Section II

c) Section III

Figure 10.1 Author transcription of 'Hedwig's Theme' by John Williams from *Harry Potter and the Sorcerer's Stone*

choral voices also. As one can see from the example, the music itself evokes the fantastic by including the metaphorically less-grounded lilting rhythms of triple metre, melodic chromaticism, tritones – in particular the A sharps occurring at the end of each section of this E minor melody and the tritones (labelled TT) within the diminished chords – and several alternatives to standard harmonic expectations.

Similarly, *The Chamber of Secrets* includes twenty-three separate statements of 'Hedwig's Theme'. Again, three sections of the theme align with images to signify magical events and cue critical moments in the drama, though the third section is heard more often than in the first film. As in the first film, the performance of the theme usually includes instrumental signifiers of the fantastic. Figure 10.2 shows an alternative, more ominous-sounding bass line and harmonic progression used in the second section (with sustained strings, during the opening titles) that reflects a darker tone in the second film. Otherwise, the music itself is the same and continues to include musical codes for the fantastic.

The role of 'Hedwig's Theme' is markedly reduced in *The Prisoner of Azkaban*, although it continues to cue important magical and dramatic events. 'Hedwig's Theme' occurs only eight times – that is, only six times in the body of the film plus once more during both the opening title and end credits – and is reduced to the first section, a reduction that the subsequent composers follow.[28] Nevertheless, the melody, harmony and instrumentation remain the same as in the first films.

A new theme, 'Double Trouble', which is melodically related to the third section of 'Hedwig's Theme' (see Figure 10.1c), aligns with film images to signify the absurd, medieval and mischievous aspects of the magical world and is heard seven times during the third film, more often than 'Hedwig's Theme' itself. 'Double Trouble' also includes chromaticism and unusual harmonies and is performed on early wind instruments to signify the medieval. The first phrase of this theme is provided in Figure 10.3. However, another new theme, representing Harry's emotional world (entitled 'A Window To The Past' on the soundtrack CD), is the most often-heard theme in the third film, occurring

Figure 10.2 Author transcription of 'Hedwig's Theme', section II, with a more ominous-sounding bass line for *The Chamber of Secrets*

Figure 10.3 'Double Trouble' (first phrase) from Williams (2004: 17). Words and music by John Williams. © 2004 Warner-Barham Music, LLC. All rights reserved. Used with permission.

eleven separate times, not counting repeats. Clearly stated, 'Hedwig's Theme' shares the spotlight with two other themes that signify the medieval landscape and Harry's emotional world, thus supporting the idea that the role of magic has relaxed in order to emphasize the emotional core of the film.

Striking changes occur to 'Hedwig's Theme' in *The Goblet of Fire*. After the opening titles, the theme cues an important dramatic event on only one occasion: Harry's journey by train to Hogwarts.[29] In both cases – the opening title and the journey to Hogwarts – only the first section is used. At just 15 seconds, the length of these two musical cues is also much shorter than the similarly placed cues in the preceding films, which range from 40 seconds to more than two minutes. Although the first statement includes shimmering cymbals, neither of the statements includes celeste, harp or voices.[30] Moreover, Patrick Doyle makes changes to Williams's original melody and rhythm that result in a grounded duple rather than lilting triple metre, less chromaticism, fewer tritones and harmonic progressions that follow, rather than diverge from, listener expectation, reinforcing the emphasis on the familiar rather than on the fantastic. Figure 10.4 shows the melody and harmony for the first occurrence, with asterisks to indicate melodic pitches that are different from Williams's original. No other musical theme takes over as a signifier of the fantastic within the score as a whole. However, the most often-heard leitmotif is one that signifies Voldemort and the rise of evil, supporting the idea that the relationship between non-diegetic music and magic is disrupted in this film, except for the portrayal of Voldemort's return to power.

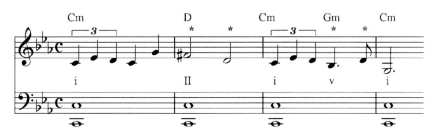

Figure 10.4 Author transcription of 'Hedwig's Theme' from the opening title in *The Goblet of Fire*

Like the third film, the fifth film, *The Order of the Phoenix*, includes eight statements of 'Hedwig's Theme' to signify magical events and to cue narrative progress. Some, but not all, deployments of the theme use instrumental signifiers for the fantastic, such as celeste, harp and windchimes. All of the occurrences use only the first section of Williams's original melody with the chromaticism and triple metre and some less usual harmonies reinstated, though Hooper sometimes concludes the theme with his own variation. As in the fourth film, the most prominent statements are heard during the opening film titles and during Harry's journey by train to Hogwarts. In the first example (Figure 10.5a), the lack of harmonic rhythm makes the triple-metre melody sound dreamlike, as does the gradual slowing and fading during the final pitches, an allusion to the second section of Williams's original theme.[31] In other words, the music helps the viewer to enter Harry's dreamlike fantasy world, much as Harry will enter the world of magic in the film.[32] In the second statement (Figure 10.5b), the ostinato harmony in the first section imitates the movement of train wheels, while the call-and-response melody sequence carries the listener away much as Harry is carried away to Hogwarts. This provides another example of how Hooper uses musical movement to represent visual movement. No other single theme usurps 'Hedwig's Theme' in its number of occurrences but many of the

a) opening title

b) the journey to Hogwarts

Figure 10.5 Author transcription of 'Hedwig's Theme' in *The Order of the Phoenix*

new themes – including 'The Flight Of The Order', 'Dumbledore's Army', the Patronus theme and 'The Kiss' – relate to Harry's joyful, emotional experiences.

Conclusion

Fans are passionate about the *Harry Potter* books and, following suit, the *Harry Potter* films have also attracted significant attention. They appeal to people for different reasons and at different levels and many have strong opinions about which films represent the story best. While fans of the novels may bring many interpretations to the story, film directors have imposed narrower interpretations on each film, based on what each believes the narrative is really about. Within the *Harry Potter* film franchise, four different director/composer collaborations have created four very different interpretations of the story. Similarly, the music demonstrates different possibilities for the representation of magic and fantasy within a single fantasy-film series.

Rowling's novels establish a direct relationship between music-making and magic, but the films do not; instead, the film-makers include varied relationships between non-diegetic music and magic. I have shown how this changing dramatic relationship illustrates and explains the significant aesthetic differences between the films: although magic is at the core of Rowling's *Harry Potter* narrative, the films feel individual because each director/composer collaboration made its own decisions about the degree to which fantasy should drive the story, and these decisions are reflected in the distinctly different musical soundtracks. Although the film images and dialogue always include some magic (by virtue of Rowling's original design), it is the *Harry Potter* film music that truly guides the imaginations and emotions of viewers in order to realize the fantasy – whatever degree of fantasy is represented, that is.

When the music from the first two films is organized to emphasize fantasy in traditional, theatrical ways, the approach elevates imagination and escapism and portrays the magical world as more different from and more appealing than our own. When the music from the third film enriches the fantasy with music that slips between source and non-diegetic sound and emphasizes new themes that highlight Harry's emotional world, the approach integrates real human struggles into the world of fantasy and portrays the magical world as different from but just as complex as our own. Additionally, this approach allows viewers to experience the magical world, rather than simply witness it. When the music from the fourth film emphasizes the familiar with source music but does not emphasize magic except for the rise of evil, the approach recontextualizes the fantasy realm as a realistic world in which human dramas play out and in which evil is real and threatening. When the fifth film, much like the third, dramatizes the fantasy with sounds that slip between source and non-diegetic music and elevates new themes to highlight Harry's emotional experiences, the approach (re)recontextualizes the human drama into the fantastical realm and portrays the magical world as an appealing parallel landscape.

The examination of changing dramatic approaches to the musical representation of magic serves as a reminder of the ways that image is manipulated with the addition of music and of the malleability of musical meaning in general. Although the technical changes that I relay in my analysis may not be perceived in the same way or in as much detail by every filmgoer, they clearly account for some of the aesthetic differences that fans and critics have publicly stated in discussions of the films as representations of Rowling's fantasy novels. Furthermore, all cinema is fantasy to a degree, and this study also reminds us that the world of film provides a way for viewers to play out the way they relate with others and the world they live in – either magical or Muggle. Moreover, the traditional role of film music is to light the course of imagination and reveal the emotion within the narrative. In the case of the *Harry Potter* films, filmgoers are able to play out and respond to different parts of their imaginations and emotions over the course of the series because each set of film-makers uses music to guide the interpretation of the fantasy world in a different way.

Notes

1. Early fan discussions on fan sites such as *MuggleNet* and *The Leaky Cauldron* often focused on the magical aspects of Harry's wizarding world. For a history of the popularity and marketing of the series, see Susan Gunelius (2008). For a history of censorship and criticism of the magic in the books, see Suman Gupta (2003: 17–18). Also see Richard Abanes (2001), Connie Neal (2001), and 'The Potter Phenomenon', *BBC News*, 18 February 2003 (http://news.bbc.co.uk/2/hi/entertainment/820885.stm; accessed 16 March 2008), for discussions on religious perspectives and problems with the series.

2. For instance, see Roger Ebert, 'Harry Potter and the Sorcerer's Stone', *Chicago Sun Times*, 16 November 2001 (http://rogerebert.suntimes.com/apps/pbcs/dll/article?AID=/20011116/REVIEWS/11116031/1023; accessed 10 August 2010); and Roger Ebert, 'Harry Potter and the Chamber of Secrets', *Chicago Sun Times*, 15 November 2002 (http://rogerebert.suntimes.com/apps/pbcs.dll/article?AID=/20021115/REVIEWS/211150304; accessed 12 March 2009). For *The Prisoner of Azkaban*, see Eugene Novikov, 'From Page to Screen: Harry Potter and the Prisoner of Azkaban', *Cinematical.com*, 11 June 2008 (http://www.cinematical.com/2008/06/11/from-page-to-screen-harry-potter-and-the-prisoner-of-azkaban/; accessed 12 March 2009). Mike Newell's assessment of *The Goblet of Fire* as a thriller in his liner notes for the CD is also reflected in reviews of the film, such as those by Manohla Dargis, 'The Young Wizard Puts Away Childish Things',

New York Times, 17 November 2005 (http://movies.nytimes.com/2005/11/17/
movies/17pott.html; accessed 17 December 2005); and Kenneth Turan, '*Harry Potter
and the Goblet of Fire* movie review', *Los Angeles Times*, 17 November 2005 (http://
www.calendarlive.com/movies/turan/cl-et-harrypotter18nov18,0,410738.story;
accessed 10 March 2008). For *The Order of the Phoenix*, see Neil Yates's emphasis
on the psychological, emotional aspects of the story as noted in his interview
with Steve Daly, 'Harry the 5th', *Entertainment Weekly*, 13 July 2007 (http://www.
ew.com/ew/article/0,,20046055,00.html; accessed 29 March 2009); and reflected in
reviews by Wally Hammond, 'Harry Potter and the Order of the Phoenix', *Time
Out* (London), 11–17 July 2007 (http://www.timeout.com/film/reviews/82039/
harry-potter-and-the-order-of-the-phoenix.html; accessed 11 November 2009); and
Peter Travers, 'Harry Potter and the Order of the Phoenix', *Rolling Stone*, June 29
2007 (http://www.rollingstone.com/reviews/movie/15087359/review/15289225/
harry_potter_and_the_order_of_the_phoenix; accessed 11 July 2007).

3. These are among the adjectives used by reviews in the online magazine *Music
from the Movies* (http://www.musicfromthemovies.com).

4. For instance, Owen Gleiberman writes, "The fourth flick offers more magic,
[but] feels less magical." Gleiberman, 'Harry Potter and the Goblet of Fire
Movie Review', *Entertainment Weekly*, 6 November 2005 (http://www.ew.com/ew/
article/0,,1131187,00.html; accessed 17 December 2005).

5. Yates and Hooper continued to collaborate for the sixth instalment, *Harry Potter
and the Half-Blood Prince* (2009). The last instalment in the epic, *Harry Potter and
the Deathly Hallows*, is split into two films (2010 and 2011), directed by David
Yates with music by Alexandre Desplat.

6. Other epic adventures (e.g., the *Indiana Jones* films and the *Lord of the Rings* trilogy)
have maintained the same director and composer throughout. Similarly, while
some *Star Wars* episodes employed different directors (for *The Empire Strikes Back*
and *The Return of the Jedi*), John Williams composed scores for the entire saga,
re-using themes and maintaining a consistent style throughout. Other series (e.g.,
Superman) have hired new orchestrators and arrangers to work with previously
composed themes, thus contributing to a perception of musical continuity. The
production strategy of changing director/composer teams for high-profile film
series may be an emerging trend, as observed more recently in the *Twilight* saga.

7. I address this example and others from the novels in greater detail in the chapter
'Folklore and Vernacular Traditions at the Nexus of Music and Gender', in Webster
(2009), in which I argue that the social structures established by music events
in the novels are disrupted or altered in the film versions.

8. However, an alma-mater sounding march is heard in the musical soundtrack
at the end of the same scene as it appears in the film. Additionally, the words
of the Hogwarts school song described in the first book are performed with a
unified melody in a deleted scene included as an 'extra' on the DVD of *The Goblet
of Fire*.

9. Music is still used to soothe the three-headed dog in the film, but the relationship
between music and magic is less clear because a harp is already playing when

Harry and his friends arrive on the scene. Because we do not see how a character uses magic to create music, or vice versa, the music-to-magic relationship is only implied, rather than explicit, for the viewer.

10. These include well-known musicians from British rock bands: Jarvis Cocker and Steve Mackay (Pulp); Phil Selway and Johnny Greenwood (Radiohead); Jason Buckle (All Seeing I); and Steven Claydon (Add N to (X)).

11. Ian Q. Hunter (2007: 154), for example, argues against the need for literary fidelity in his discussion of the complexity of fantasy literature in relation to film adaptations.

12. Thanos Fourgiotis (1992), 'John Williams Interview', *Cinema Magazine* (http://www.cswu.cz/johnwilliams/interview/jw-cinema.html; accessed 9 June 2006).

13. The strategy for establishing music as a signifier of magic in *Harry Potter* is similar to the strategy that James Buhler (2000: 37) describes as linking music and the production of myth in *Star Wars*.

14. For instance, Tchaikovsky used the harp in his ballets *Swan Lake*, *Sleeping Beauty* and *The Nutcracker* to support supernatural characters, places and events. Similarly, he used celeste to accompany the dance of the Sugar Plum Fairy in *The Nutcracker*. See Thérèse Hurley (2007) and Roland John Wiley (1985). Harp, celeste and choral voices have also been irrevocably established as aspects of magic in fantasy cinema in scores such as Danny Elfman's *Edward Scissorhands* (1990), as discussed by Janet K. Halfyard (2004: 32–3).

15. Although music is not entirely absent from the Dursleys' non-magical home in the second film, *The Chamber of Secrets*, the pattern is generally the same: scenes without magical events generally do not include non-diegetic music, while scenes with magical events (and scenes in the magical world) generally do.

16. See J. Jensen and D. Fierman, 'Inside Harry Potter', *Entertainment Weekly*, 14 September 2001 (http://www.ew.com/ew/article/0,,254808,00.html; accessed 17 September 2007).

17. Following the arguments presented by Johnson and Larson (2003) and Larson and VanHandel (2005) regarding the metaphors of musical motion, waltz-tempo triple metre may be perceived as less grounded, illogical or irrational when compared with the expectations of duple metre. Furthermore, the use of a waltzing triple metre has long been used to suggest the irrational realm – from Violetta's waltzes in Verdi's *La Traviata* to the waltzes in Elfman's *Edward Scissorhands* – through the association of this metre with the body and dance (McClary, 1991: 17). Halfyard (2010) examines the use of augmented fourths as a traditional signifier of the supernatural realm, while McClary discusses how the use of chromaticism in classical music often depicts madness or genius, but not the normative realm (*ibid.*: 82), and how standard harmonic progressions relate to the notion of 'musical reason', thus conversely suggesting that unusual harmonies suggest irrationality, or a lack of reason (*ibid.*: xv). This clearly relates Harry Potter's wizarding world as a realm apart from reason and rational, normative experience.

18. See Lizo Mzimba, 'Alfonso Cuarón: The Man behind the Magic,' *Newsround*, 28 May 2004 (http://news.bbc.co.uk/cbbcnews/hi/tv_film/newsid_3758000/3758101.stm; accessed 11 January 2009).

19. Another notable example of this strategy occurs when Harry accidentally inflates his Aunt Marge. The non-diegetic waltz that accompanies Aunt Marge's inflation changes to a diegetic tango heard while Dudley Dursley watches a dancer and her blow-up partner on television, then makes a transition again to a non-diegetic waltz as Harry gazes at a magical photo of his parents dancing. The continuity of dance music creates segues between these magical and mundane events while also suturing the disparate images to emphasize the spectrum of Harry's emotional experiences of family.

20. See, for example, the liner notes by Patrick Doyle, *Harry Potter and the Goblet of Fire* (2005), performed by the London Symphony Orchestra, conducted by James Shearman, Warner Bros. 49631 [CD]. Newell's intentions are also discussed in 'British Director Tackles *Goblet of Fire*', *Associated Press*, 21 November 2005 (http://www.cnn.com/2005/SHOWBIZ/Movies/11/21/mike.newell.ap/index.html; accessed 22 November 2005); and 'Harry Potter Director, Mike Newell, Talks to Ian Nathan about the Goblet of Fire', *Evening Standard*, 27 October 2005 (http://www.highbeam.com/doc/1G1-138022255.html; accessed 22 November 2005).

21. Only source music dances are in dancelike triple metre. Otherwise, the music does not include the codes for the irrational or fantastic found in the previous films.

22. Certainly, non-diegetic music accompanies other exciting, action-oriented scenes, such as when Harry outwits a dragon, but in these cases the musical underscore stops for periods of time to make way for other source sounds rather than scoring continuously.

23. This leitmotif for inner emotions is heard clearly in the 'Harry In Winter' track on *The Goblet of Fire* soundtrack CD, while the music for the graveyard scene specifically is found in 'Voldemort' on the same CD.

24. See Steve Daly, cited in note 2.

25. This seems to be an inverse relationship to Rowling's novels, in which descriptions of music result in magic.

26. I count entrances of the theme at least a phrase in length, but not continuations of the theme. If one counts the occurrence of each of the theme's three sections, regardless of whether another section has just been heard, there are over forty statements of the theme throughout the film.

27. Not all of the following transcriptions of the film soundtrack by me are congruent with those found in published solo piano scores, since published scores typically only provide John Williams's original (simplified, non-orchestral) version of 'Hedwig's Theme'.

28. A portion of the third section of 'Hedwig's Theme' is also stated in the last narrative scene before the credits.

29. The theme is also used on one other occasion to accompany an overhead shot of Hogwarts Castle, though this is not a critical moment in the drama. Furthermore,

because this is the first film in the series to eliminate 'Hedwig's Theme' from both the ending scenes and the end credits, the importance of magic is not summarized at the bookends of the film as it is in the previous films.

30. Celeste can be heard in the transition between the first statement of the theme and the next phrase of music, but is not in the foreground of sound, nor is it used as a signifier for magic.

31. The subsequent phrase of the theme reintroduces the more customary harmonic rhythm of the theme.

32. Fans of the film also know that dreams play an important role in the plot of *The Order of the Phoenix*.

References

Abanes, R. (2001), *Harry Potter and the Bible*, Camp Hill, PA: Horizon.

Buhler, J. (2000), '*Star Wars*, Music, and Myth', in J. Buhler, C. Flinn and D. Neumeyer (eds), *Music and Cinema*, Hanover, NH: Wesleyan University Press, pp. 33–57.

Gorbman, C. (1987), *Unheard Melodies: Narrative Film Music*, Bloomington: University of Indiana Press/London: BFI.

Gupta, S. (2003), *Re-reading Harry Potter*, New York: Palgrave Macmillan.

Gunelius, S. (2008), *Harry Potter: The Story of a Global Business Phenomenon*, New York: Palgrave Macmillan.

Halfyard, J. K. (2004), *Danny Elfman's Batman: A Film Score Guide*, Lanham, MD: Scarecrow Press.

Halfyard, J. K. (2010), 'Mischief Afoot: Supernatural Horror-Comedies and the *Diabolus in Musica*', in N. Lerner (ed.), *Music in the Horror Film: Listening to Fear*, New York: Routledge, pp. 21–37.

Hunter, I. Q. (2007), 'Post-classical Fantasy Cinema: *The Lord of the Rings*', in D. Cartmell and I. Whelehan (eds), *The Cambridge Companion to Literature on Screen*, Cambridge: Cambridge University Press, pp. 154–66.

Hurley, T. (2007), 'Opening the Door to a Fairy-tale World: Tchaikovsky's Ballet Music', in Marion Kant (ed.), *The Cambridge Companion to Ballet*, Cambridge: Cambridge University Press, pp. 164–74.

Johnson, M. L., and Larson, S. (2003), ' "Something in the Way She Moves": Metaphors of Musical Motion', *Metaphor and Symbol*, 18(2), 63–84.

Kalinak, K. (1997), *Settling the Score: Music and the Classical Hollywood Film*, Madison: University of Wisconsin.

Kassabian, A. (2001), *Hearing Film: Tracking Identifications in Contemporary Hollywood Film Music*, London: Routledge.

Larson, S., and VanHandel, L. (2005), 'Measuring Musical Forces', *Music Perception*, 23(2), 119–36.

McClary, Susan (1991), *Feminine Endings: Music, Gender, and Sexuality*. Minneapolis: University of Minnesota.

Neal, C. (2001), *What's a Christian to Do with Harry Potter?* Colorado Springs: WaterBrook, 2001.

Rowling, J. K. (1997), *Harry Potter and the Sorcerer's Stone*, New York: Scholastic.

Rowling, J. K. (1998), *Harry Potter and the Chamber of Secrets*, New York: Scholastic.

Rowling, J. K. (1999), *Harry Potter and the Prisoner of Azkaban*, New York: Scholastic.

Rowling, J. K. (2000), *Harry Potter and the Goblet of Fire*, New York: Scholastic.

Rowling, J. K. (2003), *Harry Potter and the Order of the Phoenix*, New York: Scholastic.

Rowling, J. K. (2005), *Harry Potter and the Half-Blood Prince*, New York: Scholastic.

Rowling, J. K. (2007), *Harry Potter and the Deathly Hallows*, New York: Scholastic.

Smart, M. A. (2004), *Mimomania: Music and Gesture in Nineteenth-century Opera*, Berkeley: University of California Press.

Webster, J. (2009), 'The Music of Harry Potter: Continuity and Change in the First Five Films', PhD dissertation, University of Oregon.

Wiley, R. J. (1985), *Tchaikovsky's Ballets*, Oxford: Oxford University Press.

Williams, J. (2004), *Selected Themes from the Motion Picture* Harry Potter and the Prisoner of Azkaban – *Piano Solos*, arr. B. Galliford, E. Neuburg and T. Edmondson, Van Nuys, CA: Warner-Barham.

11 Superconductors

Music, Fantasy and Science in The Sorcerer's Apprentice

Janet K. Halfyard

The Sorcerer's Apprentice (John Turteltaub, 2010) is one of the many films that owe their existence in significant part to the success of the *Harry Potter* franchise. All of these films might be looked on as a variation on Joseph Campbell's concept of the hero's journey: the hero is called to adventure, crosses the threshold to the underworld, undergoes trials in order to complete a quest, and then returns to the world, hopefully successful in his mission and bestowing a boon upon us that makes the world a better place for all (see Campbell, 1949). For Harry Potter and his imitators, the structure of the narrative presents an apparently normal boy (occasionally a girl) who learns he has extraordinary powers and a great destiny. Thus called to adventure, he crosses from the everyday world into the metaphorical underworld of myth and magic to complete a quest that invariably entails defeating some terrible evil; his success ensures a safer world for all of us.

It would be hard to argue that *The Sorcerer's Apprentice* is a great film: the plot skates so close to the completely unoriginal that it could easily have been an outright failure, and many critics were not especially kind to it. Tim Robey in the UK's *Daily Telegraph* described is as "an unsubtle ... lunge at the mainstream zeitgeist" but allowed that it was "passably diverting".[1] The most frequent criticisms in reviews were its predictability and obvious debt to *Harry Potter*. Nonetheless, a number of elements in the film allow it to explore some unusual and genuinely interesting narrative territory around the relationship between science and magic, and much of this interest is created through sound, a combination of scoring, popular music, sound design and musical intertextuality.

Intertextuality

The very premise of this film places music centrally within the narrative from the outset thanks to the film's title: 'The Sorcerer's Apprentice' (*L'Apprenti sorcier*) is a symphonic poem written in 1897 by Paul Dukas, based on a poem by Goethe, itself based on a second-century AD Greek text by Lucian. The piece's popularity in the twentieth century was ensured by Disney's 1940 film *Fantasia*, in which Leopold Stokowski introduces and conducts the Dukas while its story is acted out in animated form by Mickey Mouse as the apprentice. The 2010 film is also a Disney production and this makes possible the detailed narrative and musical allusions to *Fantasia* and Dukas that might otherwise have been prevented by copyright issues. In fact, one suspects that the title of the film and the *Fantasia* allusions may well have come first, with a modern-day magical plot built around them in a way not dissimilar to the way the films of the *Pirates of the Caribbean* series (2003–11) – also produced by Jerry Bruckheimer – were built around the long-standing Disney theme-park ride of the same name.

At the very centre of the film (one hour into its two-hour duration) is a set piece that recreates the *Fantasia* animation, with the protagonist, Dave (Jay Baruchel), in the role of Mickey Mouse. In *Fantasia*, Mickey has been instructed by the sorcerer to fill a great vat with water. The sorcerer leaves and Mickey uses the wizard's book of magic and pointed hat to cast a spell on a broom so it will do the work for him. The broom sprouts arms and begins work while Mickey falls asleep; on waking he finds he does not know how to make the broom stop, even though the vat is now full. In desperation he takes an axe and chops the broom to pieces, but each broken piece of wood then regenerates into a new broom with arms and buckets, and this army of workers continues to fetch water until the sorcerer's workroom is entirely flooded. The sorcerer returns in the nick of time to save Mickey from drowning and gets rid of both brooms and water. All of this is played out to Stokowski's rendition of Dukas: at the end of the sequence, we see Mickey 'out of character' talking to him. There is also an internal musical allusion in the way that Mickey's gestures when casting the spell and directing the broom mimic those of a musical conductor. In his dream sequence, he very obviously takes on the role of a conductor with stars and comets as his orchestra.

When translated into the 2010 film, there are numerous musical and visual connections. Visually, the size, shape and appearance of the sorcerer's spell book are repeated by the *Incantus*, the book the wizard Balthazar (Nicholas Cage) gives to Dave and from which he extracts the fateful clean-up spell; both Dave and Mickey wear red hooded tops; both use conducting gestures when directing their spells; and although Dave mostly brings mops to life, their shape mimics the shape of the brooms in *Fantasia*. Dave attempts to chop a mop into pieces but fails (although the mop is clearly frightened); and Balthazar, like *Fantasia*'s sorcerer, returns just in time to save Dave from near-certain death with the same simple gesture of dismissal.

Musically, what is written for this scene by Trevor Rabin uses the main theme from the Dukas and effectively composes a fantasia on the music of *Fantasia*. One might wonder why the film-makers did not simply use the Dukas in the same way that *Fantasia* did, but the Dukas is far longer than would have been appropriate for the sequence and using even part of it would still have required that the scene be shot and cut to fit the music. Rabin's fantasia employs the most famous theme and musical gestures of the Dukas but writes to the edited image, allowing the entire sequence to be realized in a little over 3 minutes rather than the 9 minutes of the *Fantasia* animation. Other than this scene at the centre of the film, however, the Dukas theme is not used in the score, although it does reappear in the end credits.

Apart from the film's title and this sequence, the film really has nothing in common with the *Fantasia* episode or with the Dukas piece, and on one level inserting this scene into the film might seem slightly gratuitous, a beside-the-point in-joke; intertextual, perhaps, but not really bringing anything to the audience's understanding of the film in any wider sense. The text of *Fantasia* is alluded to but what, if anything, that allusion means is rather less clear. This sets it apart from other cinematic and televisual allusions where the significance of the intertextual reference normally serves a clear function, whether that is humour or a more serious level of commentary on the text. In the opening of an episode from Season 3 of *The Simpsons*, 'Bart's Friend Falls in Love' (Fox, 7 May 1992), Bart and Homer re-enact the sequence from the opening of *Raiders of the Lost Ark* (Steven Spielberg, 1982) in which Indiana Jones steals an artefact before escaping from a huge rolling ball and a tribe of angry natives; and the comic allusion is made both more accessible and funnier by the use of John Williams's 'Raiders March' theme for Bart's escape. The musical and narrative idea of Indiana Jones and his heroic doings are intertextually superimposed over the image of Bart and his mischief, and this is where the humour lies, as well as in the absurdity of images and juxtapositions. The notoriously overweight Homer falls down the stairs and effectively transforms into the huge stone ball that threatened to crush Indiana Jones as he made his escape in Spielberg's film; Bart reaches back under the closing garage door to grab his baseball cap, recreating Indiana reaching for his trademark hat as an ancient door slides down behind him, thus making even more specific the reading of Bart as intrepid hero by allusive association with Jones. In *Platoon* (Oliver Stone, 1984), the allusion to the tragic and unnecessary deaths of other American heroes, which Samuel Barber's 'Adagio for Strings' (1936) brings to the death of Elias, adds both meaning and poignancy to the film. The scene and its music are still powerful without this additional level of meaning, but that wider reading is nonetheless available to those who recognize and are aware of the cultural meanings that have accrued to the Barber.[2]

In many respects, the allusion in *The Sorcerer's Apprentice* to *Fantasia* and Dukas operates on exactly the same level as the relationship between the film and theme-park versions of *Pirates of the Caribbean*: there is no actual meaning to be drawn from the intertextuality, and the act of recognition itself (whether of *Pirates*'s dog with keys in its mouth, or *Apprentice*'s mop being threatened with an axe) is the end that these allusions serve. This is not to say that recognition itself does not serve any function: there is a clear level of viewing (and listening) pleasure to be gained from the process of recognizing allusions such as these but, in the same way that the allusions to the theme-park ride in *Pirates* are utterly without further significance and therefore have no impact on the reading of a viewer who has not been on the ride, so too anyone who does not know *Fantasia* is not excluded from any further reading of the 2010 film that would be available to a viewer who is familiar with the 1940 sequence (and it is no longer a well-known film, being rarely broadcast and a collector's item even in DVD format). Nonetheless, the allusion is present; and if it adds no specific meaning to the narrative overall, it still has importance as the *raison d'être* of the 2010 film. This central sequence, therefore, becomes an *hommage*, a playful recreation that offers pleasure to the viewer in its own right and additional pleasures to those who recognize – musically, visually or both – that this sequence acknowledges the origins of the current narrative.

Science versus magic; science as magic

Science generally gets a bad press in fantasy films. Alex Worley has said, "If a fantasy film ever elucidates its magic through scientific reasoning it ceases to be fantasy" (2005: 11), and any attempts to explain magical events through science usually occur when characters are in denial, attempting to rationalize, contain and control their exposure to the supernatural. Moreover, the evil scientist is a stock character of the fantasy genre: the forces of science are often set against the forces of the fantastic, such as the conflict between the genuinely 'super' Mr Incredible and the scientifically enhanced Buddy (aka Syndrome) in *The Incredibles* (Brad Bird, 2006), or the episode in *Lara Croft Tomb Raider: The Cradle of Life* (Jan de Bont, 2003) where the intrepid explorer seeks to obtain a magical artefact to prevent it falling into the hands of evil scientists who wish to use it as a weapon. In *Spider-Man* (Sam Raimi, 2002), Peter Parker may establish his credentials as a nerd by being good at science, but he pursues a more artistic career in photography, while his nemesis, Norman Osborn, is an archetypal mad scientist who uses himself as an experimental subject and transforms into the Green Goblin. Although its eponymous doctor is more misguided than truly evil, Katherine Fowkes identifies *Frankenstein* as a hybrid narrative in which fantasy is combined with gothic horror, one of its key ideas being the "potentially dehumanizing effects of science and technology" (2010: 20). Even where there is no intention to do harm, it would seem that science itself – and the power it offers – will corrupt those who pursue it.

The idea of science as evil extends beyond fantasy cinema, however, into culture at large in a way that conflates science and black magic. The central thesis of Glen Scott Allen's book, *Master Mechanics & Wicked Wizards* (2009), is that Americans "love engineers, seeing them as pragmatic 'master mechanic' everymen producing useful inventions for their communities" but "loathe theoretical scientists, seeing them as aristocratic 'wicked wizards' cut off from family and community and bent on world domination' (Davis, 2010: 115). Allen positions the figure of the evil scientist in the wider cultural terms of how American culture came to distrust science during the twentieth century, citing a 1933 article by Read Bain entitled 'Scientist as Citizen': "Scientists ... more than any other single factor, threaten the persistence of Western Culture ... They are ... workers of Black Magic, weavers of weird spells, progenitors of destruction" (Read Bain, 1933, quoted in Allen, 2009: 76).

There appears, then, to be a fairly clear cultural connection between the assumed evils of science and the potential evils of magic; in this construction, it is the potential for magic's power to be used for self-serving, world-dominating destruction that is allied with science's potential to be used to similar ends.

However, *The Sorcerer's Apprentice* takes a more subtle approach to this construction of the relationship between science and the fantastic. In the process it manages to create a true fantasy narrative in which science is an important component but one which does not undermine the essentially fantastic nature of magic.

Initially, the film seems to occupy traditional fantasy territory very comfortably. It starts with a flashback to the distant past, where the wizard Merlin battles the evil sorceress Morgana le Fay (Alice Krige), who is attempting a spell named the Rising. This will awaken an army of the dead: like all evil scientists/ wicked wizards, Morgana seeks world domination. Although she kills Merlin, she is trapped in a device, the grimhold, along with one of Merlin's three apprentices, Veronica (Monica Bellucci). The other two apprentices are the treacherous Horvath (Alfred Molina), who has gone over to Morgana's camp, and Balthazar, who now takes on the task of finding the 'prime Merlinian', Merlin's true successor in sorcery and the only one who can vanquish Morgana. Before dying, Merlin grants his apprentices (including, apparently, Horvath) extended life and youth until such time as Morgana is finally defeated.

So far, so fantastic. It takes Balthazar more than a thousand years to find his prime Merlinian, eventually encountering him – a ten-year-old boy named David Stutler (Jake Cherry) – in 2000. Things go rather badly wrong and Balthazar and Horvath are sucked into a magical urn that does not release them for another ten years. When we next encounter the grown-up Dave in 2010 (on the day they escape their mystical prison), we find him as a college physics major. A central element of the film from this point on is his personal science project, which uses an array of Tesla coils to generate plasma bolts that evoke nothing so much as early science-fiction cinema: elaborate metal coils, emitting what look like lightning bolts, that seem to belong firmly in the territory of the mad scientist.[3] It is through Dave, then, that science first enters the film. It forms the ground against which he attempts to understand and reconcile himself with magic and the means by which he ultimately finds his full potential as a sorcerer. Dave himself is the pivotal character in whom science and magic coexist as equally powerful aspects of his fantastic abilities and it is this which eventually gives him the edge that the prime Merlinian needs in order to overcome Morgana.

The positioning of Dave as a scientist and the connection that is drawn between this and his abilities as a sorcerer is nonetheless one of the most anti-fantastic notions of the film, taken in the wider context of how science and scientists are generally constructed in such narratives. Balthazar makes an explicit connection between science and magic in an awkwardly expositional speech (delivered at breakneck speed by Nicholas Cage) in which he causes a parking ticket to spontaneously combust. When Dave asks whether sorcery is science or magic, Balthazar enigmatically replies, "Yes and yes"; and with the combusting parking ticket demonstrates how a sorcerer can make fire by willing molecules to vibrate faster, using knowledge of the physical properties of matter in order to manipulate them, thus neatly eliding scientific knowledge with magical application.

This would appear to deny magic a fantastic nature: it can be explained in an apparently scientific manner, although it lapses back into fantasy with the idea that sorcerers use telekinetic mind control in order to manipulate matter into apparently magical responses and, oddly like Ming the Merciless, using a ring as the focus for this. The quasi-scientific explanations abound: Balthazar explains that the ring projects the electrical energy of the sorcerer's nervous system into the physical world and insists Dave should wear what the younger sorcerer describes as 'old man shoes' with leather uppers and soles, because the rubber soles of his usual sneakers will 'block the current'. The ring's function is later understood and explained by scientist Dave in a way that adds another layer of intertextual punning in reference to the gestures of Mickey Mouse in *Fantasia* – it acts as a conductor. When Horvath starts to kill other sorcerers and steal their rings to add to his own, Dave realizes that rather than giving him more power as such, they are making Horvath a better conductor, and this becomes the key to how Dave will defeat him. He rigs up a Tesla coil on the bonnet of Balthazar's car, which he then drives to the final confrontation. When Horvath raises his ring-laden staff to strike at Dave, Dave fires the coil, and the plasma bolt it emits is automatically drawn towards the staff and Horvath as the best conductor available, so eliminating one of the two major enemies our heroes are facing.[4]

Likewise, Dave uses science alongside magic to defeat Morgana. Having lost his ring to Horvath in an earlier scene, he discovers that, as the prime Merlinian, he can still perform magical acts without the ring – he himself has now become the 'best conductor'. He appears to try to attack Morgana with a string of magically made plasma bolts. She simply allows them to pass through her with no ill effect – but we see that Dave is in fact throwing these at a small building behind her: the door opens, and we see, amidst the cables and electrical junction boxes, a mop, brought to life and now helping Dave with his endgame. Cables snake out of the building and, as Morgana attacks Dave, he divides his energies between defending himself against her and directing the cables, which wind themselves up and around the various lamp posts surrounding the park. Thinking herself triumphant, Morgana declares that Dave may have Merlin's powers but he does not have his strength or skills. "You are weak", she gloats. "But I'm not alone", he replies. "I brought a little science with me." His animated mop pulls the switch on the electrical junction box and unleashes the improvised Tesla array, which bombards Morgana with plasma bolts of such intensity that she is annihilated.

Her defeat demonstrates that his command of magical and scientific power is greater than hers: it is still clearly just as destructive. However, a final scene points to the idea that this power, whether magical or scientific, is neutral and that it is the ends that its human users put it to that make it a force for either good or evil. Balthazar lies apparently dead from one of Morgana's plasma blasts; Dave announces that if she could kill him like that, maybe he can be brought back to life in the same way. Using plasma bolts as a magical defibrillator, he reverses Morgana's act by performing an identical action but with good intent instead of evil. Thus he creates the *eucatastrophe*, the good catastrophe that Tolkien identified as a central aspect of fantasy and its happy endings, the "sudden and miraculous grace" that celebrates the "joy of deliverance" from the *dyscatastrophe* of Balthazar's death (see Tolkien, 1966: 86).

Music, magic, sound and science (and love)

The basic musical strategy of the film is not unusual: this is a hybrid score, involving extracts of some dozen pre-existing popular-music tracks alongside an orchestral score. The popular music is strongly associated with Dave's love interest, Becky (Teresa Palmer), and her identity is established through the popular music she plays. The orchestral score occupies a great deal more of the soundtrack and is strongly thematic: there are two themes, to be discussed below, associated with Dave and Balthazar, and an additional 'quirky' theme that plays to the humour of their relationship with each other. Horvath is associated with a falling two-note motif characterized by low-pitched, heavily textured music including a variety of extreme scraping and sliding sounds that position him as abnormal and obviously evil. Morgana has her own theme, a chromatically rising four-note motif usually sung *détaché* by female voices, the rising contour of the theme evoking the Rising spell she aims to cast;[5] and Veronica, Balthazar's largely absent love interest (she spends most of the film inside the grimhold with Morgana), is nonetheless made present in the musical score with a lyrical guitar theme that evokes a suitably archaic lute.

Various sonic elements also support the narrative in expected Hollywood ways. All the evil characters – Morgana, Horvath and Drake Stone (Toby Kebbell)[6] – have English accents, playing to a long-established Hollywood tradition of associating evil with Europe and especially the English, whose colonial past always provides a handy metaphor for power-hungry evildoers seeking to undermine wholesome American values. All the good characters have American accents: logical enough for Dave and Becky but profoundly illogical for Balthazar, who must logically be English or at least European if he was Merlin's apprentice circa 700 AD.[7]

One of the principal sounds of the film is the very distinctive noise of the Tesla coils themselves and the Teslas are a key element in the way that the three most important thematic elements of the narrative – magic, science and love – are brought together in a score and sound design that are remarkably unified, so allowing these narrative elements to be unified in turn.

The Teslas are in fact the first piece of sound design we hear, although it is unlikely that the audience would be aware of it: in the opening credits, the Disney credit sequence does not use the standard 'When You Wish Upon A Star' music but a specially composed cue. The listening ear attributes the unfamiliar electronic sound that occurs as the Disney signature appears on screen in front of the enchanted castle to the visual shimmer surrounding the logo. Then, as lightning repeatedly strikes the ground and finally a tree in Bruckheimer's own production credit, it is matched each time with a harsh electronic buzz that later in the film is identified as the sound of a firing Tesla coil.

Practically the first thing we learn about twenty-year-old Dave (whom we meet around 10 minutes into the film) is that he is working on a Tesla-coil project. He has built an array of several Tesla coils in a disused subway station, although the ultimate goal of his experiment is never revealed: this is simply 'science' in popular cultural terms and Dave is a self-described science nerd. Having some useful and explicable outcome to the project is not necessary to the plot and so none is given. However, shortly after he tells us of his science project, he meets Becky, his soon-to-be love interest. Where he loves science, she loves music and has her own show on the college radio station. Later, in his lab working with the Tesla array, he tunes in to her show and as he fires up the coils, she announces that "This is Becky Barnes ... hoping that music is all around you" before playing 'Secrets' by OneRepublic. In reality, the sound of the Tesla coils would be far too loud for Dave to be able to hear the song but, in the fantasy of the film, he not only hears it but realizes that indeed music is all around him: the sounds produced by his Teslas are specific pitches that are harmonizing with the melody of the song. In a subsequent scene, he brings Becky back to his lab, and persuades her to get into the Faraday cage from which he then operates the array. He taps a few keys on his computer and the Teslas come to life, playing a fragment of Stevie Wonder's 'Superstition' – itself perhaps a sidewise acknowledgement of a plot that detaches magic from superstition and attaches it instead to science, because he cuts this fragment off very quickly.[8] He then taps a few more keys, and the Teslas now play 'Secrets'. This immediately takes on the role of being his and Becky's song. She is the one who knew it, the one who loves music, but he demonstrates his feelings for her by giving the song back to her mediated by the science that he loves, as represented by the Teslas. This, then, is the first concrete gesture towards the rehabilitation of science as a force that can be used for good in that Dave can use it to make a gesture of sincere emotion, which Becky receives with a certain amount of wonder and a clear return of affection. Becky and her music have changed Dave and his relationship with science. As he tells her in this scene, "Two years I'm down here working with them and they're making their own music and it was lost on me, I was never able to appreciate it – until I met you."

At this point, the Tesla music merges with the actual song in the soundtrack. There is a distinct blurring of the musical diegesis as we know we are hearing the music of the song from the Teslas but we can now also hear the original track with its lyrics. Whether the song is now diegetic, extra-diegetic or metadiegetic is unclear, but it is established as the Dave/ Becky love theme of the film and recurs at the end when they are reunited after the final battle.

Alongside this principal popular-music track, there is also a score from one of Bruckheimer's regular composers, Trevor Rabin. Rabin's principal theme is associated with the forces of good magic as represented by Dave and Balthazar. In its usual form, it is perhaps best described as the 'Ring' theme. We first hear it when the dying Merlin gives his dragon-shaped ring of power to Balthazar, to be passed on to the prime Merlinian; and we hear it next when Balthazar gives the ring to ten-year-old Dave and it 'recognizes' him – the dragon spontaneously animates and coils itself around Dave's finger (see Figure 11.1). While the ring is the first association of this theme, it is also therefore Dave's theme, representative of his destiny as the prime Merlinian and of the magical power that he later learns to focus through the ring. However, his association with this theme goes deeper and extends into other parts of the narrative and the film's music, because the theme is evidently derived in part from the song 'Secrets' and specifically from the part of the song that Dave arranges for his Teslas, the cello introduction rather than the sung melody. The cello plays a simple broken chord pattern (see Figure 11.2) which provides a ground bass that underlies the entire song, both verses and chorus.[9] On first hearing, this is quite different from the 'Ring' theme: it is in a major key, apart from any other consideration. The 'Ring' theme is, however, easily found within it. If the broken chords are rendered as a series of two-note chords, then these dyads spell out the rising and falling minor thirds of the 'Ring' theme; and the harmony of the first two bars of the theme (see Figure 11.1) is a simple reversal of the harmony in the first two phrases of the song, as can be best demonstrated by rendering the first and third bars (omitting the repeated bar) of the 'Secrets' figure as dyads in C major (Figure 11.3).

Figure 11.1 Author transcription of the 'Ring' theme from *The Sorcerer's Apprentice* (2010), composed by Trevor Rabin

Figure 11.2 Author transcription of broken chords in 'Secrets' from *The Sorcerer's Apprentice* (2010), composed by OneRepublic

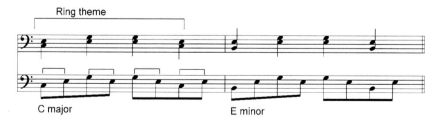

Figure 11.3 'Ring' theme derived from 'Secrets' chords

Music, therefore, unites the two aspects of Dave's trajectory through the narrative: a single musical idea on the one hand provides the musical territory that unites him with Becky and on the other establishes his destiny as wielder of Merlin's Dragon Ring and the power that it implies he possesses. Occurring in a popular-music form, it speaks to his youth and the way he is able to appropriate music to communicate with Becky. Alchemistically transmuted by Rabin into orchestral underscore, the same musical idea functions in the well-established manner of classical Hollywood scoring to position him as the central character of the drama. Even here, though, that transformational process reflects back towards the song: there is one moment in the film where the 'Ring' theme is used not for Dave but for Becky. In fact, it is Becky who saves the world: Dave and Balthazar are unable to stop Morgana from casting the Rising spell, and we see evil Morganian sorcerers the world over beginning to rise from their tombs and coffins. It is Becky, overcoming her fear of heights, who climbs the satellite tower on top of a skyscraper and kicks a satellite dish out of alignment, so breaking the threads of Morgana's technologically enhanced spellcasting and causing the reanimating sorcerers to collapse back into dust. As Becky achieves this, we hear the 'Ring' theme briefly but distinctly scoring her actions, and the theme completes a particular journey here, from its origins in her music via Dave's association with the ring and with magical power, and now back to Becky as she momentarily becomes a somewhat unwilling but significant narrative agent.

This moment notwithstanding, the 'Ring' theme is primarily concerned with the idea of magical power and Dave's destiny as Morgana's nemesis: but power itself is of little use without agency. A second theme, clearly derived from the first phrase of the 'Ring' theme with its rise and fall of a minor third, is associated with Balthazar early on in the film (Figure 11.4). We hear this secondary theme on numerous occasions involving Balthazar: as he begins his quest; as he escapes from the urn and strides off in search of Dave; as he swoops down on the eagle gargoyle he has enchanted into flight and rescues Dave; and on other occasions where his actions drive the narrative forward. He is the prime narrative agent of most of the film, the character whose quest to find the prime Merlinian and so defeat Morgana propels the story towards its conclusion; but in the latter part of the film, as Dave starts to both control and accept his powers, the 'Agency' theme is also used in connection with his

Figure 11.4 Author transcription of the 'Agency' theme from *The Sorcerer's Apprentice* (2010), composed by Trevor Rabin

actions. The first occurrence is when he uses his powers to arrest Horvath's daggers in mid-flight, just as they are about to hit Balthazar; and in Dave's ultimate confrontation with Morgana, the 'Agency' theme provides both a drum ostinato and an accompaniment to the 'Ring' theme, so bringing the two ideas of power and agency together for the final battle (see Figure 11.5).

The final moments of the battle, however, become sonically rather more interesting than this reasonably straightforward layering of the closely connected musical ideas concerning power and agency. As Dave unleashes his improvised Tesla coils on Morgana, they naturally produce sounds – and just as earlier on in the film they happened to produce harmonies to 'Secrets', now they contribute to several clear renditions of the 'Ring' theme in perfect harmonic synchronization with the underscore. If there was some ambiguity as to where 'Secrets' lay within the diegesis when Dave played it to Becky on the Teslas, the knots that one might tie oneself in trying to account for the sudden diegetic appearance of a non-diegetic musical theme at this point are formidably complex. This is, I would argue, one of the most satisfyingly fantastic moments of the film: in the moment that the Teslas start to participate in the 'Ring' theme, not only are science and magic unified – quite literally, operating in harmony – in order to defeat Morgana, but sound and music are unified with them and with each other as part of a diegesis-defying spell. Again, as with Becky apparently appropriating the 'Ring' theme shortly before this, there is a sense of the music completing a journey: emerging into the diegetic soundworld of the narrative, the 'Ring' theme signifies the

a) agency rhythm as ostinato to 'Ring' theme in final battle

b) 'Ring' theme combined with 'Agency' theme

Figure 11.5 Author transcription of 'Ring' and 'Agency' themes in combination from *The Sorcerer's Apprentice* (2010), composed by Trevor Rabin

final realization of Dave's destiny. His science and his magic come together through the Teslas as they realize the musical theme representing his power. In effect, the 'Ring' theme itself, emerging from the Teslas, destroys his – and the world's – great enemy.

Conclusion

Music was always going to have a distinctive place within this film: its origins in the *Fantasia* animation and Dukas's original programme music made this unavoidable, and the centrepiece of the film provides an entertaining allusion to its musical and visual forebears. However, despite this immediate musical agenda, it is in the intricacies of the story itself and in its differences from *Fantasia* that the music and sound design of the film succeed in being genuinely imaginative and innovative. By virtue of the relationship between score, song and Tesla coils, music acts as a mediator between science and emotion on one hand, allowing Dave to defy his science-nerd role to get the girl; and between science and magic on the other, allowing him to conquer evil by being both scientist and magician. The narrative uses music to rehabilitate the idea of the scientist in a Hollywood film, making him an unambiguous hero rather than the wicked, world-dominating villain of popular imagination.

Notes

1. T. Robey, 'The Sorcerer's Apprentice, review', *The Telegraph*, 12 August 2010 (http://www.telegraph.co.uk/culture/film/filmreviews/7941372/The-Sorcerers-Apprentice-review.html; accessed 31 December 2010).
2. The 'Adagio for Strings' was used at the funerals of both Franklin D. Roosevelt and John F. Kennedy and has gained the status of a national symbol of mourning in the USA. It was played in many memorial services following the September 11 destruction of the World Trade Center in 2001.
3. In the 1930s Nikola Tesla claimed to have invented an electromagnetic device he called the 'teleforce' that the press of the day immediately dubbed a death ray, although this was a quite different device from the Tesla coil. However, it may explain why the image of contraptions emitting bolts of plasma has such resonance in the imagery of early science-fiction cinema.
4. I can only speculate on what went on in the development process that started with the Mickey Mouse episode in *Fantasia* and resulted in this film, but I cannot help but hope that the idea of combining science and magic within the narrative derived in some part from the intertextual pun of Mickey Mouse as conductor in *Fantasia* and the idea of conductors in physics. The featurettes accompanying the DVD and Blu-Ray releases discuss the relationship of science and magic in the film but not any specific connection between this aspect of the narrative and *Fantasia*.

5. This theme strongly resembles Balthazar and Dave's 'quirky' motif in terms of the pitches used but the rhythm, articulation, instrumentation and overall effect are very different.

6. Drake Stone acts as a direct correspondent to Dave Stutler (down to their initials) in terms of both Balthazar and Horvath having youthful sidekicks/apprentices. However, Horvath, just like the Joker in Burton's *Batman* (1989), murders his own sidekick when it suits his purpose.

7. Veronica, whom we meet properly only in the final scene of the film, has a European accent which might logically connect her to the Morganian side, but she is such a minor character overall that this does not disturb the otherwise consistent use of accent.

8. Tesla music is a real phenomenon, produced by using a solid-state Tesla coil with a midi controller. The Tesla music in the film is not quite accurate – it would be impossible for Becky and Dave to have any kind of conversation whilst the music was playing – but the production of plasma filaments that can be made to resonate at specific pitches is firmly based in fact.

9. Song and theme reveal their compositional origins in their use of key: 'Secrets' is in D major, with the broken chords therefore lying fairly comfortably across the cello's natural tessitura, employing the open G, D and A strings. The 'Ring' theme's home key is normally E minor, the most natural key for the guitar, with open E, G and B strings. The guitar is Rabin's main instrument as a player and a key timbre in most of his film scores, not least this one.

References

Allen, G. S. (2009), *Master Mechanics & Wicked Wizards: Images of the American Scientist as Hero and Villain from Colonial Times to the Present*, Amherst: University of Massachusetts Press.

Campbell, J. (1949), *The Hero with a Thousand Faces*, Princeton: Princeton University Press.

Davis, D. (2010), 'Book Reviews: Allen, Glen Scott. *Master Mechanics and Wicked Wizards*', *Studies in Popular Culture,* 32(2), 115–18.

Fowkes, K. A. (2010), *The Fantasy Film*, Chichester: Wiley-Blackwell.

Tolkien, J. R. R. (1966), *The Tolkien Reader*, New York: Ballantine.

Worley, A. (2005), *Empires of the Imagination*, Jefferson, NC: McFarland.

Index

CPSIA information can be obtained at www.ICGtesting.com
Printed in the USA
BVOW04s2308300614

357709BV00006B/33/P

9 781781 791004